The Abusive Partner

An Analysis
of Domestic Battering

The Abusive Partner

An Analysis
of Domestic Battering

Edited by

Maria Roy

Founder and President of
Abused Women's Aid in Crisis, Inc., New York

VNR VAN NOSTRAND REINHOLD COMPANY
NEW YORK CINCINNATI TORONTO LONDON MELBOURNE

Copyright © 1982 by Van Nostrand Reinhold Company Inc.

Library of Congress Catalog Card Number: 81–13008
ISBN: 0–442–25647–7

Manufactured in the United States of America

Published by Van Nostrand Reinhold Company Inc.
135 West 50th Street, New York, N.Y. 10020

Van Nostrand Reinhold Publishing
1410 Birchmount Road
Scarborough, Ontario M1P 2E7, Canada

Van Nostrand Reinhold Australia Pty. Ltd.
17 Queen Street
Mitcham, Victoria 3132, Australia

Van Nostrand Reinhold Publishing
Molly Millars Lane
Wokingham, Berkshire, England

15   14   13   12   11   10   9   8   7   6   5   4   3   2   1

Library of Congress Cataloging in Publication Data

Main entry under title:

The Abusive partner.

    Includes index.
    1. Wife abuse—United States.   I. Roy, Maria.
HV6626.A17   362.8'3   81–13008
ISBN 0–442–25647–7   AACR2

To my husband, Dr. P. K. Roy,
who knows the true meaning of partnership.

Foreword

As a performer in the theater and motion pictures, I am appalled by the extent to which the media consistently and irresponsibly perpetrates, and thereby glorifies, violence as being a normal part of the social climate of our society. As a woman and as a human being, I abhor violence. Because I know how deeply affected I am by having to witness gratuitous brutality and insidious cruelty, I find it impossible to accept roles in which I am called upon to portray such attitudes. I am referring to beatings and torture, not historically fascinating villainesses, of which I've played a few!

There is a recurring nightmare that I have experienced all through my life since as far back as I can remember. It is so vivid and it arouses such a sense of indescribable terror that to awaken from it is a blessed relief. The theme of my dream is that I am being chased by someone who is going to hurt me and I will be unable to defend myself because I do not have the strength or power to get away. I have discussed this dream with others and find it is a common one, and that I am not unique in my own experience of it. Luckily for me, this is just a nightmare; not a reality. But how unfortunate for the millions of battered women in the world whose real lives are filled with violence!

Maria Roy has been a virtual one-woman crusade to promote public awareness of the crucial problem of Domestic Violence. In 1975, she founded the first specialized social-service agency for battered women in New York State—*Abused Women's Aid in Crisis,* Inc. She has spoken out on every possible occasion on TV and radio generating public awareness of the need for more federal and state legislation to support the service programs which are so desperately needed to provide counsel, relief, and indeed shelter for those women and their children who are driven from their homes in fear of their very lives.

She compiled and edited the first comprehensive study on wife beating, *Battered Women: A Psychosociological Study of Domestic Violence.* The book provides invaluable guidelines for organizers of community social services, and excellent source information for educators, legislators, lawyers, police officials, and the clergy. This book has been hailed as the best and most valuable anthology dealing with the problem of domestic violence. It contains documented essays and studies on a topic that many of us would rather not know about, but must face up to as a shocking reality on every social level of our society.

Now she has addressed herself to the understanding and treatment of the abusers themselves. In *The Abusive Partner,* Ms. Roy presents a complete study of the psychosociology of abusive behavior, the problem's current status, medical, environmental, and criminal justice aspects, and finally treatment. Her chapter on trend analysis is by far the best study done on the subject to date. It will serve as a building block for future research. This analysis, as it stands, is one of the most valuable contributions to the field.

As for the book, it is a landmark publication and the most important resource on the subject to date. It should be required reading for everyone who wants a better understanding of the batterer. Lasting solutions can only be found by understanding the total picture. This total picture must, then, include a keen comprehension of the abusive partner, and a willingness to offer the support and assistance necessary for change.

Angela Lansbury

Preface

Let this book be an aid to those who abhor violence against women and who seek lasting solutions. Let this book be an inducement for those abusive partners who repudiate their own acts of violence and who want to change their behavior and improve their relationships.

While continuing the struggle to provide refuge, resources, and information to the millions of battered women in the world today, the time has come to begin to create and implement complementary services for the millions of batterers who are inflicting the physical harm. These services should not replace services for battered women; this would be counterproductive. One does not preclude the other; both can and should coexist.

A total approach that provides assistance to the batterers and the victims can only lead to a marked reduction in the incidence of violence.

For every one batterer who stops abusing his partner, there is a battered woman who ceases to be his victim.

MARIA ROY

Contents

The Abusive Partner

An Analysis
of Domestic Battering

Part I The Psychosociology of Abusive Behavior

"... violence occurs when a person cannot live out his need for power in normal ways."

—Rollo May from *Power and Innocence*

1. The Nature of Abusive Behavior

Maria Roy
Founder and President of Abused Women's Aid in Crisis, Inc.
New York

POWER AND VIOLENCE

It has been said that it is not power that corrupts, but lack of it that does. For a deep sense of powerlessness creates a need for assertion that in most cases becomes destructive aggression that can ultimately lead to violence. Violence is the end product of pent-up frustration, denial of perceived legitimate rights over a period of time, and the constant erosion of self-esteem. It is an eruption similar to the explosive outpouring of volcanic lava following a period of dormancy. It builds, reaches a peak, and then falls, rising then falling, ticking then exploding like a kind of human time bomb. Violence is, then, an expression of accumulated aggression that failed to be defused. It is related to power because it is a consequence of the absence of power—conceived and born of impotence.

Power has many facets—some positive and other negative. These facets intermingle and overlap in each person. May (1972) described the nature of power by breaking it down into five basic kinds: exploitative, manipulative, competitive, nutrient, and integrative. Everyone experiences the various aspects of power during their lifetime.

The first two—exploitative and manipulative power—are very definitely rooted in varying degrees of destruction; i.e., violence and coercion, respectively. The third form, competition, has both destructive and constructive properties; the nature of the former related to the demise of one's opponent, while the nature of the latter is related to the development of one's own skills or talents for achieving superiority over the adversary. On the other hand, both nutrient and integrative power involve the welfare of other people. While nutrient power is *for* the other person, integrative power is *with* the other person. The former concerns all of the "giving" qualities associated with parenting or befriending, while the latter concerns the interdependency of two or more parties so that they all derive power from each other and eventually grow from it. This form of power is power at its best because no one sacrifices nor is sacrificed in the process. Instead, each party gains more power, constructive change takes place, and everybody benefits. In other words, integrative power is based on the mutual interchange of power in which the power of individuals combine to produce a new form of power that did not previously exist.

Actually, the first kind of power, exploitative power, described by May (1972), is really not power at all. Rather, it is violence disguised as a form of power, for at its very essence is an extremely small and very frail self-image that is desparately yearning to be recognized, acknowledged, and fortified; a self-image so negative that it seeks to destroy itself by destroying others. It is a suicide mission of a self wanting to be noticed, attended to, listened to, perhaps even feared. Violence is not a form of power—it is its antithesis; and, as such, it screams out for a positive entity. Everything about violence is negative, and the so-called "change" that results from violence (political upheaval, torture, maiming, death) for whatever the cause, is really counterproductive and, therefore, cancels out whatever "gains" are achieved. In war there are no true victors; death and destruction are the game. The victors must get on with reconstruction and the victims learn to respect the violence which engulfed them, only to ironically initiate and inflict similar violence on others when the opportunity arises. Violence is, then, growth in reverse. It is the epitome of death. For what could be more detrimental to the health and welfare of individuals that gratuitous violence? Unlike drought, famine, disease, and accidental death, violence can be sharply curtailed by the very individuals who use it to achieve their ends. In most cases, it does not require medication or scientific research. Its control lies within the will of the individual.

There is a mistaken notion that violence is power—perhaps the ultimate form of power and the most expedient means to an end. You have only to learn to use it and your enemies will fear you and your friends will respect you. The clenched fist is a symbol of this power. In fact, the predominant message today is that violence is good, violence is inevitable, violence is power. This bill of goods is sold to us day in and day out. This message exercises a monopoly over the advantages of pacifism and love. With the scale tipped on the side of violence, equal time for nonviolence is constantly being denied. The overall effect is a public that accepts violence as a way of life; a public that employs violence as an instinctual method of problem solving or as a means to an end.

The death penalty and summary executions of political opponents are increasing worldwide. A survey was recently compiled by the secretariat of the U.N.'s Human Rights Commission comprised of 10 nongovernmental agencies that monitored human rights practices in 52 nations. The survey found that torture remains a routine practice in many countries and that the death penalty has been restored in several countries that had abolished it earlier. "The world total of executions appears to have increased during the past three or four years."

Violent crime is the focus of radio and television newscasts; the visual impact of television renders it a more effectual instrument of communication. A day does not go by without some local news station using a crime incident as the leadin story. The more gory and bizarre the details, the more "newsworthy" the item. Sensationalizing violent crime tends to objectify it into an exploitable business by the media. It sells; it is, therefore, a valuable commodity. The message of violence as power gets translated into a surrealistic filmclip more on the order of fiction than of reality.

Even more damaging is the contrived interrelationship of the reporters on some news teams. One gets a sense of this relationship as being packaged, predictable, artificial, scripted, and directed. This obvious distancing from the real horror of violence affects the viewer in a very deleterious way. The viewer becomes desensitized to violence because he is deprived of the personal and social impact that it has on the lives of the victims. Without a social context for the violence, and removed from the reality of the human condition of pain and suffering, the viewer finds it harder and harder to socialize his own aggression and establish a control mechanism to keep it under tow.

Newscasting is only one part of television broadcasting, and as such does not have an exclusive relationship to the promulgation of violence as power. But it can exert the most influence for it has the potential to do the most harm or the most good. There are other phases of television programming which are detrimental, though not equally so. Evidence is mounting that a steady diet of TV murders, rapes, and fist fights portrayed in "made for TV movies" or on late-night satires, can incite violence in real life. However, the precise relationship between TV violence and actual violence is still undefined. Psychologists and social scientists "charge that TV violence may be dangerous because it may cause children to become insensitive to violent acts and their effects" (Marioni, 1979, p. 32). Taking this a step further, TV violence does not affect just the young. It impartially influences all of its viewers, both young and old.

Pictorial advertising also influences social consciousness and tends to shape public opinion. The glamorization of violence on record-album jackets, in rock promotion, and in magazine and newspaper ads legitimizes the crimes of rape, assault, and murder. To underestimate the powerful effect that a constant barrage of violence has on society is to fail to accept the strong possibility that media violence can encourage acts of violence within the home or between strangers.

Violence permeates the world of hard-core pornography, which depicts women and children as bound, beaten, and mutilated objects of domination, manipulation, and molestation. Like rape, violent pornography has nothing to do with sex, but everything to do with power and the subjugation of its victims. The point being made is that now, more than at any other point in history, people are being subjected to a constant and consistent message of Might Is Right. The world seems to be engulfed in an ugly Reign of Terror! Advances in communication systems have made possible an extremely efficient vehicle for transmitting information. Even though the technology has evolved and become sophisticated, there is an appalling lack of development and understanding of just how powerful an instrument of social change the media can be. As with freedom, the issue of responsibility is pivotal.

True freedom does not include the right to kill wantonly, to destroy another's property, to defame or malign another's character. True freedom implies order, respect, reverence, and love. Likewise, the media have the obligation to preserve individual dignity while they uphold the truth. That is, a better, more comprehensive understanding of the responsibility that comes with the First Amendment should be a required area of study at the institutions of journalism and communication arts, in recognition of the fact that the media is the most significant instrument of change and modification which exists in the world today. Because it is so influential, it should reflect a healthy balance of opinions, ideologies, cultures, and customs. It may seem as though the media is being singled out and made the scapegoat. This is not the case. The ubiquitous nature of violence is complex; its causes and maintaining factors are therefore far from simple. Certainly a simplistic approach does not offer a satisfactory solution. There are innumerable causal and stabilizing factors which threaten personal and international peace and security. Consider that violence is condoned around the world on two major levels: the governmental level and the familial level. Sandwiched between these levels are individuals receiving messages from the government which pontificates policy from its military see of power on the one hand, and from the family which trains its members to use violence to resolve interpersonal conflicts on the other hand. Added to this is the realization that there is enough nuclear power to annihilate all forms of life as we know it on earth. Governments and individual citizenry are well aware of this threatening aspect of modern life which dictates foreign policy and shapes world opinion. Though we do not live our everyday lives being crippled by the threat of world-wide nuclear holocaust, we cannot escape its presence. We cannot ignore our deep feelings of powerlessness and helplessness at the knowledge that our fate and the fate of future generations are in the hands of a few world leaders. For some, conventional warfare seems to be a safer alternative. But it can lead to nuclear warfare. Can any nation afford to engage in warfare of any kind? True, conventional warfare seems less dangerous by comparison. But what about the risk factor of bringing such a war to a "quick and tidy" end by deployment of nuclear weaponry? True, conventional warfare seems the lesser of two evils, but remember that the nuclear age grew out of the age that preceded it, and is a logical consequence of the quest for creating better and more advanced instruments of destruction. Where will it lead? What is dangerous is a thinking which embraces war as the ultimate expression of power. Good sense avoids wars at all cost. For the reality is that war is hell and anybody who tries to hide this with isolated accounts of glory and idealism is suffering from delusion. War is death and destruction; war is violence and hatred; war is fear and deception; war is murder and rape; war is infanticide and suicide. Conventional or otherwise, it is based on principles and strategies of demolition. Today, war can mean the nullification of not just an opposing army, not just a warring tribe or nation, but the extinction of the entire human race.

Napalm, radiation, and biological agents cannot render a man any more dead than the broadsword or the crossbow, but they have added a new dimension of horror to warfare. . . . The nuclear age has done more than just enlarge our capacity for violence; it has transformed the whole context in which our reasoning and judging about it must take place. (Holmes, 1971, pp. 103–104)

And the anger mounts. And the rage builds. One is outraged; another is enraged. Outcries of, "What can I do to change all this?" can be heard. Murmurings of discontent increase in volume, become louder and louder, become loud cries, then shouts and screams of panic. Explosions occur; violent confrontations occur; gunfire is exchanged; public demonstrations become public massacres. Students are killed; pacifists are sacrificed; protestors are clubbed; police are injured. Violence is employed as a tactic to prevent violence.

What then? Retreat? Retreat to the bosom of the family? Seek peace within the home? Solace and nurturance? Ah, that this were the case. But the facts refute this. The statistics warn us that the home can be a dangerous place, perhaps even more hazardous than we would like to admit. Who can ignore the fact that within the United States alone, over two thousand children are *killed* annually by their parents and that one quarter of all murders involve relatives? Who can ignore the fact that parents and grandparents are assaulted by their offspring with greater frequency than by nonfamily members and that approximately

1.8 million* American women that is, 1 out of 26, are beaten per year by their husbands or male companions?

> Just as there are numerous forms of violence outside the family, there are also numerous forms that can occur within it. . . . Parents, children, spouses and siblings have all been known to hit, beat, or kill one another and examples can be cited of every possible form and degree of physical force being used between every possible combination of relatives. (Dobash and Dobash, 1979, p. 9)

All one has to do is read the daily accounts of such atrocities in the newspapers to become aware of their increasing incidence. Family violence hotlines and counseling centers are springing up all over the U.S.A. and around the world. These services are being inundated by calls for help. They cannot meet the need for the demand is so great. Callers want information, advice, and in some instances shelter. Violence seems to be the norm, not the exception. Again, the message is that physical bodily harm is the desirable and popular means of control because it is seemingly very effective. One generation after another has conveyed this carefully taught lesson.

> In order for the vicious cycle of violence to be broken, society needs to recognize its obligation to find solutions, to offer help and immediate protection for all the women and children who actively seek it, and to explore non-violent modes for the expression of conflict. (Roy, 1977, p. 43)

Better still, exploring ways of improving verbal communication skills for all family members might sharply reduce the need to rely on physical aggression. Everyone suffers—children, parents, grandparents, husbands, wives. The victim suffers pain and degradation. Though physical recovery may occur, the emotional scars do not disappear. Consider the 5-year-old who is beaten with a belt buckle every time he does not comply with his parents' wishes. Consider the young wife who has her eyes blackened because dinner is not ready on time; consider the elderly woman residing at her daughter's home and tied to

---

* This figure is likely to be underestimated due to the problems of under-reporting.

her bed because she does not "stay put." The aggressor, like the victim, is not left unscathed, for it hurts to kill; it hurts to injure others; it hurts to scream and shout profane threats to others. Every time someone strikes another person in anger, hatred, or jealously—whether impulsively or calculatedly—that someone loses something of himself. That someone loses his control, loses his temper, loses his self-respect, loses the commendation of friends and relatives, loses an opportunity to resolve the conflict (violence almost always compounds a problem, never simplifies it), and may even lose his freedom (if convicted or incarcerated on an assault or murder charge). As with war between nations, intrafamilial conflagration has no victors.

Mental Harm

And the people do violence to each other. Violence is not confined to the physical kind. People do violence to others every day of the week, every week of the year, year after year. The same principles of bodily harm are at work, but the injury is far more significant, for it touches the human psyche. The wounds are deep. The spirit is defiled. The damage is insidious. The victim senses that something is gravely wrong, but does not identify the source of pain as a form of violence against his person.

Take, for instance, the following examples:

- Two political candidates are running against each other. Each candidate "declares war" on the other in order to achieve victory. Instead of just being adversaries, they become combatants. Heavy artillery is used. Mud is slung. The objective is character assassination, nothing less. A fair campaign is predicted on rules of healthy competition which can be achieved by emphasizing individual strengths. If each candidate would take a stand on the issues, and report his position and his record of accomplishments, instead of maligning the opposition, then the violence of the campaign would cease to exist. The public does not recognize the violence in the campaign. The public is inured to it. The public senses that something is not quite right, but does not differentiate between violent and nonviolent competition. If it did, then it would demand the latter.

- A man has devoted his life to helping alcoholics. He has worked for 10 years and has established a program at great personal sacrifice—sacrifice to his family and economic sacrifice. But the sacrifice is not an issue, for the man sees his work as important and necessary. He is driven by a sense of mission. He mobilizes support for his cause first locally, then regionally, then nationally, and internationally. Along the way there are roadblocks and hurdles. But they don't hamper the man's spirit; they challenge him. How to raise money, find a suitable location, implement services? These problems are solvable. Hard work, insight and planning help to exchange the problems for solutions. The violence occurs when other so-called "helping" agencies "declare war" on this man's program because his agency competes for funds or challenges the establishment. One such "war" occurred in a southern town. An agency with a pristine reputation for its excellent programs for alcoholic men reported to me over its 10-year existence that it has been plagued by larger institutions competing for government and foundation money. Behind the scenes, these large bureaucracies used coercion, plagiarism, libel, and trickery to steal ideas, and coopt projects. The man's agency continues to provide extraordinary services, but at great cost to him and his staff.

- Two women are close friends for a good number of years. One has married; the other has remained single. The married woman grows to love her friend in a sisterly way—trusts her and confides in her. One day, her friend announces that she is having an affair with this woman's husband and that they want to get married. Will she please be cooperative and give her husband a divorce? Not only has this single woman been dishonest and disloyal, but she has been violent. For she has robbed her friend of her husband; she has aided and abetted a situation that led to the eventual destruction of the friend's family life. This is not to say that the husband does not share the blame and that he may have formed a similar liaison with some other woman. This is not the point. The point is that the woman's friend has done her violence. As a friend, she had the obligation to discourage any feelings or actions which would ultimately harm her friend and her friend's family. She did not, and by the virtue of the "friendship" has acted violently.

Perhaps these examples seem somewhat remote. They are meant to plant a seed—the idea that violence is something all too common existing in blatant and obvious forms like war and murder, but also taking on more subtle guises. These examples of nonphysical violence in and of themselves demonstrate a form of violence that may or may not directly lead to physical violence, but which very definitely contributes to the level of phsical violence in a society that places heavy emphasis on exploitative, manipulative, and competitive power.

ABUSIVE PARTNERS AND VIOLENCE

In a modern world that confuses violence with power, individuals, both male and female, are hard put to sort out the differences, identify its subtler forms, and reject it outright, or begin the task of eradicating it from their everyday lives. Compounding the problem for the abusive partner is a long and ugly history of abuse against women, particularly wives. This history of permitted and condoned abuse has shaped the behavior of men towards "their" women for thousands of years. The foundation of societies down through the ages has been a family with the male partner exercising the position of authority over the wife and children. In short, men today carry with them a long history of the sub-jugation and oppression of women, and what is astounding is that very few of these men are aware of this legacy, and are therefore oblivious to its effect on their own treatment of women in the twentieth century. Writer Terry Davidson, in her article "Wifebeating: A Recurring Phenomenon Throughout History" (Roy, 1977), recounts some of the more flagrant atrocities committed by husbands against their wives. Some examples include the scalding death of Fausta ordered by her husband, the Emperor Constantine, which was to serve as a precedent for the next 14 centuries.

About A.D. 1140 Gratian systemized church law in his work, the *Decretum,* which held that

> Women should be subject to their men. . . . The image of God is in man and it is one. Women were drawn from man, who has God's jurisdiction as if he were God's vicar. . . . Therefore woman is not made in God's image. . . . Adam was beguiled by Eve, not she by him. It is right that he whom woman led into wrongdoing should have her under his direction, so that he may not fail a second time through female levity. (p. 13)

This same caution was to be shared by Napoleon Bonaparte hundreds of years later when he expressed his belief that a wife should be held ac-countable for her husband's crimes and, therefore, partake in his im-prisonment. Accounts of vicious customs in the British Isles during the 1800s are replete with expressions and practices which were considered both legal and desirable at the time (Dobash and Dobash, 1979). For instance, a section of Liverpool, England, was referred to as the "kicking district" due to the flagrantly violent treatment of wives by their husbands. In fact, the common expression heard so often in conversation today, "Rule of Thumb" is derived from an amendment to a section of British common law legalizing the beating of wives by their husbands, provided that the switch or rod used be "no thicker than his thumb." The Dobashes recount a horrific disciplinary practice in Scotland for a wife who was considered to be a virago or a harridan, which was intended for public ridicule by use of a *brank,* an "iron bridle with a padlock and a spike to enter the mouth." (p. 59)

The violence against wives which was rampant in Europe seeped into American culture, particularly through a legal process that was based on British common law. Our own courts, specifically the Supreme Court of Mississippi, in 1824 upheld the husband's *Right of Chastisement* followed by similar decisions in the courts of Maryland and Massachusetts. It wasn't until 1871 that such a prerequisite was rescinded by the courts of Alabama and Massachusetts, while a similar attempt failed to pass the state legislature of Pennsylvania in 1886.

Men today, the world over, continue to carry on their ancestral tradition of employing force and brute strength to gain the respect of and domination over "their" wives or companions. The bulk of these man fall into a nonpathological category, for their behavior constitutes what is the norm. The license to abuse their partners is felt today in the tacit approval of such behavior by societies the world over. Recently in the United States and Europe some attention has been paid to this inhuman tradition. The decade of the seventies marked the beginning of a rising consciousness about the practice—a consciousness that identified the practice as problematic, abusive, and widespread. A handful of women on both sides of the Atlantic, impassioned by the prevalence of abuse in their countries, set out in pioneer fashion to blaze a trail to self-help for all of the abused wives and mothers who were not helped by the orthodox social services. It was a particularly difficult task to accomplish since the problem had not been identified or classified as a serious social problem. In addition, there was strong resistance to providing help. "Blame the victim" ideology dominated arguments against change. Some people even felt threatened by the prospect of providing abused wives with resources and alternatives. They interpreted such assistance as antifamily and contended that it would result in the family's ultimate breakup. In order to make headway, the pioneers had to persist in their efforts to improve conditions by setting up specialized services, by locating and securing funds, by keeping the public informed and aware, by challenging an insensitive legal system, by lobbying in the political arena, by joining together through local, regional, and national networks, by opening up their own homes, or by donating their own capital in some cases, and needless to say, by devoting their entire beings to a never-ending uphill battle for the cause. Many of the pioneers suffered in the process—but this was expected and they understood its inevitability. Before long, women in the United States and elsewhere were setting up hot lines and shelters. Women were helping women. Volunteers by the hundreds committed their time and their energy, and their efforts have made the difference between life and death for grassroots agencies. But the problem continues to remain unresolved. The issue, though a popular one, has not become a priority where it counts. The government does not consider the problem serious enough to warrant financial assistance on the federal level. State governments have helped somewhat, but not enough. Foundations still need to be convinced that their contribution is a good investment. Corporations haven't yet been dented; conservative boards tend to shy away from the controversial aspects of the problem. And so the provision of these dire services is thwarted. Without financial support, self-help agencies are doomed, and abused wives will be left without services.

What this does is to create a climate of indifference for the families troubled by internal abuse, and the message that the safety, health, and well-being of the abused partners and their offspring is not important enough, reinforces the behavior of the abusing partners as legitimate and really not so bad after all. This results in a tendency for abusive partners to deny their behavior or to minimize it. In short, they fail to take responsibility for their actions, reflecting the attitudes of a society which absolves the abusers of guilt and requires the victims to secure their own relief.

"A fundamental approach aimed at understanding the root causes of wifebattering could lead to the establishment of a power base that would be comprised of both men and women working together to improve conditions." (Roy, M., 1980, p. 171) This is why it is so important for men to begin to join the march for peace within the home and to resolve that abuse against women is wrong, is criminal, and that it can and should be stopped. While women continue to struggle for change, abusive men must be willing to confront their own violence. As with alcoholics, abusive partners cannot change unless they admit their problem to themselves, reject their violent behavior, and seek out help. But before this can happen, men will need to convince other men that they should and can stop the violence—and that the ultimate responsibility for stopping it is their own. Counseling groups for batterers and batterers anonymous-type organizations can begin to affect the problem at its source. Women and children are entitled to resources that ensure their safety. These resources do not break up the family. *Violence breaks up the family.* By reducing and discouraging the violence, the family is *strengthened.* Women will continue to press for alternatives such as shelters because women have been known for their endurance, particularly when it is linked to their own survival and the survival of their children.

The abusive partners need to realize that violence is not a form of power, but a negation of it. Violence does not achieve positive results and violence does not earn the respect and love of the women and children in their lives. Rather, it alienates, it isolates, it obfuscates, it wears away a relationship. It produces fear, mistrust, hatred, pain, injury, sometimes death. It does not solidify a relationship; it blows it apart. Violence, then, is the poorest means to an end, if that end be a strong and loving partnership.

Violence Is Self-Destructive

Violence is destructive to the self. One 30-year-old abusive partner described himself as being ''dead inside.'' Other abusive partners have articulated their profound feelings in the following ways:

Composite Case Example.

- I feel like there's nothing inside . . . that my emotions are blocked. I feel isolated . . . I guess this dates back to when I was 3½ years old and my mother abandoned me. I guess I have never gotten over it. The only time I can feel is when I go crazy and beat up my girlfriend, but after that I'm even more dead inside that before. The more I find myself exploding . . . strangling her or punching her in the face, the less I am in touch with any other feelings that I have. Sometimes I wonder if there's anything there besides this wild rage that percolates deep within. I often think of myself as a percolator sitting on a stove with the burner on too high. Eventually all that hot liquid will start to boil over. I can feel something when I boil over, but what I feel is so nasty, and evil, and ugly, and negative that I spend the rest of my time trying to recover from the rotten experience by denying what I have done or that I have done it.

- Who am I? What have I become? I don't want to face the harsh reality because I would rather see myself dead first than admit to myself that I am violent. That man in the mirror really doesn't exist. The only thing that is real is the violence—what's real is her broken ribs. I'm not real. I can't find myself. I won't admit that I am responsible for injuring her so I blame her for "getting to me." She gets me so mad, it's her fault that I beat her up. It's not me. Sometimes I wonder where this will all end. Maybe the only way to stop the violence is to put an end to myself. Maybe then it'll stop.

Violence Can Be Stopped

Abusive partners need not be violent forever. Many of them can help to control or completely eliminate their abusive behavior. Success can be achieved only when the abusive partner takes the ultimate responsibility for his actions and attempts to do something about them. When this happens, all things are possible. For the very first step of assuming culpability is the repudiation necessary to reverse the pattern of violence.

REFERENCES

Dobash, R. Emerson and Dobash, Russell. *Violence Against Wives: A Case Against the Patriarchy.* New York: The Free Press, 1979.

Holmes, Robert L. Violence and nonviolence. In *Violence,* Jerome A. Shaffer (ed.) New York: David McKay., 1971.

Marioni, John. The impact of tv violence on your children. *Family Weekly Special Report,* 1979, November 11. p. 32.

May, Rollo. *Power and Innocence: A Search For the Sources of Violence.* New York: W. W. Norton, 1972

Roy, Maria. A current survey of 150 cases. In *Battered Women: A Psychosociological Study of Domestic Violence.* New York, Van Nostrand Reinhold, 1977

Roy, Maria. The intrinsic nature of wife battery. *Focus on Women: Journal of Addictions and Health,* Autumn, 1980.

Part II Trend Analysis

"Violence in a house is like a worm on a vegetable."
—Hebrew Proverb

2. Four Thousand Partners in Violence: A Trend Analysis *

Maria Roy
Founder and President of Abused Women's Aid in Crisis, Inc.
New York

INTRODUCTION

The present trend analysis is based on 4000 urban and suburban cases of spousal abuse occurring in New York City and its environs. The abused partners reporting the information represent a strongly motivated or desperately impelled segment of the population who wanted to find solutions to the problems of violence in their own lives. These partners had either attempted to extricate themselves from the violent home or to bring about some positive change during the course of their partnerships. The majority of the partners had actively pursued relief by exploring many of the orthodox channels of help (police, courts, clergy, family, and friends) but were hampered because of nonexistent or inadequate options.

The present analysis endeavors to find the trends, correlations, and cross-correlations of the various components of the problem from a relatively high population of battered partners studied over a 4-year period at Abused Women's Aid in Crisis, Inc., New York.

* I am grateful to Dr. Pradip K. Roy for his help with the statistical analysis, interpretation of the data, and assistance in writing sections of this article.

METHODOLOGY

The data base of this analysis was derived from 4000 cases of urban/suburban women (married, separated, divorced, living together, dating) over a 4-year* period. Semistructured hot-line intake questionnaires, followed by on-site interviews in most instances, was the principle method of data collection.

I. Major Limitations of the Analysis:

a. The exploratory nature of the research.
b. The methodology is somewhat biased as only the strongly motivated and/or desperate partners are represented in the population.
c. No questionnaire can include all of the "hidden" independent variables in social dynamics, and therefore all conclusions made regarding the causation of violence do not include fallout or interactions from these variables (a common shortcoming of most social-science research).
d. Not all of the respondents reported every aspect of the violent confrontations, and some partially or completely avoided answering questions related to their personal histories.

II. Major Strengths of the Analysis:

a. This analysis is unique in the area of spousal violence because it probes a population which reflects a cross-section of socioeconomic groups, parental histories, and cross-cultural population.
b. This study analyzes frequency, onset, and the degree of violence, and attempts to correlate them with other components of the violent home.
c. the relevance of the population size is very important in conventional trend analysis** in ascertaining the skewedness (β_1) and the peakedness (β_2), and type (normal, beta or gamma) of a dis-

---

* January, 1976, through December, 1979, from Abused Women's Aid in Crisis, Inc.
** Hahn, Gerald J. And Shapiro, Samuel S. *Statistical Models in Engineering*. New York: John Wiley & Sons, Inc., 1967.

tribution and its trends. Since the population density is high (N = 4,000), the confidence level of a trend is higher, as is to be expected from a conventional trend analysis in physical science.

STUDY: EXPOSITION

Types of Partnerships

The bar chart (Fig. 1A) and pie chart (Fig. 1B) indicate the relative percentage of the types of various heterogeneous partnerships in the present study and demonstrate that the legal marriage type of partnership is the most dominant type (66.2%).

II. Chronological Age Groups of Partners

Chronological age groups for abusive partners were arbitrarily divided into five subclasses.
Age in years:

Class 1	Under 25 years
Class 2	26–35 years
Class 3	36–50 years
Class 4	51–60 years
Class 5	Over 60 years

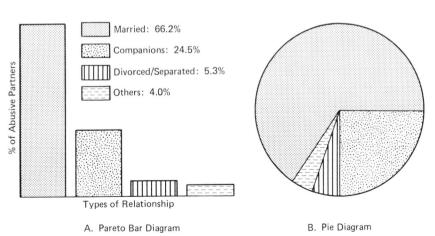

Married: 66.2%
Companions: 24.5%
Divorced/Separated: 5.3%
Others: 4.0%

% of Abusive Partners

Types of Relationship

A. Pareto Bar Diagram

B. Pie Diagram

Figure 1. Types of relationship.

From Figs. 2 and 3, it is apparent that the relative maximum occurs for Class 2 of the chronological age groups for both the female and the male population. It is to be noted from Fig. 3 that the abusive partners from Class 3 Group (36–50 years) contribute substantially (26.6%) compared to Classes 1, 4, and 5.

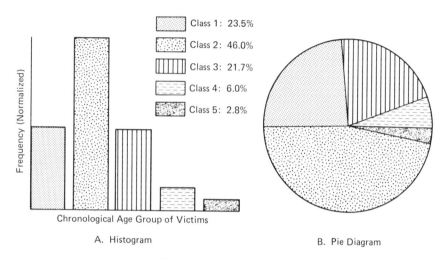

Figure 2.   Chronological age group of victims.

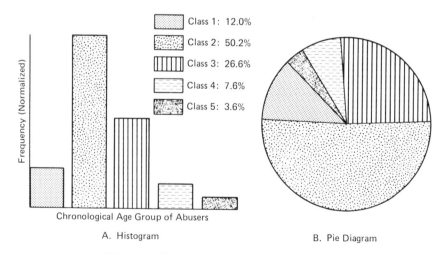

Figure 3.   Chronological age group of abusers.

III. Chronological Age Groups of Children

The following classification is based on the chronological age of the children involved in the study.

Class 1	Under 1 year of age
Class 2	1–5 years of age
Class 3	5–12 years of age
Class 4	13 years and older

The histogram and pie plot in Fig. 4 represent the relative fractions of various age groups of children indicating that the substantial population falls within Class 2 (38.9%), 3 (31.2%), and 4 (22.9%). Since the major fraction of abusive partners come from the age group 26–35 years, it is apparent that their relationships with their partners must have begun in late adolescence or early adulthood in order to account for such a high population density of children from Classes 2, 3, and 4.

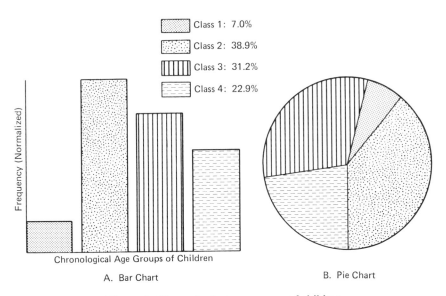

Class 1: 7.0%
Class 2: 38.9%
Class 3: 31.2%
Class 4: 22.9%

Frequency (Normalized)

Chronological Age Groups of Children

A. Bar Chart   B. Pie Chart

Figure 4. Chronological age groups of children.

There was some contribution from abusive partners in the age group 36–50 years when they have multiple children.

IV. Financial Status of the Partners

As in my previous research,* this study corroborates the significant role that money plays in the dynamics of spousal abuse. For this reason, a more detailed financial inquiry was undertaken. Figs. 5A and 5B are a Pareto plot and pie diagram, respectively, of the sources of income for the partners. Fig. 5 shows that 75% of the household finance comes from joint income of the abusive partners (44.7% of the abusers and 30.3% of the abused partners' income). The other sources of income were not derived from gainful employment. Such other sources include public assistance (17%) and assistance from relatives, pensions, and veterans benefits (8%). In some cases, both partners were working with or without public assistance and they were treated separately in calculating their relative impact. It is rather interesting to note that

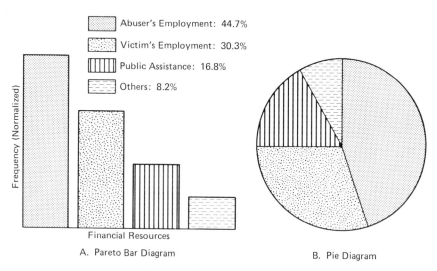

A. Pareto Bar Diagram

B. Pie Diagram

Figure 5. Financial resources.

*Roy, Maria. "A Current Survey of 150 Cases," In *Battered Women: A Psychosociological Study of Domestic Violence.* Maria Roy (ed.) New York: Van Nostrand Reinhold Co., 1977.

75% of the abusive partners hold blue-collar jobs. Also a strong trend (though not demonstrated in Fig. 5) suggests that all of the victims who act in self-defense against their abusive partner are economically independent (i.e., either have jobs or receive financial support from their families). However, the above statement does not follow the syllogism that *all* financially independent abused partners will act in self-defense. It does substantiate that a significant fraction of this group will defend themselves more frequently than those abused partners who are totally economically dependent on their abusive partners.

V. Criminal Record of the Abusive Partner

Not all of the respondents reported every aspect of the violent confrontations, and some completely or partially avoided answering inquiries regarding the criminal record of the abusers even in these strongly motivated and/or desperate victims. However, the message should be very clear that *only* 10% of the reported 4000 cases have had any past criminal record; the remainder (90%) of this enormous population of abusers have had no previous criminal record. These statistics, are rather dramatic and their implications alarming, for most of the abusers are reportedly not atypically socially deviant or hardened criminals. Rather, they are any of the everyday faces seen in the business office, the plant, at school, at the park, at church, or next door.

   Fig. 6A shows schematically the relative percentage of abusive partners having past criminal records (only 10%) and Fig. 6B is the blown-out version of the population with criminal records. It shows the relative fraction of past criminal records:*

   It is evident that a substantial proportion of the abusive partners' past criminal records are in the category of spouse abuse (44.5%) and violent crimes (14%), which usually include stabbing, hitting with an object, and shooting. A little over 8% of this population served time for their convictions for periods up to 5 years, and 6.6% were out on bail while 2.8% were released on their own recognizance (Fig. 6B) when the information was reported.

---

* Harassment of a police officer, drug possession, possession of an illegal weapon, burglary, and narcotic sales.

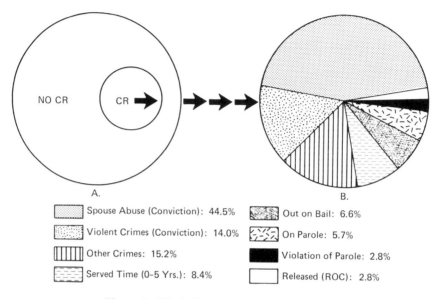

Figure 6. Criminal record of abusive partners.

VI. Duration of Partnership

Fig. 7A and 7B are the histogram and pie diagram, respectively, of the length of partnership. Duration of partnership is artificially divided into five groups based on the length of the relationship.

Class 1   0–5 years
Class 2   6–10 years
Class 3   11–15 years
Class 4   16–25 years
Class 5   26 and over

Fig. 7A shows a Pareto-type distribution: 45.9% of the population from Class 1 and 27% from Class 2, 14.25% from Class 3, and 8.7% from Class 4, and 4.2% from Class 5, respectively. This confirms the

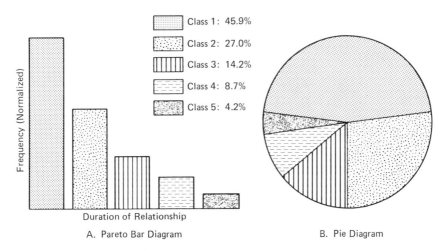

A. Pareto Bar Diagram   B. Pie Diagram

Figure 7. Duration of relationship.

previous study* which ascertained about 90% of the abuse occurs from 0–15 years of partnership.

VII. Onset of Violence

Fig. 8A is the distribution of onset of violence described as a fraction of duration of the relationship (t_R) and Fig. 8B is the corresponding pie-chart. As in the previous study, the onset of violence is characterized in Fig. 8 by four broad time segments:

1. Immediate: occurring between 0–1/10 the duration of the relationship (38.6%)
2. Early: occurring between 1/10–1/3 the duration of the relationship (34.5%)
3. Middle: occurring between 1/3–2/3 the duration of the relationship (10%)
4. Later: occurring between 2/3 of the relationship and the time when the interview was conducted (16.9%)

---

* Roy, Maria, *op. cit.*

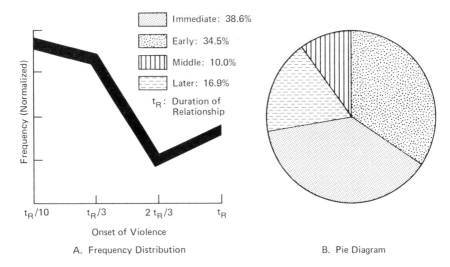

Figure 8. Onset of violence.

It is evident that in over 70% of the population studied, the onset of violence occurred in the Immediate or Early part of the partnership. During the Middle part ($1/3$ t_R to $2/3$ t_R), the distribution shows its local minimum of 10% followed by a finite increase beyond $2/3$ t_R (16.9%) which in this study indicates a major change in the abusive partnership (*viz.* a death in the family; a sudden change in financial status; a new environment).

VIII. Nature of the Abuse and the Resultant Injuries

Figs. 9A and 10A are the Pareto bar chart of the nature of abuse and the types of physical injuries incurred in abusive partnerships. Figs. 9B and 10B are the corresponding pie diagrams. The types of violence described include the following:

1. SA/Sexual Abuse (including forcible rape)
2. VA/Verbal Abuse (obscenities and personal attacks on character)
3. PA/Physical Abuse
4. PAW/Physical Abuse with a Weapon (knife, gun, foreign objects)

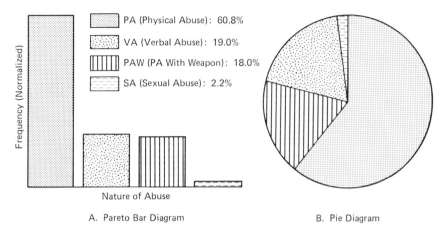

A. Pareto Bar Diagram   B. Pie Diagram

Figure 9. Nature of abuse.

Confirming the previous study,* PA dominates with 60.8% of the population, followed by VA (19%), PAW (18%), and SA with 2.2%. It is possible that some of PA and PAW are also verbally abused but that the abused partner did not report it because the physical abuse overshadowed other types of abuse.

Resulting physical injuries as a consequence of PA (with or without a weapon) indicate that 49.8% of the injuries are bruises, 23.4% include other bodily injuries including stab wounds, and 17.8% are black eyes while 9% are broken limbs. Fig. 9 does not include emotional injuries and permanent emotional scars resulting from physical abuse.

IX. Frequency of Violence

Frequency of violence was divided into four categories using the similar notations of various degrees of abuse as used in the previous study** on a scale in ascending order from LO/Less Often violent episodes occurring less than once a month, to VO/Very Often episodes occurring between 2–7 times per week. The VO category frequently includes PAW and SA. Figs. 11A and B are, respectively, the histogram and pie chart of the relative population densities of abusive partners

---

* Roy, Maria, *op. cit.*
** Roy, Maria, *op. cit.*

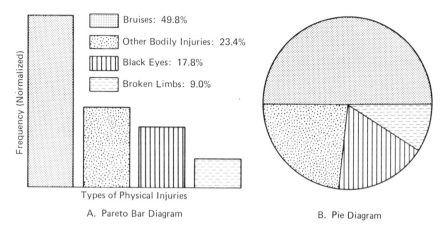

A. Pareto Bar Diagram

B. Pie Diagram

Figure 10. Types of physical injuries.

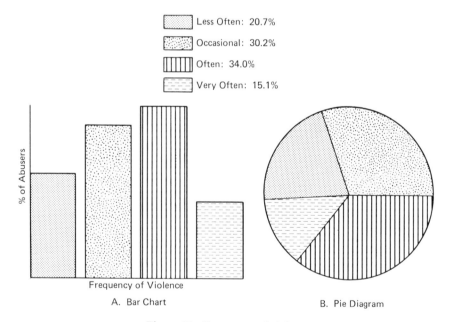

A. Bar Chart

B. Pie Diagram

Figure 11. Frequency of violence.

with various degrees of frequency of abuse. Each category contributes substantially (LO—20.7%, occasionally—30.2%, often—34%, and very often—15.1%) thus giving a rather broad Gaussian distribution in the frequency of violence category.

X. Parental Violence

Data on parental violence (Figs. 12A and 12B) are based primarily on the abused partners' reconstruction and recollection of the relevant events of their childhood. Information obtained concerning the abusers' childhood history of violence was not directly elicited from them in most cases, but rather from the information reported by the victim. Most victims garnered their information from their in-laws.

In spite of these shortcomings, the results prove to be interesting and significant. About 81.1% of the abusive partners often come from homes in which they themselves were beaten or where they had witnessed their own father abusing their mother. Comparatively, only 33.3% of the abused partners have a similar parental history of violence. These findings do not corroborate existing theories linking early exposure of violence by the victim in adult life. Also the traditional "masochistic" hypothesis regarding the victim seems to be invalid considering that 67.7% of the victims have had no previous

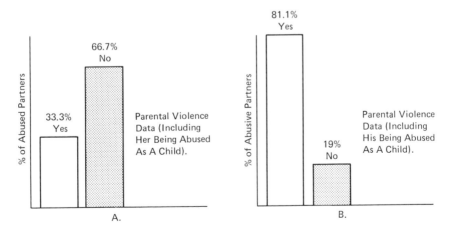

Figure 12. Parental violence.

history of either witnessing violence or being a prime target of it in their families of origin. Therefore, this huge fraction of the population definitely lacks a "built-in" past and the ensuing proclivity to accept victimization as a way of life.

XI. Drugs and Alcohol

A substantial fraction of the abusive partners are problem alcoholics (35%) and only 10% of this population is enrolled in a treatment program. In comparison, only 4% of the abused partners have serious alcoholic problems and 30% of this population are members of Alcoholics Anonymous. A similar trend exists for the abusive partners with other drug problems,* viz. 16% of the abusers have drug problems and 20% of these problem drug users sought help. On the other hand, only 2% of the victims have drug problems and 50% of this population tried to get help through drug treatment programs.

It is interesting to note that all of the abused partners who take drugs (2%) take them in conjunction with their abusive partners. In other words, the couple is addicted, and all of the victims who sought help from outside agencies did so, not alone, but with their corresponding abusive partners. Alcohol and/or other drugs seem to act as catalysts to violence, confirming my previous study. About 10% of the total number of abusive partners have concurrent alcohol and other drug problems. (This population comprises the group with a relatively shorter duration of relationship.)

STUDY: CATALYSTS AND CONTRIBUTING FACTORS FOR VIOLENCE

This study confirms the previous study on causation.** The following factors were reported in ascending order of importance as the prime variables leading to violent confrontations: (refer to Fig. 13).

---

*Drug problems reported in this study were due to morphine, heroin, cocaine addictions, and various types of hallucinogens. No one in the study reported problems related to prescriptive barbiturates even though they may have been contributing factors in some cases. (For a thorough treatment on the complex subject of substance abuse, see Robert J. Powers' article in this book.)
**Roy, Maria (ed.), op. cit.

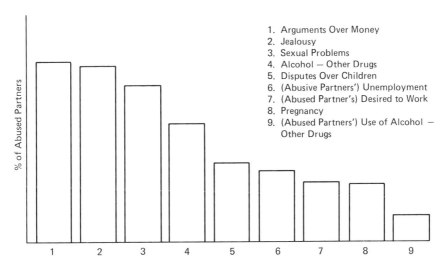

1. Arguments Over Money
2. Jealousy
3. Sexual Problems
4. Alcohol — Other Drugs
5. Disputes Over Children
6. (Abusive Partners') Unemployment
7. (Abused Partner's) Desired to Work
8. Pregnancy
9. (Abused Partners') Use of Alcohol — Other Drugs

Figure 13. Nucleating and contributing factors.

1. Arguments Over Money

Of those reported arguments over money as a factor, some indicated that lack of money due to the husband's unemployment was the basis of many arguments resulting in physical violence. Others reported that the husbands controlled all of the earned income by keeping tight reins on the budget. The wives were given just enough money to buy groceries for the family. They almost always needed to ask for spending money for their own personal items—clothes, perfumes, etc. This was the case in middle and upper middle class homes.

2. Jealousy.

Of those reporting jealously as a factor, most cited that sexual problems such as impotency, frigidity, denial, excessive demands, led to arguments in the bedroom that resulted in physical violence. In such instances, the abuser usually doubted his own virility and questioned victim's fidelity. He would therefore, discourage her from participating in activities outside the home. In extreme cases, some of the abusers even questioned the paternity of one or more of the children. A small percentage of those citing jealousy as a factor indicated that they felt threatened when victims went back to school.

3. Sexual Problems.

Of those citing sexual problems as a cause of violence, most reported that the problems began very early in the relationship (during the honeymoon period, if not sooner). The husbands' acts of brutality often caused the wives to withdraw both physically and emotionally. The women expressed a feeling of alienation from their husbands—a feeling of worthlessness. This low self-esteem resulting from the violent acts made sexual intimacy for the women very difficult. In addition, many women related that their husbands constantly accused them of infidelity and adultery. A smaller percentage reported that their husbands had problems with sexual identity, having had previous or concurrent sexual relationships with men.

4. Alcohol.

Of those citing alcohol-other drugs as a precipitant to violence, a large proportion indicated that their husbands beat them when drunk. Very often drinking was used by the husband to "numb" the anger. Paradoxically, alcohol as a depressant of function breaks down inhibitions and thereby increases rather than decreases the anger or the mechanism for controlling it.

A small proportion reported that their husbands were drug addicts— using heroin, cocaine, or barbiturates.

5. Disputes over Children.

Of those citing arguments over the children, most indicated that their husbands resented parental responsibilities, both emotional and financial. They usually had arguments over disciplining the children—often when the husband would beat one of the children. The wives felt that their husbands regarded children as a threat to the relationship because the children would "rob" them of their wives' affections.

6. Husband's Unemployment.

Of those citing unemployment as a precipitant to violence, many indicated that this added stress to a relationship that had already gone awry. The lack of employment increased already existing feelings of insecurity about the husband's virility, self-worth and productivity.

7. Wife's Desire to Work Outside the Home.

Of those citing a wish to secure work, as a precipitant to violence, many reported that this was a problem when the husband rated his occupational and/or educational status as lower than his wife's. Others stated that their husbands refused to permit them to seek employment, because "a wife's place is in the home, and a husband's responsibility it as the breadwinner of the family."

8. Pregnancy.

Of those citing pregnancy as a precipitant to violence, many reported that an unplanned pregnancy put a great strain on the relationship. Many indicated that the husbands were jealous toward the unborn newcomer and resented the intrusion. Pregnancy, occurring in a relationship already troubled by sexual problems, unemployment and deep-rooted personal problems, caused additional frustration and resulted in explosive bursts of anger and physical abuse.

9. Wife's Use of Alcohol—Other Drugs.

Of those citing alcohol or other drugs as a precipitant to violence, many indicated that their husbands beat them to keep them in line and to make them stop drinking.

CONCLUSIONS

Recently, there has been a growing body of research on battered partners which has described their special unmet needs and suggested possible solutions. However, studies on the abusive partners are practically nonexistent to date, though the need to understand the problem of violent partnership as a whole is great. This thesis attempts to satisfy this need by offering a complementary overview of the problem while deconvoluting the relative impact of various components of abusive partnerships. This analysis reveals the following trend:

1. Most abusive partners are between 26–35 years of age with a substantial number falling between the 36–50-year category.
2. A high population of children are between ages 1 through 13. Since most abusive partners are between 26–35 years of age, their relationship with their partner most likely began during late adolescence or early adulthood.
3. Most partnerships are supported by joint incomes derived from gainful employment, usually blue-collar jobs.

    All of the victims who acted in self-defense were gainfully employed, though all those who were employed did not necessarily defend themselves.
4. Most abuse occurs during the first 15 years of partnership.
5. Ninety percent of the abusive partners *do not* have criminal records, demonstrating that the typical batterer is law abiding and not criminally deviant in all other aspects of his life. A high percentage of the criminal population were convicted of spouse abuse, though only a very small percentage served time for their crimes.
6. In over 70% of the population, the violence occurred immediately or very shortly after the partnership began.

    Any major changes in the steady state of the partnership such as a sudden death of a close relative, loss of a job, unsatisfactory relocation, caused a change in equilibrium and was noted to increase the level of violence in relationships of long duration.
7. Most abuse is the physical type without use of weapons, with the bulk of ensuing injuries mostly described as bruises. Physical abuse with a weapon occurred in 18% of the population and tended to result in stab wounds in most cases.
8. Over 80% of the abusive partners have a positive history of childhood abuse or have witnessed abuse against their own mothers, while only a little more than 33% of the abused partners have similar histories, tending to invalidate traditional the-

ories which attribute the endurance of the victims to masochistic pathologies.

9. About 35% of the abusive partners have alcoholic problems with only 10% of them in treatment programs, while only 4% of their partners had similar problems with alcohol abuse and 30% of them in treatment programs.

10. While 16% of the abusive partners have other drug-related problems, 20% of them sought help. On the other hand, only 2% of the abused partners reported similar problems with other drugs and 50% of them sought help. When the victim had a drug problem, her abusive partner also had a drug problem and when help was sought, it was done so as a couple.

In conclusion, this trend analysis, while not accounting for the many hidden variables and their interactions in the social dynamics of violent partnerships, contributes a unique fundamental basis on which to build new studies.

Part III   Contributing Factors

Man must evolve for all human conflict a method which rejects revenge, aggression and retaliation. The foundation of such a method is love.''

—**Martin Luther King, Jr.,**
Speech accepting Nobel Peace
Prize, December 11, 1964

''Nonviolence and truth (Satya) are inseparable and presuppose one another. There is no god higher than truth.''

—**Mahatma Gandhi,** from True
Patriotism: Some Sayings
of Mahatma Gandhi, 1939

''All violent feelings produce in us a falseness in all our impressions of external things which I would generally characterize as the 'Pathetic Fallacy'.''

—**John Ruskin** from *Modern
Painters,* 1888.

3. Alcohol, Drugs, and Partner Abuse

Robert J. Powers, Ph.D.
Chief, Alcohol Rehabilitation Program,
Veterans Administration Medical Center,
East Orange, N.J.

Irwin L. Kutash, Ph.D.
Faculty Member, New York Center for Psychoanalytic Training,
Clinical Assistant Professor of Psychiatry,
New Jersey College of Medicine and Dentistry

Are alcohol and drugs important contributors to partner abuse? According to a great number of research studies, there is a very frequent association of substance abuse and violence between partners. Appleton (1980) surveyed 30 battered women in a hospital emergency room and found that 87% reported more than moderate drinking by their partners prior to battery, and 13% identified more than moderate drug use. In a project for battered women, Carlson (1977) interviewed 101 women who reported that 60% of their partners abused alcohol and that 21% abused other drugs. Ten percent of the women acknowledged abusing alcohol themselves, while 5% reported abusing drugs. Roy (1977) reviewed 150 cases randomly selected from over 1000 cases at AWAIC (Abused Women's Aid in Crisis). Approximately 85% of the violent partners had an alcohol and/or other drug problem. In numerous other surveys of partner abuse, high percentages of alcohol or drug use were found (Bayles, 1978; Gayford, 1975; Gelles, 1972; Walker, 1979).

Clearly alcohol and drug use are highly associated with abuse between partners. An important question is whether alcohol or drugs cause partner abuse. Alcohol and drugs are not causally related to partner abuse in terms of being necessary or sufficient conditions for the violence. Substance use is not a necessary condition, in that a great proportion of violence occurs in the absence of alcohol and drugs. Substance use is not a sufficient condition, for alcohol and drugs are very often used without violent occurrence. Recently, several authors have suggested that alcohol and drugs are best considered as contributors or "triggers" for spouse abuse, rather than causes (Fleming, 1979; Martin, 1976; Pizzey, 1974). As contributors to partner abuse, alcohol and drugs may interact with other influences, such as financial loss or disruptions in plans, to bring forth violent episodes.

The primary purpose of this chapter is to examine contributors to partner abuse involving alcohol and drugs. The primary factors to be considered are: drug type (alcohol is classified as a drug), premorbid personality, personality interactions, dosage levels, "set" or expectancies, and "setting" or environmental context. A brief description will now be given of each of the factors just mentioned that may contribute to partner abuse. The potential influence of each factor will then be described in detail for each of four main classes of drugs: depressants, stimulants, narcotics, and hallucinogens.

Drug type is a key variable. Different classes of drugs may have markedly different psychoactive effects. Hoffman (1975) differentiates four primary classes of drugs: depressants, stimulants, narcotics, and hallucinogens. Depressants, which are therapeutically used mainly for their calming effects, consist of barbiturates (such as Seconal and Nembutal); sedative-hypnotics (such as Quaalude and Placidyl); tranquilizers (such as Thorazine, Librium, and Valium); and alcohol (which has no recognized therapeutic use). Stimulants are used to combat depression, reduce appetite, and, paradoxically, to calm hyperactive children. The stimulants include amphetamines (such as Dexedrine); cocaine; antidepressants (such as Elavil and Tofranil); and convulsants (such as strychnine). Narcotics are used in the relief of pain (e.g., Morphine, Demerol, and Heroin) and as cough suppressants (e.g., Codeine). Hallucinogens have been used in psychotherapy with mixed results, and include LSD, PCP, mescaline, and marijuana.

Premorbid personality has a vital effect on the relationship between substances and partner abuse. An individual in harmony with himself and his environment is less likely to seek drug effects. With inadequacies in ego functioning, an effort to alter internal experience becomes more likely. Also, however, with increasing impairments in ego functioning, there often are increased difficulties in integrating the psychoactive effects of drugs and in regulating aggressive drives. Hence, inadequacies in premorbid personality may well lead simultaneously to greater utilization of drugs and to greater potentiality for violence once substances are abused. Some premorbid personality types clearly associated with violence and substance abuse include antisocial personalities, passive-aggressive personalities, and explosive personalities. Psychotics, such as paranoid schizophrenics, and depressed individuals with potential to turn aggression inward also can be included in this group.

Personality interactions may be an important factor. In many instances of partner abuse, the premorbid personality of the abusive individual is an overwhelming factor, while the personality dynamics and the actions of the partner have very little influence. In many other instances, however, partner abuse is produced largely by conflicts that arise within the relationship. Substance use may aggravate the conflicts by disrupting established personality balances or adjustments between partners. Substance use may additionally impair functioning in coping with the conflicts, thereby increasing the likelihood of aggressive or violent confrontations.

Drug dosage is often a key factor, in that different pyschoactive effects may well occur with dosage variations from low to high levels. Closely related to drug dosage are frequency and methods of use. Frequent or chronic use of a drug may cause a cumulative effect, serving to intensify psychoactive experiences. Similarly, methods of use which facilitate the drug's entrance into the bloodstream, as in subcutaneous and intravenous injections of narcotics, also tend to heighten psychoactive effects.

Mental set regarding a drug entails an individual's prior experience with the drug and his expectancies about its use. An understanding of likely drug effects and a nonapprehensive attitude toward them may well reduce the likelihood of negative reactions, such as aggression. This is especially true for hallucinogens and amphetamines.

Setting includes the cultural and physical environments, as well as immediate events which may act as "triggers" for violent acts. The cultural environment may involve propensities toward both substance use and violence in certain socioeconomic and ethnic groups. The physical environment may include deprivations leading to discomfort and frustration, which in turn can lead to anger and aggression. The immediate events or "triggers" precipitating an aggressive outburst may range from seemingly mild occurrences, such as burnt toast, to intense verbal or physical attacks by the partner.

Drugs in each of Hoffman's (1975) four classes may be directly related to episodes of partner abuse. A review will now be provided of each class of substances—depressants, stimulants, narcotics, and hallucinogens—with particular attention given to factors that moderate the expression of aggression and violence: premorbid personality, personality interactions, dosage, set, and setting. One caution, however: Although, for the sake of clarity, we evaluate drugs under the heading of these separate variables, in clinical occurrence these variables interact in almost all cases, so that aggressive or violent behavior is most often multidetermined.

DEPRESSANTS

The primary central nervous system depressants are alcohol, barbiturates, nonbarbiturate sedative-hypnotics, and tranquilizers. The depressants have been considered responsible for more violence against partners than any other substances (Goldstein, 1975). One might expect that the sedative or hypnotic effects of the depressants would calm and reduce aggressiveness. Frequently, that is the case. Many patients of the authors have stated that they regularly use alcohol and other depressants for their calming effects. The patients have stated that when they begin experiencing strong hostile feelings toward their partner, they may often take a drink or perhaps a sedative to "settle down." Unfortunately, alcohol and other depressants also may have disinhibitive effects and may impair cognitive functioning, which may then contribute to partner abuse. Alcohol has been found to have a particularly high association to partner abuse. The effects of alcohol will now be discussed in detail, followed by a briefer discussion of the other depressants.

Alcohol

The use of alcohol dates at least from the Babylonian period and has been found in a majority of cultures throughout the world. In the United States the use of alcohol has been prominent since the earliest colonial settlements; and, as Benjamin Rush observed in 1786, it was frequently related to aggressive and violent behavior (Paredes, 1976). Recently several surveys have indicated a strong relation between alcohol use and both assaultive and nonassaultive crimes. Wolfgang (1958), for instance, examined Philadelphia police records of 588 homicides and found that alcohol had been present in 54% of the offenders and in 53 percent of the victims. Voss and Hepburn (1968) analyzed Chicago police records of 395 homicides and noted that alcohol was evidenced in 53% of the cases. Nicol and his colleagues (1973) found that men appearing before courts, as well as men in prisons, often have a history of heavy alcohol use.

Premorbid Personality.   Several authors point out the importance of personality tendencies as contributors to partner abuse, in addition to the effects of alcohol. Hanks and Rosenbaum (1977) studied the interpersonal relationships of 22 alcohol-abusing men and the battered women with whom they had been living. They found that the men usually had a propensity to violence before establishing relationships with the women. In the relationships, the men frequently expressed intense negative feelings, such as rejection or inadequacy; had begun drinking, and had then become assaultive. Lenore Walker (1979) drew upon over 120 interviews with battered women and concluded that alcohol generally was only a component in battering episodes, not a precipitating cause. Frequently the men beat the women whether or not they had been drinking. However, the most violent physical abuse occurred from men who were consistent drinkers. Shainess (1977) describes personality types with a particular propensity for partner abuse: the obsessive-compulsive, the passive-aggressive, and the sadistic personalities. Shainess concludes that alcohol and drugs increase the likelihood of violence in each of the personality types.

Alcohol has disinhibitive and cognitive effects which may have differing influences, depending upon premorbid personality characteristics. In persons with rigid, moralistic tendencies or obsessive-compulsive traits, hostile impulses may build up from repeated resentments or frustrations and explode in violent outbursts. Persons with such tendencies have been described as "Dr Jekyll and Mr. Hyde" personalities (Symonds, 1978). An individual may appear exceedingly well mannered and controlled, especially in public; but then have episodes of violent temper and rage. Frequently these individuals turn to alcohol to seek relief from their inner tensions and anger. The result may be a temporary calming effect; but the disinhibitive and cognitive effects of the substance create a high potential for violence.

Alcohol's disinhibitive effects may weaken restraints on emotions and "release" aggressive impulses. Alcohol's cognitive effects may impair such vital processes as perception, judgment, and memory. Distortions in perception increase the likelihood that a partner's remarks or actions will be misunderstood, leading to increased resentments. When anger is experienced, impairments in judgment decrease the probability that the person will accurately predict the negative consequences of aggressive actions. Limitations in memory interfere with ability to recognize explosive situations and use coping skills to diffuse anger before violence occurs. Consequently, under the disinhibitive influences of alcohol, there is an increased likelihood of a sudden discharge of aggression, possibly with little or no warning. Also, with the cognitive impairments from alcohol, there is a greater probability of an escalating sequence of aggressive remarks or actions which progresses unchecked to violence.

In passive or passive-aggressive individuals, strong repressions also may exist over the direct expression of aggression. Again, alcohol may disinhibit aggressive impulses and additionally may impair abilities to appropriately channel aggression. Several laboratory studies have documented the disinhibitive effects with such individuals. Tamerin and Mendelson (1969) and McNamee, Mello, and Mendelson (1968) conducted studies in which chronic alcohol abusers were allowed full access to alcohol for extended periods. The subjects were observed to be very passive, as well as uncomplaining and anxious to please, during the predrinking phase of the studies. Under the influence of alcohol, the subjects became demanding and aggressive. There were frequent complaints regarding the experimental situation, and in the Tamerin and Mendelson study especially, there was much hostile, "hyper-masculine" behavior.

In aggressive or sadistic individuals, alcohol paradoxically may at times calm or reduce aggressiveness, but at other times may lead to increased aggression. When the aggressive individual becomes more passive with alcohol use, the relaxing and euphoric effects of the drug may help the person to overlook frustrating and negative feelings, such as rejection and inadequacy. Menninger, Mayman, and Pruyser (1963), in their description of five levels of personality dyscontrol, note that highly aggressive individuals commonly use alcohol to maintain control over threatening impulses. Unfortunately, the calming influence of alcohol is quite tenuous. Frustrating or challenging occurrences may readily result in intense outbursts of aggression or violence. In frequent close interactions between partners, the probability of provocative events is very high. Despite a partner's efforts to be cooperative, or even compliant, frustrating events may occur that lead to aggressive exchanges and then violence. Also, the individual may unexpectedly experience negative internal states, such as feelings of shame or failure. The internal states may occur relatively independent of the partner's actions and, under the disinhibitive influences of alcohol, may result in sudden aggressive outbursts.

Personality Interactions.   There are two primary groups of violence-prone relationships (Symonds, 1978). In the first, the premorbid personality structure of the abusive partner is chiefly responsible for eruptions of violence (See above discussion of premorbid personality). In the second, violence results principally from conflicts which arise within the relationship. Psychodynamic balances are often established in relationships as partners develop patterns of adjusting to each others needs. Substances may be used to help maintain or improve the balances, but often the reverse eventually occurs. Three areas of conflict which are particularly common in alcohol-involved couples are: dependency needs, control needs, and intimacy needs.

In dependency conflicts, individuals with strong dependency needs often experience great frustration, as their partners fail to be satisfactorily nurturant or fail to assume a great proportion of daily, family responsibilities. In our clinical practices, individuals have frequently been treated who resorted to alcohol both to mask feelings of frustration when their dependency needs were not met and to have an excuse for not meeting their adult responsibilities. The use of alcohol upset previously established balances in their relationships. Their partners often resented the drinking episodes and were even less nurturant and sympathetic than usual. The drinking individuals experienced increased frustration and rage, and, under the influences of alcohol, often lashed out at their partners.

Conflicts over control also may readily lead to partner abuse. Symonds (1978) provides an illustration of control conflicts in what he terms a "policeman-scofflaw marriage." One partner continually tries to correct and control the other's behavior, and views the person as a delinquent psychopath. The other person, in turn, resists the control by repeating the "delinquent" behavior. For example, a husband wishes to have the family dog kept on leash to prevent him from spoiling the neighbors' lawns, while the wife insists that the dog be a free spirit and lets the animal out to roam (Symonds, 1978). We have found similar examples in our clinical practices, such as a successful businessman, trying to have his partner maintain an "orderly" house and a tight budget. When alcohol is used, the "controller" often is enabled to act out his marginally controlled rage, resulting in episodes of partner abuse.

Intimacy conflicts principally involve concerns over sexual contact and performance. In our clinical work, several individuals revealed deep anxieties about having sexual relations, and especially about achieving an "adequate" sexual performance. The couples generally reached compromises in their sexual contacts; however, recurrent anxieties remained. Individuals often drank to reduce the anxieties, but frequently also reduced their responsiveness to their partners' sexual cues. Alcohol thus disrupted the couple's tenuous sexual adjustment, and led to frequent resentments, increased demands, and even to ridicule by the partner. The drinker frequently retaliated with abusive behavior; perhaps partially as an attempt to compensate for inadequacy feelings and to achieve dominance in at least the nonsexual sphere.

Dosage.   Moderate dosage levels of alcohol (blood alcohol content .10–.29) have been found to be associated with the greatest frequency and intensity of violence (Shupe, 1954). At low levels, disinhibition effects and cognitive impairments may be insufficient to enhance aggression. At high levels, consciousness is often so dulled and physical reactions so slowed, that there is limited ability to plan or carry out assaultive actions. Nevertheless, at high dosages, there is a particularly high risk of reactive aggression, as individuals resist attempts of others to restrain or influence them. Personnel in hospital emergency rooms readily attest to the violence potential of highly intoxicated individuals.

Set.   Expectations of alcohol-induced behavior may well lead to aggression. Gelles (1972) notes two ways in which attitudes toward alcohol may influence partner violence. First, Gelles observes that partners may inappropriately identify alcohol as a cause of violence, in order to "disavow the deviance of hitting a family member." Gelles maintains that in many cases alcohol contributes little to violent occurrences, but the partners ascribe causality to the alcohol to avoid or disavow the stigma of accepting responsibility for the violence. Second, Gelles states that persons may use alcohol as an excuse for carrying out violent acts. In particular, "individuals who wish to carry out a violent act become intoxicated *in order to carry out the violent act*" (Gelles, 1972, p. 117). Gelles is correct in stating that persons may receive less blame for drinking behaviors than nondrinking acts. Recently, Richardson and Campbell (1980) found that when husbands drank, more blame was assigned to situational factors and less to them. When wives drank, however, just the reverse occurred. Wives received more blame for behaviors when drinking than when sober. Gelles (1972) seems to overstate his further point that individuals may drink primarily as an excuse to be violent. There are many motives for drinking. Drinking as an excuse to be violent may be one of many motives, but appears likely to be a secondary motive, rather than a primary one.

Brown and associates (1980) identified six primary expectancies for the behavioral effects of alcohol: increased power and aggression; increased social assertiveness; reduced tension, enhanced sexual performances; positive transformation of experiences; and enhanced social and physical pleasure. An individual may drink primarily in hopes of achieving more power over his partner or in an effort to become more aggressively assertive with the partner. The drinking may or may not help the person realize these aims. Nevertheless, the drinking may result in disinhibition of aggressive impulses and impair cognitive functioning and thereby contribute to episodes of violence. The primary motives for drinking may be to exert greater power or influence over the partner or to be more socially assertive or aggressive. Once violence has resulted from alcohol's disinhibitive and cognitive effects, attempts may then be made to consider alcohol as the cause or "excuse" for the violent episode.

Setting. The physical environment and the nature of interactions between partners both may contribute greatly to aggression. Most violence between partners occurs in the home (Pokorney, 1965; Pittman and Handy, 1964). There is close interaction in the home and, in Western society, there also is the frequent presence of alcohol. As Bennett, Buss, and Carpenter (1969) observed, the combination of close physical proximity and the presence of alcohol, results in an increased likelihood of alcohol-associated violence, independent of the pharmacological effects of the drug.

Nevertheless, alcohol-related behaviors are important contributors to violence. A drinker's behavior may be highly frustrating or stressful to the partner and may place strains on the partner financially, emotionally, and physically. In an inebriated state, the individual is more likely to be provocative or to make unreasonable demands upon the partner. The combination of increased stress and provocative acts may readily lead to escalating series of aggressive exchanges. Gelles (1972) provides a graphic illustration of the process:

> In many of the situations where the husband returns home drunk, he demands food and sex (usually in that order). These circumstances provoke the wife who is angry that her husband has been drinking and spending budget money on liquor. The wife is also upset because she has to cook for her inebriated spouse. Finally, she often may be repulsed by the thought of having sex with her drunken husband. The wife often refuses to comply with her husband's demands or complies grudgingly. Faced with his wife's refusal to welcome him home with food and sexual favors, the husband often will berate his wife as a poor cook and as frigid. Thus the fact that the husband has come home drunk sets off primary conflict over his drinking

and secondary conflict over financial problems, the role of the wife, and sexual responsiveness. This conflict in many cases leads to violence.

Partners of drinkers also may initiate aggressive actions. The partner of the drinker may be experiencing her/his own frustrations or conflicts independent of the drinker. According to Steimentz (1978), Bach and Goldberg (1974), and others, women may be as aggressive as men in relationships. The expression of aggression may differ with men generally having learned more physical expressions of aggression and women having learned more verbal expressions (Martin, 1976). The results of aggression also may differ, in that, men generally have greater physical capacity to cause physical harm. However, when weapons are used, women can be as lethal as men. Homicide rates for husbands and wives are approximately equal (Langley and Levy, 1977). When the partner of the drinker initiates verbal or physical aggression, there may be a rapid escalation to violence; for the drinker has impaired abilities to diffuse the situation and his controls of his own aggression are likely to be quite marginal.

Barbiturates, Sedative-Hypnotics, Tranquilizers

Barbiturates were introduced medically in 1903 as Veronal (barbital) and made commercially in 1912 as Luminal (phenobarbital). The most frequently used barbiturates include: Seconal (secobarbital); Nembutal (pentobarbital), Tuinal (secobarbital and amobarbital), and Luminol (phenobarbital). Barbiturates usually are taken orally, but in abusive patterns may be injested subcutaneously or intravenously. Barbiturates may cause anxiety reduction and drowsiness, but also may bring confusion and loss of memory, and in large dosages, may have intoxicating effects similar to alcohol. They have an especially high addictive potential. Nonbarbiturate sedative-hypnotics were first developed in the 1950s and include: Quaalude (methaqualone); Placydil (ethychlorvynol); Dalmane (flurazepam); and Doriden (gluethelhimide). These drugs were created as alternatives to barbiturates and have similar effects, and also have a relatively high addictive potential. The "major" tranquilizers, such as Thorazine (chlorpromazine) and Haldol (haloperidol), are rarely, if ever, abused.

The first "minor" tranquilizers, Miltown and Equanil (meprobamates), were produced in the mid-1950s and publicized as antianxiety agents that did not cause sedation. Librium (chlordiazepoxide) and Valium (diazepam) were subsequently marketed and have become very widely prescribed. The minor tranquilizers have less estimated ability to produce disinhibition euphoria than the other central nervous system (CNS) depressants (Smith and Wesson, 1973). However, large dosages may produce euphoria and lessening of restraints, and frequent usage may lead to addiction.

Barbiturates, nonbarbiturate sedative-hypnotics, and minor tranquilizers have much in common with alcohol pharmacologically. All produce depressant effects along a continuum which defines deeper levels of unconsciousness: antianxiety, sedation, hypnosis, anesthesia, coma, death (NIDA, 1974). Alcohol, however, is far more often represented in acts of violence against partners than all the other CNS depressants. In a study of 23 women who abused barbiturates and other prescription medicines, Borgman (1973) found only rare allegations of violence against others. In a survey of housewife drug abuse, Brahen (1973) determined that only in extreme cases did aggressive behavior develop from barbiturate use. Heightened aggressiveness has been reported for "street use" of barbiturates, particular through intravenous use. In street use, however, barbiturates are often used with alcohol and other substances. Relatively few incidents of partner abuse have been reported where barbiturates were the sole drug used (Cooper, 1975; Wesson and Smith, 1977).

The much lower incidence of partner abuse associated with nonalcohol depressants appears primarily due to availability, drug action, and set; and to lesser extent to premorbid personality, dosage, and setting. Alcohol has been available in the United States since the earliest Colonial period, while other depressants were first marketed during this century. In the 1960s, there were an estimated 9 million alcoholics, as compared to 500,000 barbiturate abusers (Dutta, 1977). Since the early 1970s, there has been a sharp decline in prescriptions given for barbiturates due to negative publicity of their high potential for addiction and mortality, and particularly due to the government's reclassification of barbiturates from a Class III to a Class II substance, under the Controlled Substances Act of 1970 (Cooper, 1975). Correspondingly, there has been a steady increase in the use of minor tranquilizers, such as Librium and Valium.

Drug action may be a factor. Although alcohol and other CNS depressants exhibit great similarities in psychoactive effects, the precise mechanism of action on the central nervous system is unknown. Important differences likely exist. All CNS depressants have both disinhibitive and sedative effects. It is possible that the proportion of disinhibitive effects to sedative effects is greater in alcohol, especially for males (Barry, 1977).

Set or expectancy appears to be a critical factor. Barbiturates and other CNS depressants, besides alcohol, were initially available to the public only through prescription. The drugs were marketed as medications—as sedative or hypnotic agents—to calm anxieties and induce sleep. There was no suggestion that they should be used for social or recreational purposes. The prevailing view of the drugs as calming agents may well have affected the experiences from the drugs. In the home, the drugs have been used predominantly as medications. Although excessive use frequently occurred, the prevailing attitude has been to use the drugs for their sedative properties. By contrast, in the "street" the drugs often have been used for their euphoric and disinhibitive effects. Freqently they were used with alcohol to potentiate the disinhibitive effects of both substances. It is quite understandable then that the great majority of reports of violence with depressants is from their "street" or recreational use, not from their use in the home.

A word of caution. The available data on the relation of nonalcohol depressants to violence in the home is extremely limited. There is a possibility that there is underidentification and/or underreporting of instances where depressants contributed to partner abuse. With the increasing number and sophistication of surveys on violence in the home, the role of nonalcohol depressants, as well as other psychotropic drugs, will likely soon be more fully understood. In future surveys, attention should be given particularly to whether a substance increased irritability or quarrelsomeness, which precipitated a series of aggressive exchanges leading to partner abuse.

STIMULANTS

The most commonly used CNS stimulants include: amphetamines, cocaine, antidepressants, and convulsants. Stimulants, with the exception of depressants, have been associated with more violence against partners than any other class of substances (Goldstein, 1975). Amphetamines, in particular, have been associated with partner abuse, especially in combination with alcohol. Eisenberg and Michlow (1977) found that in 20% of wife batterings they surveyed, amphetamines were used prior to the beatings. In every case surveyed, the amphetamines were used in combination with alcohol. Amphetamines potentiate the effects of alcohol and allow the user to function under high dosages of alcohol which ordinarily would incapacitate him. The severity of assaults under a combination of amphetamines and alcohol is therefore likely to be greater than under either of the substances alone. The combination of amphetamines and barbiturates is similarly dangerous. As one heavy amphetamine user stated:

> Barbs are what make you really mean and nasty. It's the combination of the two. Once you've got enough goofers (barbiturates) so that you are ready to kill somebody, you have to shoot crank (amphetamines) so that you have enough energy to do it. It's the combination of the two that really tears your head apart. (Smith, 1972, pg. 213)

Although stimulants may contribute to partner abuse, in many instances they are used with no increase in violence (Leavitt, 1974). As in the case of depressants, stimulants may at times even alleviate aggressive feelings. Patients of the authors have indicated that when feeling frustrated or angry at their partners, they have taken stimulants to feel more confident and generally to feel better about themselves. Whether a greater or lesser degree of partner abuse results, is largely determined by premorbid personality, personality interactions, dosage levels, set, and setting.

Amphetamines

Amphetamines were first marketed in the 1930s as decongestants and soon were used to counteract fatigue and depression and to increase mental alertness. Amphetamine type substances include: amphetamine (e.g., Benzedrine); d-amphetamine (e.g., Dexedrine); and methamphetamine (e.g., Methedrine). There was little public concern about possible negative effects of amphetamines until the 1950s, with the advent of high-dosage intravenous use. Since the 1960s, widespread incidents have been reported of heightened excitability, aggressiveness, and violence (Grinspoon and Hedblom, 1975). Many other stimulants exist with properties similar to amphetamines, such as Preludin (phenmetrazine); Ritalin (methylphenidate); and Meratran (pipridrol). These substances are more expensive, less publicized, and less available than amphetamines, but differ little in other respects.

Premorbid Personality.   Aggression and violence due to amphetamine use are particularly likely in individuals with premorbid aggressive tendencies and problems of impulse control. Amphetamine users with latent schizophrenic tendencies also appear highly prone to violence associated with toxic psychosis. Ellinwood (1971) reviewed psychiatric evaluations of 13 persons who had committed homicide after taking large doses of amphetamines. Four of the individuals were noted to be highly impulsive and aggressive, even after withdrawal from amphetamines. Five were diagnosed as schizophrenic after withdrawal, and in three of these cases amphetamines had evidently precipitated the more extreme schizophrenic symptoms.

Many individuals, however, with no apparent personality abnormalities have evidenced aggression or violence during amphetamine use. In one of the earliest reports of negative effects of amphetamines, Davis (1947) found that the drug enhanced aggressiveness in apparently normal British servicemen. Connell (1958) observed hostility and aggressiveness in persons hospitalized for amphetamine-induced paranoid psychosis and noted that several of the persons showed normal personalities and backgrounds after withdrawal. In a review of the literature, Grinspoon and Hedblom (1975) discovered numerous reports of amphetamine-related aggression and violence in manifestly normal individuals. They concluded that personality disorders involving abnormal aggressivenes, lack of impulse control, unstable object relations, or paranoid tendencies may be exaggerated by amphetamines and result in violence. However, they emphasized that violence may also occur during amphetamine use by individuals with no evidence of premorbid personality disorder.

Personality Interactions.   Partner abuse may arise from many interdynamic conflicts in amphetamine using couples. In our clinical experience, a common center of conflict in these couples has been the need for a sense of competence and, at times, dominance, within the relationship. Amphetamine abusers who become abusive toward their partners often have a high premorbid aggressiveness which reflects poor personality integration and poor impulse control. The individuals have an extremely low sense of adequacy and self-worth and seek relationships in which the partner is more competent and dominant. The abusive individual desperately wants acceptance and recognition by the partner. However, when the individual achieves successes, such as promotions at work, the partner often feels threatened. As a consequence, the partner may undercut the individual's sense of achievement through not recognizing the accomplishment and in a variety of ways of "putting down" or diminishing the person. The abusive individal may turn to amphetamines and other psychoative substances in search of feelings of confidence and self-worth. Frustrations and resentments toward the partner remain, however, and under the influence of drug effects, episodes of aggressiveness and violence often occur.

Dosage.   Individuals may differ greatly in their reactions to the same dosage levels of amphetamines. Dosages as low as 40 milligrams have produced psychotic effects in nonexperienced users, while some experienced users have taken dosages of up to 5000 milligrams without toxic reactions (Smith, 1969).

Typically, low dosages of amphetamines will alleviate fatigue, facilitate assertiveness, enhance mental alertness, and promote feelings of mastery and self-confidence. Low-dosage use, however, may also engender aggressiveness in the form of easy irritability and hostile attitudes and may lead to use of higher dosages. High-dosage intravenous usage may produce a "rush" (comparable, metaphorically, to a pleasurable electric shock), fascination with one's thoughts and actions, and feelings of supreme mastery and confidence. But with such intravenous usage the likelihood of extreme aggressiveness or violence is particularly great.

Characteristic of high-dosage, intravenous use is the cyclic pattern of "runs" in which there are frequent amphetamine injections over 2-to 5-day periods. Initially, a "run" produces considerable euphoria and rapid, decisive thoughts and actions. These effects diminish after a few hours, however, and the user must take another dose to recapture them. With repeated injections, thoughts often become perseverative, and actions frequently become mechanical and repetitive. The user maintains a hyperactive state, however; he usually does not sleep during a run and shows only brief moments of calm or peace. This hyperactive state may lead to a form of aggression or violence that Carey and Mandel (1968) term a "reaching out." In the words of an official whom they interviewed:

> One of the main problems we've got to face is this damned aggressiveness. These amphetamine users, they're all this way. This is the common denominator. I've seen guys that pop fifty 10-milligram pills or shoot some Meth and they're just all over—they can't stand still—they just can't keep from doing things and they're jumping around all the time. If they've got something in their hand they'll hit you without realizing what they're doing and they'll—if they've got a flashlight they're likely to go like that (swings) and hit you with it. (p. 169)

As the run continues, the user may develop increasing suspiciousness and feelings of being watched, which evolve into delusions of persecution. Violence may then occur as a defensive reaction to imagined danger. Some person or event may be perceived as threatening, and the user may well react with force.

The user rarely eats during the run, and the combination of little nutrition and sleep may eventually result in physical exhaustion or a "crash." After the run, the individual may sleep for a day or more. Upon awakening, he is likely to be extremely irritable and depressed. Heated arguments may occur, and blows exchanged, over minor incidents (Carey and Mandel, 1968). In order to offset his negative feelings, the individual may again resort to amphetamines, and hence another run may begin. Additionally, some individuals, after coming down from the effects of the drug, particularly high doses, may commit suicide, due to the resultant depression.

Set.   An understanding and awareness of the possible effects of amphetamines can minimize the likelihood of aggression or violence. This is particularly true when paranoid ideation develops through amphetamine use. When the individual learns to expect feelings of suspiciousness, as well as delusions of persecution, he can then treat them in a "half-serious, half-humorous, game-playing" manner (Kramer, Fischman, and Littlefield, 1967). He is thus less likely to act upon paranoid feelings with assaultiveness.

Setting.   When one partner is using amphetamines, the other partner may provide support and help the user identify delusional thinking. When both partners are using amphetamines, however, the probability of partner abuse is greatly increased. The partners are less likely to be able to reassure each other, and are more prone to be provocative. Griffith (1966) describes amphetamine "parties" in which mutual grievances commonly erupted into intense arguments. Several persons would tease or "egg on" an individual, and rage reactions would then often occur. Similar aggressive interactions often occur when both partners use amphetamines in high dosages. The partners often become highly excitable, and when conflicts arise, they may be extremely caustic and belittling. Quick rage may result with one or both partners abusing the other.

Cocaine, Convulsants, Antidepressants

Cocaine is derived from coca leaves, which have been chewed for stimulant effects by South American Indians for at least 1200 years. Cocaine was isolated from coca leaves in 1860, and in the 1890s, cocaine became the first stimulant to be widely abused in the United States (Spotts and Shontz, 1980). When inhaled through the nose ("snorted"), cocaine may produce enhanced feelings of physical and mental power, along with feelings of increased self-confidence and well-being. However, the drug also may bring irritability and restlessness and, with high dosages, may cause tremors or convulsions. The drug has been associated with heightened aggression and violence, but not as commonly or with the same levels of intensity as amphetamines.

Ashley (1976) found that cocaine may be associated with irritability and verbal abuse, but rarely with physical abuse. Grinspoon and Bakalar (1976) reported similar findings and describe a woman whose husband had gone through a period of abusing various drugs, including cocaine. The woman stated that cocaine caused mainly verbal unpleasantness, while physical violence was associated with barbiturates. She viewed cocaine positively in spite of her husband's verbal abuse.

In cases where physical abuse does occur with cocaine use, premorbid personality is a predominant factor. Spotts and Shontz (1980) provided a detailed, phenomenological analysis of a sample of cocaine users. Several of the users reported having seen men become violent when using the drug, but pointed out that the "individuals exhibited the same pattern of uninhibited, antisocial behavior at all times" (p. 465). Grinspoon and Bakalar (1976) similarly conclude that "the drug can obviously exacerbate tendencies toward paranoia and violence that are already present in its users or encouraged by a criminal milieu" (p. 277).

Convulsant drugs, such as strychnine, can stimulate respiration and counteract the action of depressant drugs, but seldom are used clinically. Occasionally the drugs are placed in illicit drug preparations as unwanted substitutes for amphetamines or cocaine. Antidepressants, such as Elavil (amitriptyline) and Tofranil (imipramine), may be given to combat psychic depression. The last named drugs have relatively little abuse potential, for they have little influence in the behavior of nondepressed or "normal" persons (Julien, 1978).

NARCOTICS

The primary narcotics include: heroin, morphine, codeine, demerol, methadone, and opium. The narcotics may indirectly contribute greatly to partner abuse through heightened aggressiveness during withdrawal and through emotional stresses of the addictive lifestyle. The direct effects of the substances, however, are usually to reduce aggressiveness. The narcotics commonly produce a relaxed, drowsy state; and with intravenous injection, may initially produce a "rush" ("like a huge orgasm"), followed by a more prolonged "high" ("a profoundly heightened sense of well-being") (DeLong, 1972).

In a survey of 30 male heroin abuse patients in a Veterans Administration Medical Center, the authors found that 27 patients (90%) had been married or had lived with a woman. The mean age of the patients was 28, and the average length of the relationships was 2 years 7 months. Twenty-two of the patients with partners (81%) acknowledged having physically abused their partners, e.g., hitting them with fists or blunt objects. Twenty-six of the patients with partners (96%) reported having emotionally abused their partners, e.g., threatening them with physical harm; causing the partner's plans to fail. The patients indicated that very few instances of physical or emotional abuse occurred when they were high on narcotics. The greatest incidence of abuse occurred when they were high on other substances, particularly alcohol and barbiturates. Additionally, however, numerous violent incidents were reported for when they were in withdrawal and/or need of drugs.

Heroin

Heroin was first derived from morphine in 1874, but was not widely abused until the 20th century. At present, heroin is the most widely abused of all the narcotics. Considerable partner abuse has been reported for persons abusing heroin. Shainess (1977) emphasized that when the heroin abuser is in need of a "fix" is a time of danger for a wife and children. Shainess pointed out that the addicted person is more self-oriented, and that particularly when he is in need of drugs, others are likely to be an annoyance to him and to elicit quick rage. Taylor, Wilbur, and Osnos (1966) interviewed 16 heroin-involved couples and found that over half the heroin-abusing men had been violent toward their women. The women appeared to have accepted and resigned themselves to the violence, but appeared even more disturbed by the passive behaviors of their husbands when on drugs. The women resented bearing the full responsibilities of daily living while their husbands were "relaxed and happy in another world." (p. 589) Therefore, in addition to physical abuse, emotional abuse is particularly common in heroin-involved couples. As Taylor and associates noted, the lives of the women "were characterized by a constant series of medical, economic, legal, and social crises." (p. 589)

Premorbid Personality. Heroin abusers manifest a wide range of character traits; no single "addictive personality" has been identified. Many heroin abusers are highly aggressive and hostile, with histories of extensive antisocial and violent behavior prior to drug use (Khantzian, 1974; Wurmser, 1972). Others are fundamentally passive and unassertive, with strong withdrawal tendencies (Chein et al., 1964; Fort, 1966). For the drug abuser with heightened aggressiveness, heroin provides calming, relaxing effects, along with a sense of self-worth and competence. For the more passive, withdrawn individual, the enhanced feelings of self-worth may well be a primary incentive in the use of the drug. For both the aggressive and the passive user, the need to obtain funds for the drug typically requires considerable assertiveness and activity. The great majority of heroin users must constantly and aggressively pursue a series of demanding tasks to obtain funds for the drugs. As Preble and Casey (1969) point out:

> They (heroin abusers) are always on the move and must be alert, flexible, and resourceful. The surest way to identify heroin users in a slum neighborhood is to observe the way people walk. The heroin user walks with a fast, purposeful stride, as if he is late for an important appointment—indeed, he is. He is hustling (robbing or stealing), trying to sell stolen goods, avoiding the police, looking for a heroin dealer with a good bag (the street retail unit of heroin), coming back from copping (buying heroin), looking for a safe place to take the drug, or looking for someone who beat (cheated) him—among other things. He is, in short, *taking care of business.*" (p. 2)

If a person is severely passive and withdrawn, he is not likely to be able to maintain a heroin habit and may turn to less expensive drugs, such as alcohol or amphetamines. If the individual has less severely inhibited aggressive drives, with perhaps a passive overlay, the "hustling" life-style may provide a semistructured means or outlet for aggression. For the highly aggressive individual, the drug's effects afford brief periods of calm, while the tasks involved in obtaining the drug provide modifying, structuring influences on the expression of his aggression. However, the feelings of calm and of having structure might prevent the heroin abuser from seeking more adaptive means for the expression of aggression.

Personality Interactions.   The heroin abuser commonly seeks a partner who has strong needs to protect and nurture him. In his search, the heroin abuser often tries to recreate his original family pattern (Seldin, 1972). For a great many heroin abusers, the original family consisted of an overprotective and overindulgent mother and a passive father, who was frequently absent (Attardo, 1965; Chein and associates, 1964, Seldin, 1972). The partner of the heroin abuser often is initially attracted to the immaturity and the gentle, passive side of the individual

(Taylor, Wilbur, and Osnos, 1966). Conflicts arise, however, as the heroin abuser's demands soon strain the partner's emotional and financial resources. As Kaufmann and Kaufmann (1979) observe, "in the addict-spouse pair, there is frequently competition over who is sickest or most needy. This may be a source of many quarrels and continues when the addict is drug free." (p. 101)

If the heroin abuser marries a woman who is not part of the drug subculture, he faces added conflicts. As Seldin (1972) notes, if the heroin user "marries a woman who is 'not in the life,' he finds his antisocial values challenged. His wife and then his children present him with role expectations (for example, breadwinner) which he cannot meet. The marriage deteriorates within a very brief period of time." (p. 105)

Partner abuse frequently arises in the conflicts over being protected and nurtured. As Kaufmann and Kaufmann (1979) observed, spouses tend to provoke each other into escalating quarrels over meeting each others needs; quarrels which at times may be stopped only by pulling in a third party, such as an in-law or child. If the third party is not available, intense emotional and physical abuse may occur.

Heroin abusers have been found to be very cautious and selective with whom they associate and especially with whom they develop an intimate relationship (Saxon, Blaine, and Dennett, 1978). Once a strong commitment is established, the heroin abuser and his/her partner appear unusually willing to accept provocative and stressful behaviors from each other. In an interesting preliminary study of heroin-involved couples, Lewis et al. (1980) found a relationship between the degree of commitment between partners and their tolerance for receiving negative behaviors. The greater the commitment, the greater the acceptance of the partner's negative behaviors. Many relationships endure, therefore, despite partner abuse and the manifold stresses of the addict life-style.

Dosage.   Heroin has generally been found to reduce aggressiveness and to induce a drowsy relaxed state—a narcosis. There is some evidence, however, that under certain circumstances, there may be an increase in aggressive tendencies. Mirin, Meyer, and McNamee (1976) provided six detoxified addicts with self-regulated access to increasing dosages of heroin, on a locked ward, over a 10-day period. The investigators found that initially there was a decrease in levels of anxiety and somatic concerns, but with prolonged heroin use there was an increase in these levels. At the same time, the patients became more belligerent, negative, angry, and aggressive. It is likely that the locked-ward environment was an important factor. In home environments, the drug user may have opportunities to express or channel his aggressiveness in the demanding search for drugs. It is an important finding, however, that under certain circumstances, high anxiety levels, as well as aggressiveness, may be associated with prolonged use of the substance.

Set. Expectations regarding the pharmacological effects of heroin have little direct influence on aggression. Indirectly, an awareness of the cyclic effects of the drug may influence the occurrence of aggression by enabling the individual to avoid or to manage withdrawal symptoms. After 4 to 10 hours of abstinence, the user may experience intense agitation, restlessness, tremors, chills, and sweating. If he has not planned well to obtain a supply of drugs, or if his usual source is unexpectedly eliminated, he may act rashly to obtain a supply quickly. If, for example, he feels that his partner is voluntarily withholding drugs or money from him, anger and assault may occur (Tinklenberg and Stillman, 1970). Ironically, then, the absence of heroin—rather than the use of the drug itself—may result in aggression or violence.

Setting. Some heroin users are able to maintain their drug habit on legal or illegal earnings and thus place only moderate financial strain on the family. Other heroin users, however, exhaust their own resources and then drain the resources of the family. Deprivations in physical comforts and even necessities may result. Adequate diets may not be followed. Health care may be neglected. A general deterioration in the home environment may take place. In the context of such deterioration, frustrations and resentments often occur, leading to confrontations that readily may escalate to mutual aggressiveness and then violence.

Opium, Morphine, Codeine, Demerol, Methadone

Opium is obtained naturally from the opium poppy plant and was used as early as 3000 B.C. to treat headaches, colic, diarrhea, and other medical complaints. In the early 1800s, morphine and codeine were isolated from opium. The hypodermic needle was invented in 1856 and morphine began to be injected on a wide scale and, during the Civil War, became known as the "soldier's disease" (Julien, 1978). Demerol and methadone are wholly synthetic substances which were introduced in 1939 and 1945, respectively (Hoffman, 1975).

Opium, in its crude form, is so rarely used in the western world that it is of little concern for this chapter. Morphine has been widely prescribed for the relief of pain. Excessive use leads to addiction, and through cross-tolerance, morphine abuse often is associated with subsequent heroin abuse. Codeine is an extremely effective drug for the relief of cough and is much less potent than morphine. Due to its addictive potential, however, codeine has been replaced in nonprescription cough preparations by nonnarcotic cough suppressants, such as dextromellorphan, which have a low potential for compulsive use. Demerol is widely available commercially as an analgesic, and is probably the narcotic most frequently abused by physicians and others within the medical profession (Julien, 1978). Methadone is extensively used in the treatment of heroin abuse to override or "block" heroin's effects. In nonprescription ("nonmaintenance") dosages, however, methadone also can produce euphoria and can be addictive (DeLong, 1972).

In general, the direct pharmacological effects of morphine, codeine, demerol, and methadone is to reduce aggressiveness. When abused, the substances may indirectly contribute to partner abuse through a user's heightened irritability and aggressiveness during withdrawal and through his emotional and financial demands in maintaining his drug habit. In addition, the use of the substances may contribute to subsequent use and addiction to heroin, with all its negative impacts upon both the user and the partner.

HALLUCINOGENS

The principal hallucinogens are LSD (lysergic acid diethylamide), PCP (phencyclidine), marijuana, mescaline, DOM, Psilocybin, and Psilocyn. The hallucinogens, by themselves, are relatively rare contributors to violence against partners. Violence may occur, but usually represents a panic reaction to disturbing bodily sensations or to bizzare and grotesque images, often accompanied by paranoidal feelings. In the majority of cases, the hallucinogens either reduce aggressiveness or have little effect (Leavitt, 1974; National Commission on Marijuana and Drug Abuse, 1972). In instances where violence does occur, premorbid personality, set, and setting are especially important.

LSD

From 1943, when the psychoactive properties of LSD were discovered, until the early 1960s, there was little public concern about potential adverse reactions. During that early period, the drug was tested extensively in psychotherapy with relatively few reported negative occurrences (Cohen, 1960; Cohen and Ditman, 1963). In the mid-1960s there was a rapid growth in illicit use of LSD. This development was given considerable impetus from publicity attending use of the drug by Harvard professors Timothy Leary and Richard Alpert. In the "street use" of LSD, the drug frequently has been taken under poorly supervised conditions, in which dosage levels and drug quality were not fully known. Adverse reactions or "bad trips" from the drug were commonly reported and consisted primarily of panic reactions to the drug's effects. The user's behavior during a panic reaction was generally poorly organized but could inadvertently result in harm to himself or to others who may have been attempting to aid him. Suicides and homicides were infrequent, although some have been documented in the medical literature (Smart and Bateman, 1967).

Premorbid Personality.   Individuals with aggressive character traits and poor impulse control are especially prone to aggressive impulses and behavior while under the influence of LSD. In a laboratory setting, Klee (1963) administered doses of LSD up to 16 milligrams per kilogram (mg/kg) to several hundred volunteers who had no known history of psychiatric disturbances and who functioned well at work. He observed that some subjects felt overwhelmed by assaultive impulses and found it difficult or impossible to control their behavior; a majority of these subjects were particularly aggressive and impulsive to begin with.

In five LSD-related homicides described in the medical literature, premorbid personality disturbances were prevalent. In one case a 32-year-old male with a history of chronic paranoid schizophrenia stabbed his mother-in-law to death while he was under the influence of

LSD (Barter and Reite, 1969). In a second instance a 25-year-old female with premorbid psychotic depression killed her boyfriend with a knife 3 days after receiving LSD in psychotherapy (Knudson, 1965). In a third episode, a 22-year-old male with a paranoid character structure developed paranoid delusions under the influence of LSD and fled from the United States to Israel, where 8 days later he stabbed a stranger (Reich and Hepps, 1972). In a fourth occurrence a 22-year-old male, who was judged to have an undefined personality disorder, shot a girl friend to death 2 days after using LSD (Klepfisz and Racy, 1973). In a fifth episode a 24-year-old male, who had several previous arrests for assault during alcohol intoxication, shot a stranger to death while under the influence of both alcohol and LSD (Barter and Reite, 1969).

In at least four of the five cases just mentioned, premorbid personality appeared to play a dominant role in the occurrence of violence. Glickman and Blumenfield (1967) make the point that premorbid personality may be such an overriding factor in LSD-related homicides, suicides, and psychoses that the events would have occurred with or without the drug. Furthermore, they assert that the use of the drug may have delayed such events, through the individual's belief that the drug would help alleviate his emotional stress. With the small data base, it is not possible to confirm of deny Glickman and Blumenfield's hypotheses, but their assertions remain as alternative possibilities.

Personality Interactions. Personality interactions are an important factor in LSD-related partner abuse; however, they are usually overshadowed by the influence of dosage levels, premorbid personality, set, and setting. In our clinical work, no particular pattern of interpersonal conflict stands out as especially contributory to negative experiences under LSD. A great variety of conflicts may generate hostile, aggressive feelings. If a person has taken LSD when he is in a hostile mood, his "mental set" during drug use is liable to be adversely affected. As noted below, a negative mind "set" may readily lead to a "bad trip" and panic reactions, which may in turn lead to reactive aggression.

Dosage. In LSD dosages of .5 mg/kg and above, there commonly is an initial period, of up to a half-hour, in which somatic effects such as lightheadedness, chilliness, and nausea are experienced. Then alterations may occur in perceptions of the size and shape of objects and surroundings, and the individual may experience intense feelings of wholeness or oneness. Illusions may occur of brightly colored images, in varying patterns, moving across the perceptual field. There also may be hallucinations of beautiful objects or loving persons ("good trip") or of grotesque, terrifying demons or persons ("bad trip"). In the instance of a bad trip, ideas of reference and paranoid delusions are common (Wikler, 1976).

In a review of LSD's effects during psychotherapy, Cohen (1960) determined that adverse reactions tended to appear with dosages above 75 milligrams. A danger in the widespread use of blackmarket or "street" LSD is the possibility that someone will receive an unexpectedly high dosage of the drug. With the differing procedures used among illicit manufacturers of the drug, there may be considerable differences in drug potency. As Brecher and associates (1972) point out, an individual who has become used to the effects of a certain general dosage level may have an acute panic reaction if he takes an unusually high dosage. Just such an occurrence was suspected in one of the five homicides reported in the medical literature (Riech and Hepps, 1972).

Set. Preparedness for the LSD experience and a positive mood at the time of use are considered highly important in precluding adverse reactions. Leary, Metzner, and Alpert (1964) suggest that, before using LSD, a person take considerable time to put himself in a constructive frame of mind and in a favorable mood for the experience. Conflicts between partners are one of many possible sources of negative mind set. Long-standing or recent conflicts may leave a residue of hostile feelings of which the drug user may be only dimly or preconsciously aware. In contributing to a negative mind set, angry feeling may well add to the possibilities of a "bad trip" and panic reactions.

Setting. In unsupportive settings, there is a greatly increased likelihood of adverse reactions to LSD, perhaps resulting in injury to the user or to others. As has often been emphasized, a concerned person or guide should be present during an LSD experience, and the surroundings should be comfortable and free of interruptions (Leary, Metzner, and Alpert, 1964). In psychotherapeutic settings these conditions are generally observed. In nonpsychotherapeutic settings, when partners use LSD, many problems may arise. If the partner is unfamiliar with the drug's effects, the user may not get needed guidance and reassurance. If the partner acts aggressively to the drug user due to resentments over drug use or due to non-drug-related conflicts, the aggression may be highly disturbing. If the partner is also using LSD, the two individuals may not be able to offer guidance and reassurance when needed. If one of the partners should then develop adverse reactions to the drug, the negative responses are likely to be highly disturbing to the partner. With the occurrence of a bad trip or panic reaction, there is an increased likelihood that a person will harm himself or his partner, who may only be trying to help or restrain him. Partner abuse, then, would occur principally as an accidental or reactive consequence of the unfavorable drug experience.

PCP, Marijuana, Mescaline, DOM, Psilocybin, Psilocyn

PCP (phencyclidine) was first synthesized in 1926 and since the 1950s has been used effectively as a tranquilizer for animals. In the late 1960s, PCP was introduced in tablet form in the San Francisco drug subculture, but the drug soon lost favor due to its unpredictable adverse effects. In the 1970s, users found that smoking PCP allowed more accurate measure of dosage levels, and the drug became widely popular, principally among teen agers and young adults.

PCP has been reported to have such desired effects as a euphoric, dreamy detachment, a sense of oneness, and feelings of strength and invulnerability. Adverse reactions include: agitation, inability to speak, muscular rigidity, repetitive motor movements, gross incoordination, convulsions, stupor, and coma (Peterson and Stillman, 1978). Heightened aggressiveness and violence have frequently been reported for PCP. Most reports of violence have come from surveys of PCP users seeking emergency medical treatment for drug-induced toxic psychosis (Fauman and Fauman, 1978; Lerner and Burns, 1978; National Institute on Drug Abuse, 1978). A recent survey of adolescent PCP users in their home environments, revealed relatively low levels of aggressiveness and violence (Feldman, Agar, and Beschner, 1979).

PCP users tend to be youthful (ages 14 to 25) and to have never married. At present, therefore, the opportunities for partner abuse with

PCP appear to be far fewer than for most other psychoactive substances. Possibly there is greater use of PCP in adult populations than current surveys indicate. Perhaps in the future, PCP use will spread more extensively to adult populations. Currently, however, PCP, by itself, appears to have only moderate potential as a contributor to partner abuse.

Marijuana, mescaline, DOM, Psilocybin, and Psilocyn are all in current use in the United States. Marijuana is a mixture of crushed leaves and flowers of the hemp plant, *cannabis sativa,* and was used as early as 2700 B.C. Mescaline (peyote) is also an ancient drug, having been used in religious rites of the Aztecs. The peyote plant is a cactus with a small crown or "button" which is dried to form a hard brown disc, and then is ingested orally. DOM (also known as STP) is a synthetic compound very similar to mescaline. Psilocybin and psilocyn are obtained from mushrooms and have a long history of sacramental use in South America. The "magic mushrooms" are far less potent than LSD, but have similar psychoactive properties. Recent investigations of marijuana, mescaline, DOM, psilocybin, and psilocyn have revealed very low associations with violence (Julien, 1978; Leavitt, 1974; National Commission on Marijuana and Drug Abuse, 1972). As in the case of LSD, the relatively rare occurrences of violence are usually panic reactions to psychoactive effects of the drug or to intrusive external stimuli.

MULTIPLE DRUG USE

The influence of alcohol and drugs on partner abuse is often compounded by the multiple use of different substances. In the last decade, the incidence of multiple drug abuse has increased dramatically (Kaufman, 1977). A recent national collaborative study concluded that nearly 2 million adult Americans now abuse a variety of nonopiate drugs (Lau and Benvenuto, 1978). A far greater number would be expected to use multiple substances on an occasional (nonabusive) basis.

Drugs may be used in combination or in sequence. When used in combination, the substances may interact to produce more frequent or more extreme aggressiveness and violence that would likely occur from any of the substances alone. Alcohol and amphetamines are particularly dangerous. The alcohol may reduce impulse control, while the amphetamines provide energy and allow the individual to be active when he otherwise would collapse (Ellinwood, 1971). Barbiturates and amphetamines are a similarly potent combination, while LSD and amphetamines are also especially dangerous together. The amphetamines intensify and prolong the psychoactive effects of LSD and produce so many more panic reactions than LSD alone that the combination is commonly referred to as the "death trip" (Hoffman, 1975). One primary cause of the panic reactions is the muscular tremors and general physical agitation induced by the amphetamines. LSD and alcohol are not commonly used together, but the potential for violence is high when the disorienting effects of LSD are combined with reduced impulse control from alcohol. The potential hazards when they are taken together is well illustrated in the homicide described by Barter and Reite (1969), referred to earlier. In illicit drug preparations, PCP is often substituted for other hallucinogens, and at times for amphetamines and cocaine (Peterson and Stillman, 1978). The unfamiliar or unexpected effects of PCP may create panic reactions, depending especially upon dosage levels and the other substances included.

Certain drugs may interact to reduce the likelihood of aggression and violence. Heroin may be taken with amphetamines or cocaine (the traditional "speedball") to increase the "rush" from the heroin and to take the edge off the adverse effects of amphetamines such as hyperexcitability and tremors. Heroin may be used with alcohol to heighten the "high" from both drugs and may have calming effects on aggressiveness elicited by the alcohol alone. This last combination, however, is highly dangerous to the user, for the joint depressant effects of the substances greatly increase the potential for drug overdose and death. Just such effects were indicated in the deaths of rock stars Jimi Hendrix and Janis Joplin (Brecher et al., 1972).

Sequential use of drugs may reflect many factors, such as availability or cost of the drugs, curiosity, peer influences, or changing needs of the user. When one drug is used instead of another, there may be a change in the potential for partner abuse. As may be noted in the above reviews of depressants, stimulants, narcotics, and hallucinogens, one drug may have a greater or less potential for increased aggressiveness and violence than other drugs, depending especially upon premorbid personality, personality interactions, dosage levels, set, and setting. Additionally, individuals may use one drug in attempting to withdraw from another drug. For example, amphetamine or heroin users often use alcohol to offset extreme irritability, physical discomfort, or depression during amphetamine or heroin withdrawal. But persons who give up or "kick" amphetamines or heroin often become highly dependent on alcohol. Hence, the long-range effects may be a continuance or even an increase in aggressiveness or violence.

SUMMARY

Alcohol and drugs contribute to partner abuse through complex interactions of drug type with premorbid personality, personality interactions, dosage levels, "set," and "setting." The depressants and stimulants have the greatest influence on partner abuse, with alcohol being particularly influential. The narcotics have many indirect influences through withdrawal effects and the frequent emotional and financial strains of maintaining a drug habit. The hallucinogens have relatively little effect on physical abuse between partners. PCP has been often reported to create aggressive and violent outbursts, but, at present, the drug is most widely used by young people, who have not established marriages or continuing partner relationships.

Multiple drug use abuse is a major problem. The use of different substances in combination or in sequence has become common, and the interactive effects of the substances may be greater than their effects individually. Particularly dangerous combinations are: alcohol and amphetamines; barbiturates and amphetamines; alcohol and barbiturates; LSD or PCP and amphetamines. The use of multiple substances increases the difficulty of gauging the psychoactive effects. This is particularly true for illicit drug preparations, where dosage levels are often unknown and where certain substances, such as PCP, are often substituted for others. Unfamiliar or unexpected psychoactive effects may create panic reactions leading to reactive aggression.

There are two major groups of violence prone marriages. In the first group, partner abuse is principally due to the premorbid personality of the abusive individual. Substance use at times may alleviate aggressive tendencies. But under certain conditions of dosage, set, and setting, substance use may well heighten aggressive and violent behaviors. In the second group, partner abuse is produced by conflicts which arise within the relationship. Substance use may aggravate the conflicts by disrupting established balances or adjustments by which each partner's needs are met. Substance use may additionally impair functioning in coping with the conflicts, thus increasing the likelihood of aggressive or violent confrontations.

Although alcohol and drugs have frequently been identified in episodes of partner abuse, much additional research is needed on both the incidence of different substances used and the contributory influences of premorbid personality, personality interactions, dosage, set, and setting. An important additional focus for future research, is the use of alcohol and drugs by the partner of the abusing individual. Impressions from interviews with battered partners indicate extensive use of psychoactive substances. Barbiturates and other tranquilizers are particularly common. Abused partners frequently appear to be self-medicating themselves to attempt to cope with the stress of aggressive and violent occurrences, or with the continuing threat of such episodes. The use of psychoactive substances as coping mechanisms may lead to habituation and addiction, but also may delay a person from taking more direct action in either changing or disengaging from abusive patterns. Information is needed, therefore, on what particular substances are used by the battered partner, and in what specific contexts.

The literature on partner abuse is growing rapidly. The perspectives in the above chapter are intended both to set forth current understandings on the potential influences of alcohol and drugs and to stimulate future investigations. In the 1970s, much important work was done in drawing attention to the greatly neglected problem of partner abuse. In the current decade, it is anticipated that continued advances will be made in identifying the roles of the multiple influences on partner abuse; particularly the role of alcohol and drug use.

REFERENCES

Appleton, W. The battered woman syndrome. *Annals of Emergency Medicine,* 1980, **9,** 84–91.

Ashley, R. *Cocaine: It's History, Uses, and Effects.* New York: Warner Books, 1976.

Attardo, N. Psychodynamic factors in the mother-child relationship in adolescent drug addition: A comparison of mothers of schizophrenics and mothers of normal adolescent sons. *Psychotherapy and Psychosomatics,* 1965, **13,** 249–55.

Bach, G. R. and Goldberg, H. *Creative Aggression.* New York: Avon Books, 1974.

Barry, H. Alcohol. In *Drug Abuse: Clinical and Basic Aspects,* S. N. Pradhan and S. N. Dutta (eds.), St. Louis: C. V. Mosby Co., 1977.

Barter, J. T., and Reite, M. Crime and LSD: The insanity plea. *American Journal of Psychiatry,* 1969, **126**, 531-37.

Bayles, J. A. Violence, alcohol problems and other problems in disintegrating families. *Journal of Studies on Alcohol,* 1978, **39**, 551-53.

Bennett, R. M., Buss, A. H., and Carpenter, J. A. Alcohol and human physical aggression. *Quarterly Journal of Studies on Alcohol,* 1969, **30**, 870-76.

Borgman, R. D. Medication abuse by middle-aged women. *Social Casework,* 1973, **54**, 526-32.

Brahen, L. S. Housewife drug abuse. *Journal of Drug Education,* 1973, **3**, 13-24.

Brecher, E. M., and Editors of *Consumer Reports. Licit and Illicit Drugs: The Consumers Union Report on Narcotics, Stimulants, Depressants, Inhalants, Hallucinogens, and Marijuana—Including Caffeine, Nicotine, and Alcohol.* Boston: Little, Brown & Co., 1972.

Brown, S. A., Goldman, M. S., Inn, A., and Anderson, L. R. Expectations of reinforcement from alcohol: Their domain and relation to drinking patterns. *Journal of Consulting and Clinical Pyschology,* 1980, **48**, 419-26.

Carey, J. T., and Mandel, J. A San Francisco Bay Area "speed scene." *Journal of Health and Social Behavior,* 1968, **9**, 164-74.

Carlson, B. E. Battered women and their assailants. *Social Work,* 1977, **22**, 455-60.

Chein, L., Gerard, D. L., Lee, R. S., and Rosenfeld, E. *The raod to H: Narcotics, Delinquency, and Social Policy.* New York: Basic Books, 1964.

Cohen, S. Lysergic acid diethylamide: Side effects and complications. *Journal of Nervous and Mental Disease,* 1960, **130**, 30-40.

Cohen, S., and Ditman, K. S. Prolonged adverse reactions to lysergic acid diethylamide. *Archives of General Psychiatry,* 1963, **8**, 475-80.

Connell, P. H. *Amphetamine Psychosis.* London: Oxford University Press, 1958.

Cooper, J. R. (ed.) *Sedative-Hypnotic Drugs: Risks and Benefits.* Rockville, Md.: National Institute on Drug Abuse, 1977.

Davis, D. R. Psychomotor effects of analeptics and their relation to "fatigue" phenomena in air-crew. *British Medical Bulletin,* 1947, **5**, 43-45.

Delong, J. V. The drugs and their effects. In *Dealing with Drug Abuse: A Report to the Ford Foundation,* P. M. Wald and P. B. Hutt (eds.), New York: Praeger, 1972.

Dutta, S. N. Sedative-Hypnotics. In *Drug Abuse: Clinical and Basic Aspects,* S. N. Pradhan and S. N. Dutta (eds.), St. Louis: C. V. Mosby Co., 1977.

Eisenberg, S. E. and Micklow, P. L. The assaulted wife: Catch 22 revisited. *Women's Rights Law Reporter,* 1977, **3-4**, Newark, N.J., Rutgers University School of Law.

Ellinwood, E. H. Assault and homicide associated with amphetamine abuse. *American Journal of Psychiatry,* 1971, **127**, 1170-75.

Fauman, M. A. and Fauman, B. J. The psychiatric aspects of chronic phencyclidine use: A study of chronic PCP users. In *Phencyclidine (PCP) Abuse: An Appraisal,* R. C. Peterson and R. C. Stillman (eds.), Rockville, Md.: National Institute on Drug Abuse, 1978.

Feldman, H. W., Agar, M. H. and Beschner, G. M. *Angle Dust: An Ethnographic Study of PCP Users*. Lexington, Mass.: Lexington Books, 1979.

Fleming, J. B. *Stopping Wife Abuse: A Guide to the Emotional, Psychological, and Legal Implications for the Abused Woman and Those Helping Her*. Garden City, N.Y.: Doubleday/Anchor Books, 1979.

Fort, J. P., Jr. Heroin addiction among young men. In *Narcotic Addiction*, J. A. O'Donnell and J. C. Ball (eds.) New York: Harper & Row, 1966.

Gayford, J. J. Wife battering: A preliminary survey of 100 cases. *British Medical Journal* (January 1975), pp. 194-197.

Gelles, R. J. *The Violent Home: A Study of Physical Aggression Between Husbands and Wives*. Beverly Hills, Cal.: Sage Publications, 1972.

Gerson, L. W. Alcohol-related acts of violence: Who was drinking and where the acts occurred. *Journal of Studied on Alcohol*, 1978, **39**, 1294-96.

Glickman, L., and Blumenfield, M. Psychological determinants of "LSD reactions." *Journal of Nervous and Mental Disease*, 1967, **145**, 79-83.

Goldstein, J. H. *Aggression and Crimes of Violence*. New York: Oxford University Press, 1975.

Griffith, J. A study of illicit amphetamine drug traffic in Oklahama City. *American Journal of Psychiatry*, 1966, **123**, 560-69.

Grinspoon, L. and Bakalar, J. B. *Cocaine: A Drug and its Social Evolution*. New York: Basic Books, 1976.

Grinspoon, L., and Hedblom, P. *The Speed Culture: Amphetamine Use and Abuse in America*. Cambridge, Mass.: Harvard University Press, 1975.

Hanks. S. E., and Rosenbaum, C. P. Battered women: A study of women who live with violent alcohol-abusing men. *American Journal of Orthopsychiatry*, 1977, **47**, 291-306.

Hoffman, F. G. *A Handbook on Drug and Alcohol Abuse: Biomedical Aspects*. New York: Oxford University Press, 1975.

Julien, R. M. *A Primer of Drug Action*. San Francisco: W. H. Freeman & Co., 1978.

Kaufman, E. Polydrug abuse or multidrug misuse: It's here to stay. *British Journal of Addictions*, 1977, **72**, 339-47.

Kaufmann, P. N. and Kaufmann, E. From multiple family therapy to couples therapy. In *Family Therapy of Drug and Alchol Abuse*, E. Kaufmann and P. N. Kaufmann (eds.), New York: Gardner Press, 1979.

Khantzian, E. J. Opiate addiction: A critique of theory and some implications for treatment. *American Journal of Psychotherapy*, 1974, **28**, 59-71.

Klee, G. D. Lysergic acid diethylamide (LSD-25) and ego functions. *Archives of General Psychiatry*, 1963, **8**, 461-74.

Klepfisz, A., and Racy, J. Homicide and LSD. *Journal of the American Medical Association*, 1973, **223**, 429-30.

Knudsen, K. Homicide after treatment with lysergic acid diethylamide. *Acta Psychiatrica Scandinavica*, 1965, **Supplement 180**, 389-95.

Kramer, J. C., Fischman, V. S., and Littlefield, D. C. Amphetamine abuse: Pattern and effects of high doses taken intravenously. *Journal of the American Medical Association*, 1967, **201**, 305-09.

Langley, R. and Levy, R. C. *Wife beating: The Silent Crisis.* New York: Simon & Schuster Div. of Gulf & Western Co., 1977.

Lau, J. P. and Benvenuto, J. Three national estimates of prevalence of nonopiate drug abuse. In *Polydrug Abuse: The Results of a National Collaborative Study,* D. R. Wesson, A. S. Carlin, K. M. Adams, and G. Beschner (eds.), New York: Academic Press, 1978.

Leary, T., Metzner, R., and Alpert, R. The psychedelic experience: A manual based on the Tibetan book of the dead. New York: Citadel Press, 1964.

Leavitt, F. *Drugs and Behavior.* Philadelphia: W. B. Saunders Co., 1974.

Lerner, S. E. and Burns, R. S. Phencyclidine use among youth: History, epidemiology, and acute and chronic intoxication. In *Phencyclidine (PCP) Abuse: An Appraisal.* R. C. Peterson and R. C. Stillman (eds.), Rockville, Md.: National Institute on Drug Abuse, 1978.

Lewis, R. A., Filsinger, E. E., Conger, R., and McAvoy, P. (Arizona State University.) The quality of love relationships among heroin-involved couples. Paper presented at the First World Congress of Victimology, Washington, D.C. August, 1980.

Martin, D. *Battered Wives.* New York: Simon & Schuster Div. of Gulf & Western Co., 1976.

McNamee, H. B., Mello, N. K., and Mendelson, J. Experimental analysis of drinking patterns of alcoholics: Current psychiatric observations. *American Journal of Psychiatry,* 1968, **124,** 1063–69.

Menninger, K., Mayman, M., and Pruyser, P. *The Vital Balance.* New York: Viking Press, 1963.

Mirin, S. M., Meyer, R. E., and McNamee. H. B. Psychopathology, craving, and mood during heroin acquisition: An experimental study. *International Journal of the Addictions,* 1976, **11,** 525–44.

National Commission on Marijuana and Drug Abuse. *Marijuana: A Signal of Misunderstanding.* Washington, D.C.: U.S. Government Printing Office, 1972.

National Institute on Drug Abuse (NIDA). *Phencyclidine—PCP: Report Series 14, No. 2.* Washington D.C.: U.S. Government Printing Office, 1978.

National Institute on Drug Abuse (NIDA). *CNS Depressants: Technical papers, Number 1.* Rockville, Md.: National Clearinghouse for Drug Abuse Information, 1974.

Nicol, A. R., Gunn, J. C., Gristwood, J., Foggitt, R. H., and Watson, J. P. The relationship of alcoholism to violent behavior resulting in long-term imprisonment. *British Journal of Psychiatry,* 1973, **123,** 46–51.

Paredes, A. The history of the concept of alcoholism. In *Alcoholism: Interdisciplinary Approaches to an Enduring Problem.* R. E. Tarter and A. A. Sugerman (eds.), Reading, Mass.: Addison-Wesley, 1976.

Peterson, R. C. and Stillman, R. C. Phencyclidine: An overview. In *Phencyclidine (PCP) Abuse: An Appraisal.* R. C. Peterson and R. C. Stillman (eds.), Rockville, Md.: National Institute on Drug Abuse, 1978.

Pittman, D. J. and Handy, W. Patterns in criminal aggravated assault. *Journal of Criminal Law, Criminology, and Police Science,* 1964, **55,** 462–70.

Pizzey, E. *Scream Quietly or the Neighbors Will Hear.* London: If Books, 1974.

Pokorny, A. D. Human violence: A comparison of homicide, aggravated assault, suicide, and attempted suicide. *Journal of Criminology, and Police Science,* 1965, **56,** 488–97.

Preble, E., and Casey, J. J., Jr. Taking care of business: The heroin user's life on the street. *International Journal of Addictions,* 1969, **4,** 1–24.

Reich, P., and Hepps, R. B. Homicide during a psychosis induced by LSD. *Journal of the American Medical Association,* 1972, **219,** 869–71.

Richardson, D. C. and Campbell, J. L. Alcohol and wife abuse: The effects of alcohol on attributions of blame for wife abuse. *Personality and Social Psychology Bulletin,* 1980, **6,** 51–56.

Roy, M. A research project probing a cross-section of battered women. In *Battered Women: A Psychosociological Study of Domestic Violence,* M. Roy (ed.), New York: Van Nostrand Reinhold Co., 1977.

Saxon, S., Blaine, J. D., and Dennett, C. P. Compulsive heroin use and interpersonal orientation. *International Journal of the Addictions,* 1978, **13,** 349–58.

Seldin, N. E. The family of the addict: A review of the literature. *International Journal of the Addictions,* 1972, **7,** 97–107.

Shainess, N. Psychological aspects of wifebattering. In *Battered Women: A Psychosociological Study of Domestic Violence,* M. Roy (ed.), New York: Van Nostrand Reinhold Co., 1977.

Shupe, L. M. Alcohol and crime: A study of the urine alcohol concentration found in 882 persons arrested during or immediately after the commission of a felony. *Journal of Criminal Law and Criminology,* 1954, **44,** 661–64.

Smart, R. G., and Bateman, K. Unfavorable reactions to LSD: A review and analysis of the available case reports. *Canadian Medical Association Journal,* 1967, **97,** 1214–21.

Smith, D. E. Analysis of variables in high dose methamphetamine dependence. *Journal of Psychedelic Drugs,* 1969, **2,** 132–37.

Smith, D. E. and Wesson, D. R. *Uppers and Downers.* Englewood Cliffs, N.J.: Prentice-Hall, 1973.

Smith, R. C. Compulsive methamphetamine abuse and violence in the Haight-Asbury District. In *Current Concepts in Amphetamine Abuse,* E. H. Ellinwood and S. Cohen (Eds.), Rockville, Md.: National Institute of Mental Health, 1972.

Spotts, J. V. and Shontz, F. C. *Cocaine Users: A Representative Case Approach.* New York: The Free Press, 1980.

Steinmetz, S. K. The battered husband syndrome. *Victimology: An International Journal,* 1978, **2,** 499–509.

Symonds, M. The psychodynamics of violence-prone marriages. *American Journal of Pyschoanalysis,* 1978, **38,** 213–22.

Tamerin, J., and Mendelson, J. H. The psychodynamics of chronic inebriation: Observations of alcoholics during the process of drinking in an experimental group setting. *American Journal of Psychiatry,* 1969, **125,** 886–99.

Taylor, S. D., Wilbur, M., and Osnos, R. The wives of drug addicts. *American Journal of Psychiatry,* 1966, **123,** 585–91.

Tinklenberg, J. R., and Stillman, R. C. Dug use and violence. In *Violence and the Struggle for Existence.* D. N. Daniels, M. F. Gilula, and F. M. Ochberg (eds.), Boston: Little, Brown & Co., 1970.

Voss, H. L., and Hepburn, J. R. Patterns in criminal homicide in Chicago. *Journal of Criminal Law, Criminology, and Police Science,* 1968, **59**, 499–508.

Walker, L. E. *The Battered Woman.* New York: Harper & Row, 1979.

Wesson, D. R. and Smith, D. E. *Barbiturates: Their Use, Misuse, and Abuse.* New York: Human Services Press, 1977.

Wikler, A. Drug dependence. In *Clinical Neurology,* Vol. 2, A. B. Baker and L. H. Baker (eds.), New York: Harper & Row, 1976.

Wolfgang, M. E. *Patterns in Criminal Homicide.* Philadelphia: University of Pennsylvania Press, 1958.

Wurmser, L. Methadone and the craving for narcotics: Observations of patients on methadone maintenance in psychotherapy. *Proceedings of the 4th National Conference on Methadone Treatment,* 1972, **4**, 525–28.

4. Effects of Environmental and Nutritional Factors on Potential and Actual Batterers

Alexander G. Schauss, M.A.
Director, American Institute for Biosocial Research,
Tacoma, Washington

A careful review of the related literature on battering reveals relatively scant attention to nutritional and environmental factors involved in the etiology of battering. In recent years, studies have been conducted to supercede anecdotal reports of the importance of considering nutritional and environmental factors on potential and actual battering behavior.

Various nutritional and related biochemical imbalances, particularly of neurohormones, and environmental sensitivities, can indirectly or directly contribute to battering behavior. There is no doubt that societal values and expectations play a strong role in battering behavior. However, one must begin to wonder why an increasing number of battering cases continue to come to the attention of social-service and law-enforcement agencies in the face of an increasing awareness of this problem by the public. Of even greater concern to the clinician should be the question of why certain batterers continue to violate their mate in spite of sometimes substantial therapy and supportive services.

DIAGNOSING FOR PHYSIOLOGICAL FACTORS

A number of studies appearing in the *Archives of General Psychiatry* clarify the reasons why a complete physiological screen of the potential or actual batterer, and even, at times, the victim, might be of considerable value to understanding some of the dynamics contributing to unwanted behavior. Three studies reported in 1978, 1979, and 1980, in the *Archives of General Psychiatry,* and confirmed in similar studies reported in the *British Journal of Psychiatry* and the *Lancet,* indicate that there may exist an unrecognized medical illness in seriously mentally ill individuals, either directly causing or greatly exacerbating their symptoms.[1-6] Although this may not seem to relate directly to batterers, experience at the American Institute for Biosocial Research in Tacoma, Washington, has indicated that a complete physiological workup of actual or potential batterers can be of significant value in over 43% of such referrals. As reported by Richard C. Hall, et al., in the *Archives of General Psychiatry,*[3] the Institute's experience has confirmed the value of the 34-panel automated blood-chemistry analysis and routine urinalysis. However, several emergent diagnostic techniques have been proven to complement and even isolate factors normally overlooked by both the blood or urine screens, namely, hair trace mineral and metal analysis, and a complete computer-analyzed nutritional evaluation. Using a combination of the above-mentioned techniques, along with a complete physical examination, can prove highly valuable in uncovering those physiological factors directly or indirectly contributing to some battering behavior.

As reported in the *American Journal of Clinical Nutrition*[7] and other studies, hair is a cellular product excreted by the body capable of revealing valuable data about the metabolic balance of an individual. Studies have shown the hair to be reflective of a person's nutritional environment, including absorption of protein, carbohydrate, fat, vitamins, and particularly, minerals and toxic metals.[8,9] Whereas blood values inform the health professional what is in the blood, hair analysis provides a record of how the body uses, stores, and disposes of some essential and nonessential elements. More importantly, the technique is noninvasive, inexpensive, and, in the case of heavy metals, more reliable than blood tests in chronic cases. This is not true in acute transient cases. Two problems still remain in hair analysis: validity data is limited and interpretation can be difficult for untrained behavioral and medical scientists.

Hair specimen sampling is done by cutting a gram of hair from the nape area of the head and having the sample analyzed by a licensed laboratory. Such labs dissolve the hair specimen into a liquid which is evaluated by an argon-supported inductively coupled plasma technique allowing for analytical atomic emission spectroscopy.[10] Using an atomic emission polychromator, quantitative elemental analyses by plasma emission spectroscopy can be used for determining the levels of between 20 and 25 elements for diagnostic studies. Knowing the levels and ratios of these elements in the body can provide a valuable adjunctive tool to understanding the total body chemistry of an individual. This diagnostic tool, in conjunction with a complete computer analyzed nutritional intake study and other physiological assessment techniques, can provide valuable information about both the existence of a serious biochemical imbalance and its possible etiology.

A nutritional intake study evaluates the dietary consumption patterns and estimated nutrient intake as compared to nutrient data requirements derived from current nutritional-medical literature.[11] These comparisons, when considering for the individual's height, weight, age, gender, and activity level, result in a discussion guide recommending dietary modifications.[12-19] In comparing our analysis of over 600 normals to batterers, we have found a consistent pattern of either nutrient intake deficiencies or overconsumption malnutrition. The following case histories will illustrate the value of both the hair trace mineral and metal analysis and computerized nutritional intake study.

In a client who objected to having a blood analysis performed, a hair trace mineral and metal analysis, nutritional intake evaluation, medical and psychiatric history, and physical examination were completed. This male, aged 26, was referred to us for evaluation by his wife because of incessant ''wife-beating,'' which had become progressively more serious prior to referral. An interview revealed a polite and socially skillful male. He had recently completed several months of group therapy at a local program for abusive spouses. Although he learned various coping skills in these sessions, he admitted to losing his temper more frequently, particularly toward the end of each week. For 5 years, he and a brother had been managing a successful motorcycle shop. He enjoyed repairing motorcycles and automobiles and considered himself a "grease monkey." He drank a considerable amount of coffee and smoked more than two packs of cigarettes a day. His intake of alcohol was minimal, except toward the end of the week, when "his nerves felt tingly." He used no drugs except for an occasional aspirin.

Hair analysis revealed significantly elevated levels (toxic range) of lead (50 ppm), mercury (5.9 ppm), cadmium (2.8 ppm), and aluminum (37 ppm). While his iron level was found to also be elevated, his zinc, sodium, and potassium levels were significantly low. The latter two elements would suggest adrenal stress and impairment. All of these element imbalances were found to be of clinical value, particularly the elevated levels of the heavy metal neurotoxins, lead, cadmium, mercury, and aluminum. Later intracellular blood studies confirmed these findings.

Just as syphilis was once the "great imitator" of various disease states, so lead is known to cause a virtually unlimited number of cellular perturbations.[20] Signs and symptoms of lead toxicity include: depression, insomnia, fatigue, nervousness, irritability, dizziness, confusion, disorientation, anxiety, temper tantrums, impaired adrenal gland function, and fearfulness.[21,22] Subclinical mercury toxicity can induce: nervousness, insomnia, loss of memory, lack of self-control, irritability, anxiety, loss of self-confidence, depression, fatigue, headaches, emotional instability, and forgetfulness.[22] Cadmium's primary symptoms are fatigue and hypertension, while aluminum is, in rare cases, related to hyperkinesis, senile dementia, and even psychosis. Clearly, the impact of elevated levels of several of these neurotoxins could have a direct bearing on the husband's behavior.

This batterer's computerized nutritional intake analysis revealed other significant factors. In comparison to the Recommended Dietary Allowance (RDA),[23] his dietary intake was deficient in folic acid, manganese, and Vitamin A. Further, he was found to be below the optimum intake levels for riboflavin (Vitamin B_2), pyridoxine (Vitamin B_6), biotin, magnesium, Vitamin E, inositol, Vitamin C, thiamine (Vitamin B_1), pantothenic acid, niacin, para-aminobenzoic acid (PABA), molybdenum, Vitamin B_{12}, bioflavinoids, vanadium, and fiber. Both the three nutrients found to be below the RDA and 11 of the 15 nutrients below the optimum levels have been determined by researchers to be involved in central nervous system functioning.[24-26] He was found to have an excessive intake of refined carbohydrates, cholesterol, sodium, protein, and calories. His refined carbohydrate consumption included 28 teaspoons of refined sugar per day.

He was first instructed to call upon the local environmental health department to inspect his premises for the levels of lead, mercury, cadmium, aluminum, and other harmful elements and compounds. They discovered his place of work to contain unsafe levels of both lead and cadmium. His employer was given 30 days to improve conditions for his employees. It was further suggested to the husband to abstain from the ingestion of foods from lead-soldered cans, since it had been suggested by studies at the California Institute of Technology's ultra-clean environmental testing center that lead concentrations in such contaminated food was as much as 10,000-fold above that found in uncanned foods.[20]

With the cooperation of his spouse, the husband's diet was modified to enrich the levels of missing nutrients through a combination of more natural unrefined and unprocessed foods and nutritional supplements. The supplements utilized were particularly of the "detoxifying" types, including: Vitamin C, because of its demonstrated ability to enhance the body's natural affinity to eliminate neurotoxins;[27] selenium and zinc, which bind up cadmium and mercury; and, the sulfhydryl rich amino acids, methionine, cysteine, and cystine. These latter nutrients are quite rich in beans, eggs, onions, and garlic.

Careful monitoring of his urinary excretion levels of the heavy metal neuro-toxins, indicated progressively more and more of the heavy metals leaving his body. In turn, he reported less anxiety, more restful sleep, and a more controlled temper. Within 3 weeks of commencing treatment, his wife reported a dramatic improvement in their relationship. He returned to therapy 1 month after treatment. After 1 year, he has not physically abused his wife once. Retesting of his tissue levels, through hair analysis, 9 months after treatment, revealed that his lead, mercury, cadmium, and aluminum levels were all markedly improved, only cadmium remaining at an undesirably elevated level. As a sidelight, many of the employees at the motorcycle shop reported an increased sense of well-being within 2 months after steps were taken by the owner and management to improve the working environment according to guidelines of the Occupational Health and Safety inspector for the Environmental Health Department.

In three years of using hair trace mineral and metal analysis and the computerized nutritional intake study, in combination with the other mentioned diagnostic techniques, frequent significant findings have been made. Another example would be the following case.

This subject was a male, 20 years of age, referred to the Institute for rage reactions, the last three resulting in physical abuse of his wife of 2 years. She was considering divorce and felt that the Institute's evaluation would be the last resort before formally filing separation papers. Her husband completed a full physical examination, including hair analysis, nutritional intake evaluation, blood analysis, and urinanalysis. Because he had reported nine of ten common symptoms associated with nutritionally induced chronic endocrinopathy on the Nutrition Behavior Inventory,[28] he was given a glucose tolerance test of 6 hours. Blood was drawn whenever reported symptoms appeared. (This is not commonly done by most physicians, who prefer to draw a blood sample only on the hour. Unfortunately, this often misses the more severe blood-sugar drops, therefore missing a significant finding). A diagnosis of reactive hypoglycemia resulted. Twenty minutes after blood was drawn at 4 hours, his blood sugar dropped from 84 to 48. During this period, he became increasingly agitated and difficult to manage. At one point, he made a threatening gesture at one of the nurses in the clinic. When a male attendant entered the room, he returned to his chair. A few minutes later, he threatened the nurse with bodily harm "when she went home." At the conclusion of the test, he swore that he never said anything to the nurse and could think of no reason for having so acted. In a previous work, this author has reported on countless medical and scientific references involving acts of violence in which the perpetrator reported a complete loss of memory of the violent act.[29] Since reference to such "temporary amnesia" was found in medical journals persistently beginning in 1869 to the present, in six languages, it appears that this phenomena is more than the efforts of the perpetrator to play "dumb." In several infamous cases reported in both the United States and Great Britain, lawyers have successfully provided clinical proof that the assailant went through a period of temporary amnesia, during which time the heinous crime was committed. More recently, O'Banion and Greenberg have videotaped such remarkable changes in personality and emotional lability during single-subject studies to measure the behavioral effects of various foods.[30] Selecting individuals with sensitivities to specific foods, they were offered either nonreactive or a combination of reactive and nonreactive foods in alternating 6-day cycles. Behavioral and physiological measures were taken during these phases. Their data indicated a strong functional relationship between both behavioral and physiological changes and the varied diets.

The man's dietary intake evaluation revealed 15 nutrients below the RDA: Vitamin D, niacin, calcium, copper, iodine, Vitamin A, thiamine, pyridoxine, magnesium, manganese, Vitamin E, riboflavin, folic acid, potassium, and zinc. Additionally, he was below optimum levels for 19 other nutrients, including: valine, PABA, inositol, selenium, vanadium, bioflavinoids, isoleucine, methionine, Vitamin K, Vitamin B_{12}, phosphorous, nickel, lysine, threonine, pantothenic acid, biotin, Vitamin C, chromium, and molybdenum. His diet was found to be high in refined carbohydrates and fat. Since he reported no abuse of refined sugar (confirmed), the possibility of a sensitivity to either food(s) in his diet or a chemical(s) or a combination of both, was not ruled out. However, an analysis of his hair test results revealed a significant finding that relates to hyperaggressive and hyperkinetic behavior.

His hair analysis found a very high copper level of 91 ppm with evidence of associated zinc deficiency. Our research confirms the findings of Pfeiffer et al.[24] and Schroeder[31] that significantly elevated copper levels with associated zinc deficiency in tissue, such as hair, is related to hyperaggressive and hyperkinetic behavior. We have seen this in numerous children so labeled taking Ritalin[R]. Once the copper levels were returned to normal through zinc therapy, medication was eliminated and normal behavior exhibited. Frequently, the rage reactions diminished within 2 weeks and stopped within 1 month after treatment. Therefore, a program of zinc therapy was initiated. Once begun, a copper blood serum analysis revealed elevated levels. Zinc compounds are frequently used in this type of treatment since zinc and copper are antagonists. The higher the zinc level, the lower the copper. However, this should not be done by other than a trained health professional because the copper level can be driven too low resulting in too low a copper level, which can also result in hyperkinesis and (more rarely) in aggressive behavior.

Within 3 weeks the husband reported a marked improvement in behavior and a heightened sense of well-being. His Nutrition Behavior Inventory score had dropped significantly. Six months after treatment began, a second hair analysis revealed a copper level of 35 ppm, well within the normal range. Although only speculative, it was believed that he absorbed excess levels of copper from copper plumbing in his home due to insufficiency of zinc and other micronutrients in his diet. Diet modification shortly after zinc therapy commenced resulted in a more balanced nutrient-rich diet.

When evaluating a case, it is essential to attempt to relate the emergence of the abusive behavior with some change in activity or modification in lifestyle. Although many examples can be offered, one case sufficiently illustrates this point.

A husband came to the Institute threatening to send his wife to a state mental hospital because "she was losing her mind." Earlier in the week she had assaulted him with a butcher knife shortly after he arrived home from work. He became frightened by her actions since he knew she was taking Valium. The Valium was prescribed to her several weeks earlier by their family physician to "calm her nerves." We discovered during the course of the interview that he had brought her a coffee percolator approximately 3 months earlier. Interestingly, he suddenly realized that there might be a connection between the two. He called his wife at home and asked her how many cups of coffee she thought she was drinking a day. She replied, "between 15 and 20 cups." He wondered aloud whether this was not the cause of her problem. He recalled that she normally would not consume more than 3 or 4 cups of caffeinated coffee a day. We agreed that he might have discovered the cause and urged him to remove the percolator, consult his doctor, because from experience we knew that sudden caffeine withdrawal could result in severe headaches. After 3 days without coffee, he called to report that his wife was back to normal and had "given up coffee for life." I mention this seemingly obvious case history because we have constantly seen professionals neglect the possibility of caffeinism in the etiology of battering or many other behavior disorders. This continues to be true even though the relationship between anxiety and caffeinism have been reported in such periodicals as the *American Journal of Psychiatry, Journal of the American Medical Association, Science,* and the *New England Journal of Medicine.* Medication is no substitute for eliminating an offending food or beverage.

MULTIPLE ETIOLOGIES

As indicated earlier, and in other chapters of this book, battering behavior presents a complex interaction of physical, mental, and societal factors. In order to elucidate a more complex case involving several physiological problems, the following case history is presented.

There is a subspecialization emerging in the field of clinical allergy known as clinical ecology. This specialized branch of medicine treats those individuals suspected of having adverse reactions to environmental substances and foods causing multiple symptoms, none of which are acute. A combination of double-blind studies and well-documented clinical research is providing increasingly impressive evidence of the possibility that an entire host of behaviors might be influenced *directly* by a cerebral allergic response to foods or environmental substances.[32-38] The complexity of this field of study becomes clearer after learning that in many cases the response pattern varies from individual to individual just as much as the offender food or substance. In some cases, more than fifty foods *and* numerous environmental substances, such as, phenols, hydrocarbons, and natural gas, have been food to provoke allergic responses in the same individual.

MacKarness describes one particular case in England of a mother who repeatedly abused her children.[33] Child Protective Services eventually removed the mother from the home and placed her in a sanitarium after she had thrown one child through a closed window from the fifth floor. Just prior to her receiving a lobotomy, MacKarness intervened and was able to test this mother for sensitivities to various foods and chemicals. Through a series of tests, he was able to isolate seven offending foods. Within days after eliminating these foods from her diet, her behavior improved markedly. She was returned to her family and after 12 years continued to display normal behavior.

A Case of Cerebral Allergic Response

A couple was referred to the Institute for abusing *each other*. A working equilibrium had been achieved between the spouses through frequent alteration of the passive and aggressive roles. The husband occasionally suffered from delusional jealousy, depression, anxiety attacks, and violent tempers. The wife willingly admitted that often she would provoke the attacks, but reasoned, "I also hit him back equally as hard!" The couple had been in therapy for nearly 20 months. The therapist, upon inquiry by our staff, would not even consider the possibility that a physiological problem might exist contributing to their abusive behavior. The therapist felt that therapy was at a crucial stage and would suffer from any false assumptions the couple would make due to our suggestion that nonpsychosocial factors might be a contributing factor. We left the decision to pursue the matter further with the couple who felt that although therapy had been helpful, recent events had indicated clearly to them the need to explore other avenues.

The couple proceeded to describe the most recent acts of violence. Each exhibited a pattern suggesting the possibility of cerebral allergic response. In each case, the husband had gone through a period of fasting in which he would not eat any food or nourishing beverage in a 16–20 hour period. He would have several cans of beer and by evening began to act erratically and eventually, without provocation, assault his wife.

The wife described the most recent incident as follows:

John took me to his brother's house that day. They were drinking beer most of the day. If I asked him to eat something he told me to get lost. About an hour and a half we left his brother's his driving became wild. He was catching the gravel and moving into other people's lanes when turning a curve. When I asked him to slow down, he started to curse at me. Finally he hit me across the face with his open hand. I punched him back and started to cry. This really upset him so he started to speed up even more. I asked him to let me out because I thought he was gonna kill us both. Finally he slammed on his brakes which caused him to lose the trailer. Then he started to really hit me hard across the face and arms. As soon as he stopped I jumped out and told him I was gonna walk home. He told me not to come home because he would kill me. I walked about a mile down the road and he came behind me and tried to run me over on the shoulder. I ran. He jumped out of the car and caught me. He hit me several more times with his fist. I tried to hit him back but he was like crazy. I got away and called the police. When I got home, he was calm and acted like nothing had happened.

On another occasion he did the same thing, except when I threatened to call the cops, he grabbed me by the throat and started choking, while holding my mouth and nose closed with his other hand. He nearly killed me. I think that day he also drank a few cans of beer and had nothing to eat. Each time he had gotten this wild and crazy it was between 7:00 or 7:30 P.M. and 10 P.M. at night.

John was tested for food allergies and was found to have a severe reaction to wheat, corn, and potatoes. All three are commonly used in making alcohol, particularly corn. It was later learned that he had a history of fighting after he drank either liquor or beer.

There are many ways to have an individual tested for cerebral allergic responses. It has been our experience that a clinical ecologist should be consulted whenever this is feasible. These doctors have diagnostic tests, such as the radioallergen absorbent test (RAST), and techniques, such as intradermal testing or sublingual testing, that help to "unmask" the suspected offending foods or chemicals. Sheinkin and Schacter, both psychiatrists, offer many methods to unmask food and chemical allergens in their book, *The Food Connection*.[34] Some are easy and can be done at home, while other methods require qualified professional assistance. In general, most methods have their weaknesses and strengths. Each is thoroughly discussed in their book.

STUDIES CONFIRM PHYSIOLOGICAL PROBLEMS

At the Santa Barbara, California, branch of the American Institute of Family Relations, Mary Jane Hungerford, Ph.D., has found that in nearly 75% of the cases she sees involving serious marital discord, particularly wife-beating, the abuser clinically reveals an abnormal blood glucose level upon glucose-tolerance testing. In many, a sudden drop in blood sugar triggers violent impulses or even suicidal depressions. Such symptoms as depression, anxiety, and uncontrollable tempers, she has found, show the most marked improvements after dietary restrictions or adjustments have been made. She reports that within several weeks after commencement of a nutrition education program, 80% of the couples report a significant improvement in their relationship.

At the Behavior Research Institute, Peacham, Vermont, William J. Lederer, M.D., Ph.D., has examined 312 couples experiencing serious marital crises. In 57% of these cases, at least one spouse was discovered to have a treatable biochemical imbalance that could later be demonstrated to provoke the negative behavior.[39] This was particularly true if the problem involved a sensitivity to a food(s). After eliminating the offending food(s) from the individual's diet, the person would normally report a heightened sense of well-being and improvements in their relationship with their spouse. However, when the offending food was reintroduced into the diet, a worsening of behavior and coping skills would appear, usually within hours and, in some cases, minutes.

Some of the most common problems Dr. Lederer discovered in the couples were: cerebral allergic reactions to offending foods, particularly, milk, wheat, refined sugar, coffee, chocolate, house dust, corn, eggs, yeast, alcohol, citrus fruits, peanuts, and tomatoes; nutritionally induced chronic endocrinopathy; improper levels of vitamins and minerals; elevated levels of neurotoxins; and either plain malnutrition or overconsumption malnutrition.

Dr. Lederer sees that the biochemical imbalances are treated to enable the couple to be more responsive to therapy. Therafter the couples are placed in a 5-week course to modify their own behaviors. That is, they reduce the old, rehearsed negative behavioral exchanges with more satisfying exchanges.

Working with Dr. Don D. Jackson, Dr. Lederer studied another group of 278 young and middle-aged couples with troubled relationships.[40] The majority of these couples were characterized as suffering from a *fatigue-irritability-irrational-behavior syndrome*. This syndrome they found to be common in couples experiencing constant discord, while none existed among a control group of couples with satisfying relationships. The symptoms associated with this syndrome are: fatigue, depression, unpredictable temper tantrums, moodiness, forgetfulness, insomnia, headaches, anxiety, irritability, crying spells, indigestion, compulsive eating, pain in muscles and back, difficulty in concentrating, and sensitivity to noise and light. The latter two symptoms are interesting as they are reported by Michael Lesser, M.D., a psychiatrist, as related to deficiency levels of Vitamin B_2 and B_6.[25]

What are we to make of these findings and the many physiological factors that have been suggested as possibly related indirectly or directly in the battering behavior? Of most importance is the need to be open-minded to the possibility that nutritional and/or environmental factors could be contributing to the problem. But to do this intelligently, it will become necessary to study the literature in their field further. The significant amount of knowledge that has been accumulated in recent years indicating the role nutrition and other physiological factors can play in abnormal behavior should no longer be denied or disregarded. Any program or clinician that attempts to improve the behavior of a batterer should develop methods for gathering information that could indicate when to consider biochemical imbalances as an area for further evaluation. An option would be to locate trained health professionals in the community who have had experience with these areas. If none exist, the professional can seek training through professional groups such as the Society for Clinical Ecology, Huxley Institute for Biosocial Research, or courses similar to those provided by the American Institute for Biosocial Research at various universities. This new training and knowledge should then be integrated into the clinician's existing armamentarium of approaches and resources for dealing with potential and actual batterers.

REFERENCES

1. Hall, R. C. W., Popkin, M. K., and DeVaul, et al. Physical illness presenting as psychiatric disease. 35: 1315–20. *Archives General Psychiatry,* 1978.
2. Koranyi, E. K. Morbidity and rate of undiagnosed physical illness in a psychiatric clinic population. *Arch. Gen. Psychiatry,* 1979, 36: 414–19.
3. Hall, R. C. W., Gardner, E. K., and Stickney, S. K., et al. Physical illness manifesting as psychiatric disease: II. *Arch. Gen. Psychiatry,* 1980, 37: 989–95.
4. Maguire, G. P. and Granville-Grossman, K. L. Physical illness in psychiatric patients. *British J. Psychiatry,* 1968, **115:** 1365–69.
5. Marshall, H. Incidence of physical disorders among psychiatric in-patients. *British Med. J.,* 1949, 2: 468–70.
6. Herridge, C. F. Physical disorders in psychiatric illness: A study of 209 consecutive admissions. *Lancet,* 1960, 2: 949–51.
7. Gershoff, S., and McGandy, R., et al. Trace minerals in human and rat hair. *Am. J. Clinical Nutr.,* 1977, **30:** 868.

8. Hopps, H. The biologic bases for using hair and nail for analyses of trace elements. *Trace Substances in Environmental Health,* 1974, **VIII:** 59–73, University of Missouri.

9. Bland, J. Hair tissue mineral analysis: An emergent diagnostic technique. Bellevue-Redmond Medical Laboratory, Washington, 1979.

10. Fassel, V. A. Quantitative element analyses by plasma emission spectroscopy. *Science,* October 13, 1978, **202:** 183–91.

11. Recommended Dietary Allowances, National Academy of Sciences, National Research Council, Washington, D.C., 8th ed., 1974, and 9th ed., 1980.

12. Schneider, H., Anderson, C., and Coursin, D. *Nutritional Support of Medical Practice.* Hagerstown, Md.: Harper & Row, 1977.

13. *Nutrition Review's Present Knowledge in Nutrition,* 4th ed. New York: The Nutrition Foundation, 1976.

14. Underwood, E. *Trace Elements in Human and Animal Nutrition,* 4th ed. New York: Academic Press, 1977.

15. Prasad, A. *Trace Elements in Human Health and Disease,* Vols. I and II, New York: Academic Press, 1976.

16. Kelsay, J. A review of research on effects of fiber intake on man. *Am. J. Clin. Nutr.,* 1978, **31:** 142–59.

17. Frolich, W. and Asp, N. Mineral bioavailability and cereal fiber. *Am. J. Clin. Nutr.,* 1980, **33**(11): 2397–98.

18. *Diet related to killer diseases,* IV. Hearings before the Select Committee on Nutrition and Human Needs of the United States Senate, Washington, D.C.: U.S. Government Printing Office, 1977.

19. Astrard, P. and Rodahl, K. *Textbook of Work Physiology,* 2nd ed. New York: McGraw-Hill Book Co., 1977.

20. Settle, D. and Patterson, C. C. Lead in Albacore: Guide to lead pollution in Americans. *Science,* March 14, 1980, **207:** 1167–76.

21. Schauss, A. G. *Diet, Crime and Delinquency.* Berkeley, Cal.: Parker House, 1980.

22. *Clinician's Guide to Toxic Metals: Sources, Occupational Exposures, Signs and Symptoms.* Hayward, Cal.: Mineralab, 1979.

23. *Recommended Dietary Allowances.* Washington, D.C.: National Research Council, National Academy of Sciences, 9th ed., 1980.

24. Pfeiffer, C. *Zinc and Other Micro-Nutrients.* New Canaan, Conn.: Keats Publishing Co., 1978.

25. Lesser, M. *Nutrition and Vitamin Therapy.* New York: Grove Press, 1980.

26. Lonsdale, D. and Shamberger, R. J. Red cell transketolase as an indicator of nutritional deficiency. *A. J. Clin. Nutr.* 33(2): 205–211, 1980.

27. Corwin, A. H. (Emeritus Professor of Chemistry, John Hopkins University) Chelation: A lecture demonstration. *13th Advanced Seminar of the Society for Clinical Ecology, San Diego, Cal., October 28, 1979.*

28. Schauss, A. G. *Diet, Crime and Delinquency.* Berkeley, Cal.: Parker House, 1980, pp. 21, 22, 54, 98–100.

29. Schauss, A. G. *Orthomolecular Treatment of Criminal Offenders.* Berkeley, Cal.: Parker House, 1978.

30. O'Banion, D. R., Greenberg, M. R. Behavioral effects of food sensitivity. (Department of Psychology, North Texas State University, Denton, Tex.). In Press.

31. Schroeder, H. *Trace Elements and Man.* Old Greenwich, Conn.: Devin-Adair, 1978.

32. Rapp, D. J. *Allergies and Your Family.* New York: Sterling Publishing, 1980.

33. MacKarness, R. *Eating Dangerously: The Hazards of Hidden Allergies.* New York: Harcourt, Brace Jovanovich, 1976.

34. Sheinkin, D. and Schacter, M. *The Food Connection.* New York: Bobbs-Merrill Co., 1980.

35. Mandell, M. and Scanlon, L. W. *Dr. Mandell's 5-Day Allergy Relief System.* New York: Thomas Y. Crowell, 1979.

36. Breneman, J. C. *Basics of Food Allergy.* Springfield, Ill.: Charles C. Thomas, 1978.

37. Roth, J. *The Food/Depression Connection: Dietary Control of Allergy-based Mood Swings.* Chicago: Contemporary Books; 1978.

38. Mandell, M. Cerebral Reactions in allergic patients. In *A Physicians' Handbook on Orthomolecular Medicine.* R. J. Williams, and D. K. Kalita, (eds.), Elmsford, N.Y.: Pergamon Press, 1977.

39. Lederer, W. J. *Marital Choices.* New York: W. W. Norton Co., 1981.

40. Jackson, D. D. and Lederer, W. J. *The Mirages of Marriage.* New York: W. W. Norton Co., 1968.

5. Pornography and Woman Battering: Dynamic Similarities

*Frances Patai**
Faculty member of LaGuardia Community College (CUNY),
coeditor Rape *and* Child Abuse,
and organizer for Women Against Pornography

How do pornography and woman battering share similar dynamics and why is the latter a logical expression of the former? How do both create and reflect a society's patriarchal principles, institutions, and values?[1]

"Pornography," for the purposes of this chapter, is not to be confused with "erotica," which deals with *mutual* sexual pleasure between equals. Pornography, then, is written or pictorial depiction of women as objects for exploitation, sexual abuse, and repression. Pornography is not harmless diversion, but an industry which earns more than $6 billion a year through systematically *eroticizing violence* against

---

* The writer wishes to acknowledge the substantial contribution of the women in Women Against Pornography in the development of much of the philosophy and many of the analyses presented herewith. The dedicated members of Women Against Pornography should be credited with the worthwhile aspects of the article; the flaws are the author's.
[1] For detailed studies of the causal relationship between pornography and woman abuse, see Laura Lederer's *Take Back the Night.*

women by producing and marketing images of men humiliating, battering, and murdering women for sexual pleasure.

Pornography's messages and myths are:

1. Pain is glamorous;
2. Women are passive—willing collaborators in their own victimization;
3. Women cannot and should not be independent, self-directed people;
4. It is appropriate for men to define women's sexuality and behavior;
5. Men are entitled to constant and unconditional access to women's bodies.

Similar messages and myths also support woman battering as acceptable behavior:

1. Battered women want to be mistreated; this is a sign of love;
2. Battered women are masochists who feel that they deserve to be victimized;
3. Battered women are passive, submissive, and exclusively dependent on their assaultive partners;
4. Wives, as property of their husbands, should be dominated by them;
5. Marriage permits men to beat their wives.

The word, pornography, comes from the Greek, "pornographos," from "porne," meaning prostitute or female captive, and "graphein," to write—thus writings about prostitutes. Pornography is about power imbalances using sex as a weapon to subjugate women. In pornography, the theme is assailant vs. victim.

FBI statistics note that woman battering is one of the most frequently occurring crimes in the nation—a beating occurring every 18 seconds. Sociologists estimate that as many as 2 million American wives are beaten annually by husbands.[2] Parents United reports that one out of every four girls in the United States is sexually abused. The Department of Justice reports that there is a rape every 3 minutes. It is estimated that 1.2 million children under 16 years of age are involved yearly in the commercial sex industry.

The connection between the ideology of pornography, and the acceptance of and the battering of women can be seen in the following examples of pornography in the media.

1. Linda Wertmuller's "Swept Away," a movie whose plot deals with an independent woman being systematically physically and verbally abused until she is reduced to a passive, sexual slave who craves more abuse and loves the tormentor. This film was received as an amusing comedy and played to enthusiastic audiences all over the world.
2. Brian de Palma's "Dressed to Kill," which portrays women as sexual playthings only—to be raped, tortured, and slashed to death. The critics praised this as "... witty ... romantic ... erotic ... funny ... irresistible."
3. Record album covers centering on a woman's crotch with the caption, "Jump on it!"
4. A popular nudie magazine cover showing a naked woman being fed into a meat grinder and coming out hamburger!
5. Shoe advertisements showing a nearly naked woman falling to the ground—wounded or killed by a male gun-wielding attacker.

Pornography objectifies women by caricaturing and reducing them to a sum of their sexual parts and functions—devoid of sensibilities and intelligence. Woman battering objectifies women by reducing them to objects of possession. Both pornography and woman battering legitimize the pain inflicted on the women by objectifying the women. In addition, many women are raped and verbally assaulted while being battered. So there is often a combination of sexual assault and verbal assault with the actual physical assault—the theme of pornography.

Further examples of objectification of women in the cultural mainstream include:

- Ubiquitous jeans ads emphasizing hips and crotch.
- Magazine layouts offering female breasts as edible desserts (complete with real fruit toppings).

- A record album cover targeting a woman's bare buttocks stamped with the name of the album: "Choice Cuts."
- Magazine centerfolds of naked, trussed, ketchup-covered women rotisseried like chickens.

Objectifying the sexual anatomy of women renders them inferior and nonhuman, thus providing the psychological foundation for committing violence against them.

Sexual trivialization in pornography has its counterpart in the trivialization encountered by battered women who seek out the help of the police, the law, the medical profession, the church, the state, and social-service agencies. How many battered women have not been believed, or taken seriously, or have been told by one or more of these establishments to "Calm down . . . don't be hysterical . . work it out together (with the battering man) . . . don't leave; your place is to stay home where you belong . . . he wouldn't hit you if you hadn't provoked him . . . forgive him . . . try to be more understanding" etc.? This response reinforces an ideology which blames the victim for her own victimization.

Until about a decade ago, woman battering was considered so unimportant that accurate statistics and data were not collected. Even now, recent research shows that only one out of 270 incidents of wife-beating is reported.[3] Definitions of abuse often vary and influence record keeping. For instance, a punched, beaten women may be described in police or medical records in vague generalities as merely having been "slapped around a bit." Many of the women at the International Tribunal on Crimes Against Women held in Brussels in March of 1976 testified that when they reported sexual assaults, the authorities viewed *them* and not their assailant with suspicion, and tended to minimize their reactions by reason of female hysteria or vindictiveness. Over and over women testified to the recurrent theme of battering accompanied by sexual abuse. One woman's testimony illustrates this point.

In 1972, because of contraceptive problems, I had to be sterilized. That's when the problem of battering started . . . He came into the bedroom, called me a whore, asking me the man that I had been with that evening, and started to rip off my clothes . . . I was dragged downstairs by my hair, and beaten in the kitchen with his fists, with a knife, and with a chair across my back. My head was banged on a brick wall for a solid hour. And all he kept saying was, "You are whore. You are a whore."

Another witness noted that her husband beat her when she refused to have sexual intercourse with him because it might threaten her pregnancy.

This in a sense is like an acting out of the pornographic script. As in real life, total, unquestioning sexual access to women's bodies is a basic ingredient in pornography. A clear-cut causal relationship between pornography and the physical abuse of women has not yet been documented. However, a group of French women protesting against the proliferation of porn films such as "The Story of O" noted that the rape of one of the women in their group followed the plot of that film exactly.

Time and again women at the Tribunal testified to the common theme of rape, woman battering, and pornography as mutually coercing women to participate in their own subjugation, dehumanization, terrorization.

A Danish woman testified to the victimization and exploitation of women in the porn business by saying that pornography

...gives life to men's sexual fantasies...reduces women to passive objects to be abused, degraded, and used. I say that this is violence against women because now every woman is for sale to the lowest bidder, and for all men.

Many women revealed that the bedroom (second only to the kitchen) was usually the scene of much domestic violence originating from arguments over acting out pornographic fantasies.[4]

Violent pornography, presented as "trendy," "chic," "fun," in a glamorous, guilt-free context, and packaged in slick format is, though not proven to be, highly suspected of influencing the abuse of women in real life. In a study of 100 victims of wife battery in Erin Pizzey's shelter for battered women in London, 15% of the wives reported that their husbands "seemed to experience sexual arousal from the violence—since the demand for sexual intercourse immediately followed the assault."[5] This is not to say that men simply imitate pornography's scenarios. There are complex reasons for wanting to act out porno's scripts. The point is that *pornography (especially as it is legitimized in mainstream TV shows, ads, movies, fashion layouts, etc.) socializes some men into thinking that the maltreatment of women is erotic, sexually desirable, desired by women, and a necessary proof of virility.* Studies of peaceful cultures such as those of the Samoan and the Balinese, in which male sexual violence is almost unknown, show that violence most often is learned, not instinctive, behavior.

Research indicates that exposure to condoned portrayals of violence does indeed affect attitudes and behavior to differing degrees depending on the individual's personality, value system, environment, sexual persona, etc.[6] We know that much of our behavior is a result of exposure and socialization.[7] New behavior is often learned by copying others. Studies have shown that subjects act out and imitate the violent acts of TV characters.[8] Other experiments have produced data to indicate that when males viewed violent sexual acts in pornography, their inhibitions regarding rape and other aggressive acts were weakened.[9] Social psychologist, Edward Donnerstein, concludes from his extensive research that images of violence against women may trigger aggressive behavior against women.[10] Seymour Feshbach, professor and chairman of the Psychology Department at the University of California at Los Angeles, and co-author of *Television and Aggression* states that:

> ... findings of a series of experimental studies that my colleague, Neil Malamuth, and I have carried out in conjunction with several other collaborators have led us to conclude that the depiction of violence in pornography can have decided negative effects. Males, in particular, are prone to use violent erotica to reinterpret expressions of pain on the part of a female rape victim as indications of sexual excitement ...
>
> In brief, the message that "pain or humiliation can be fun" can be a harmful message when used to justify rape. Moreover, the juxtaposition of violence with sexual excitement and satisfaction provides an unusual opportunity for the psychological conditioning of violent responses to erotic stimuli ... when violence is fused with sex, we have a potentially dangerous form of alchemy.[11]

The male porn consumer's demand for *more* violent, sex-associated stimuli is reflected in the fact that such depictions in ads, cartoons, and story lines have increased markedly over the past 5 years in *Playboy* magazine. According to Bob Guccione, publisher of *Penthouse,* there are at present 160 clone magazines. These magazines depict women as "pets" to be mistreated at the male "owner's" whim. The child pornography market meets a demands by publishing no less than 260 kiddie-porn journals each month. With this explosion, is it any wonder that eroticized violence against women is on the increase?

SUGGESTIONS FOR CHANGE

Education on pornography and its meaning and effect on society—especially women—is essential. Women and men must examine the role pornography plays in their lives and consider what it says about women. Connections between pornography, sex, and eroticized violence against women must be made. Pornography reinforces a view prevalent in society that views women as either whores or madonnas, that sees women only as sexual objects, that confirms battered women in their suspicion that *they* must be "bad," or at fault, that their condition is somehow appropriate, or in the nature of things. We must condemn the system whose values pornography both reflects and creates.

We must establish pornography as a humanist issue. This entails confronting and changing a society which fosters and condones sexual inequalities at work or at home.

We must educate young people so that females are not socialized to be dependent and males to be dominant; most of our role models will have to be changed. Many loving, egalitarian relationships are in effect; more can be.

We must work to change the climate of opinion so that pornography is no longer viewed as socially acceptable. We must inform people that pornography is not sexually liberating, but is repressive, and that eroticizing violence and power has nothing to do with sex and love.

We must challenge existing laws that protect masculine double standards, depriving battered women of equal protection under law.

We must have more research based on a feminist perspective. Social scientists tend to reflect society's values and biases; thus they perpetuate and reinforce the very problems they are studying. As a result, both pornography and woman battering as psychosocial pathology, dangerous to women, was a concept largely ignored by many academic researchers. Feminist analyses focus on violence, not lewdness or grossness, when examining depictions of explicit sexual material.

We can support groups like Women Against Pornography, Women Against Violence Against Women, and Women Against Violence in Pornography and Media. All of these groups will send experienced speakers to organizations all over the country to present programs illustrating the dangers of pornography and its real-life acting out in woman-battering behavior. Join these groups. Combine action with analyses.

We can boycott pornographic films, magazines, and TV programs and their sponsors and advertisers.

Start at home. Women can let the men in their lives know that they object to pornography and its destructive effects on their interpersonal relationships.

Censorship of pornography is not the answer, for this would clearly constitute an infringement of First Amendment Rights. For an excellent analysis of pornography and the First Amendment, see Wendy Kaminer's "Pornography and the First Amendment: Prior Restraints and Private Actions," in Laura Lederer's *Take Back the Night.*[12]

SUMMARY

When people bond together for a common goal they can accomplish a great deal. By concentrating on changing society's rationalizations for and sanctions of woman abuse, the problem may be alleviated. The message is that beating up women—whether in pornography or in real life, is *not* fashionable, harmless, legitimate entertainment, but life-threatening and perilous to all females.

FOOTNOTES

1. Lederer, Laura. (ed.), *Take Back the Night: Women on Pornography.* New York: William Morrow & Co., 1981.
2. Reported by Professor Murray Straus, University of New Hampshire, to U.S. Commission on Civil Rights, in *New Women's Times,* Rochester, N.Y. January 5–18, 1978.

3. Steinmetz, Suzanne K. Wifebeating, husbandbeating—A comparison of the use of physical violence between spouses to resolve marital fights. In Maria Roy (ed.), *Battered Women* New York: Van Nostrand Reinhold, 1977, p. 65.

4. Russell, Diana E. H. and Van de Ven, Nicole. (eds.) *Crimes Against Women: Proceedings of the International Tribunal.* Millbrae, California: Les Femmes, 1976, passim.

5. Barry, Kathleen. *Female Sexual Slavery.* Englewood Cliffs, N.J.: Prentice-Hall, 1979, p. 145.

6. Eysenck, H. J. and Nias, D. K. B. *Sex and Violence in the Media.* New York: Harper & Row, 1978, passim.

7. Rachman, S. Sexual fetishism: An experimental analogue. *The Psychological Record,* **16,** 293–96.

8. Woodrick, C. Chissom, B., and Smith, D. Television-viewing habits and parent-observed behaviors of third grade children. *Psychological Reports,* **40,** 830.

9. Berkowitz, L. *Aggression: A Social Psychological Analysis.* (New York: McGraw-Hill Book Company, 1962). Feshbach, Seymour and Malamuth, Neal. Sex and aggression: Proving the link, *Psychology Today,* November, 1978, **XII:**6.

10. Donnerstein, Edward. Pornography and violence against women: Experimental studies. *Annals of the New York Academy of Science,* 1980.

11. Feshbach, Seymour. Mixing sex with violence—A dangerous alchemy, *New York Times,* August 3, 1980, p. 29.

12. Lederer, Laura. *Take Back the Night,* op. cit. pp. 241–47.

Part IV Special Populations

"A good portion of the evils that afflict mankind is due to the erroneous belief that life can be made secure by violence."
—Leo Tolstoy from *Confessions*, 1879.

6. Spouse Abuse in the Military Community: Factors Influencing Incidence and Treatment

Nancy K. Raiha, ACSW, CPT, U.S. Army
Assistant Chief, Social Work Service
Reynolds Army Hospital
Fort Sill, Oklahoma

INTRODUCTION

Investigation by MP Unit 10 revealed that SMITH and dependent wife SMITH became involved in a verbal altercation resulting in SMITH striking dependent wife SMITH in the face and back with a closed fist. SMITH was apprehended, advised of his rights and transported to the MP station. Dependent wife SMITH was transported to the US Army Hospital Emergency Room where she was treated for soft tissue trauma and a sore back.

The typical payday Friday night blotter entry at this Army post in Kentucky differs little in substance from a civilian report of "domestic disturbance." Somebody assaulted his wife and the local law enforcement officials were called to calm things down. Bruises, black eyes, crying children, and angry stares look the same whether a police officer wears civilian blue or Army green. Yet as we in the Armed Services, like our civilian counterparts, become increasingly aware of and concerned with the problem of spouse abuse, we realize that certain variations on the common theme of domestic violence are unique to the military. The incidence of, circumstances of, and even some of the solutions to this problem are influenced by the distinct structure and characteristics of the military community.

While most factors discussed in this paper will apply to all three major military services, the author is most familiar with the Army and will generally confine examples and observations to that branch of the service.[*]

INCIDENCE/CONTRIBUTING FACTORS

When this author and staff at the U.S. Army Community Hospital, Fort Campbell, Kentucky set up a new and somewhat unique program to meet the needs of battered spouses at this fairly isolated Army post, the widespread interest in military spouse abuse became immediately evident. Inquiries and on-site visits were received from other military bases; other Armed services; numerous civilian agencies; authors; the Department of Health, Education, and Welfare; and the Center for Women Policy Studies. This flood of inquiries appeared to stem from not only a search for new answers to the problem of spouse abuse in this particular population group, but also an interest in the military as a visible group under federal control, and a speculation that domestic violence is especially prevalent in military populations. Del Martin, for example, suggests a correlation between military experienc and marital violence in her (1976) book *Battered Wives*. Whatever the relationship between rates of abuse in military and civilian communities, it is true that certain factors inherent in military life may well tend to create a climate conducive to domestic violence.[**]

Before discussing such factors, a note of caution is in order. Considering exclusively such contributors to family stress and abuse tends to lead to an unrealistically negative view of military life. It should be remembered that many happy, well-adjusted families choose military living. There exist such positive factors as job security, steady paychecks, opportunity for upward mobility, continuing education, predictable environment, sense of camaraderie and an extensive network

---

[*] For information on the Navy program contact: Family Advocacy Office, Bureau of Medicine and Surgery: Code 3123, Department of Navy, Washington, D.C. 20372. Information on the Air Force program is available from: HQ, AFMSC–SGPC, Consultant in Social Work, Brooks, Air Force Base, Tex. 78235

[**] See Schlesinger, et al. in this book.

of support systems which will be discussed at length in the second half of this paper.

Although today's American military community includes single-parent families, those where both adults are service members, and two-parent families in which the female is the active-duty member, such nontraditional configurations are still proportionately rare. For the sake of simplicity, the discussion of contributing factors will speak mainly to the traditional nuclear family where the male parent is the service member.

Finances

As national defense has become a more popular issue in recent times, much attention has been given to the "soldier on food stamps" and to the fact that many military families fall within poverty guidelines. Military financial problems are, however, more complex than commonly understood. In most cases the level of military pay would be adequate to support a careful family in a stable situation. It is the extra financial stresses of the military life-style that can place a household in financial jeopardy. The new recruit with a family usually has no cash reserves. He joined the Army to gain steady employment. Private Doe's not-so-new car breaks down as the family moves cross-country, creating bills for motels and repair. When he arrives at the new duty station more nights are spent in motels and meals taken in restaurants while housing is located. Lower-ranking married Army personnel with less than 2 years in service usually may not live in post housing, so he must find cheap housing off post. With a trailer come deposits, rent, gas, electricity, and phone (required for his job). He must borrow against future pay. The stage is set. Future paychecks will never contain quite enough to pay the bills and put food on the table. Payments falls behind. Luxuries become nonexistent. And a small unexpected expense like a flat tire turns into a major nightmare—and perhaps the spark that turns frustration to aggression to violence.

Job Stress

The service member who is less likely to experience severe financial problems—the man with more rank and time in service—may well have to deal with more severe pressures in the work environment. Soldiers are taught that "the commander is always responsible," and a person in a leadership position on any level must ensure that his unit meets goals and performance standards, passes inspections and graded exercises, experiences few disciplinary problems, and has a high reenlistment rate. This is generally accomplished through long hours of personally overseeing every aspect of unit operations and closely monitoring leaders on the next lower level. Each commander "rates" his immediate subordinates and under the competitive military "up-or-out" system even one bad rating can be enough to label a man "average" or "below his contemporaries" and detrimentally affect future promotions and job assignments. There is no opportunity to "leave your problems at work" for the leader who must be responsible every hour of every day.

On the other end of the spectrum is the common soldier who often has little or no personal control over the job situation. Many times there is little opportunity for him to make decisions or influence policy. The vast coordination of resources involved in major troop exercises sometimes requires a unit to wait in place for hours before the next phase of movement begins. The unit member may interpret this alternation of periods of bored inactivity with sudden heavy demands for performance ("hurry up and wait") as a lack of respect for his individual needs and capabilities. Individual achievement may not be recognized on a daily basis although failure to perform acceptably can result in censure or punishment. In the peace-time Army the soldier may spend years training for a job he or she never actually performs in the combat environment. The service member whose needs for individual recognition and personal control are frustrated on the job may respond with exaggerated control needs in the home.

Intercultural Marriages

The mobility inherent in military life tends to create a "melting pot" atmosphere and dramatically increases the number of intercultural marriages. Not only do service men and women marry locals in whatever region or country they are stationed, but as more and more women are incorporated into the military, two service members from vastly different backgrounds are likely to marry. In any intercultural marriage differences in norms, values, expectations, and habits may lead to tension and conflict. Social pressures are sometimes an additional burden to an interracial couple. The foreign-born may not only have to deal with an alien environment, but also with a language barrier. Couples who are unable to communicate verbally seem more likely in some cases to resort to physical means of expressing displeasure and frustration.

Separation

Absence from the home is a fact of life for all military service members. Not every family experiences "unaccompanied tours" that mean years overseas and training exercises that may involve months away. But long hours, evening and weekend "duty" in the unit, and field training are common to all service members. In most male-headed families, wife and children adapt to such separations from their "sponsor," creating their own patterns of daily life. Even the most traditional mother assumes responsibility for finances, and rule-making. Then, it seems, just as mom and the children settle into a comfortable routine, dad comes home. The soldier may be required to be away from home frequently, but he does receive a generous amount of vacation and holiday time. So periods of absence alternate with periods where dad is home *all* the time. He feels uncomfortable and out-of-place and tries to slip back into the role of head-of-household. Wife and children, consciously or unconsciously, resent this change and cling to the *status quo*. Tension and some conflict are unavoidable.

In the smaller percentage of families where wife and children cannot adapt to the military sponsor's absence, tensions are even greater. When the wife ceases to function or children act out seriously, the absent sponsor must be brought back to the home. If this becomes a pattern the service member experiences increasing unit pressure to "put his personal affairs in order" and stop shirking duty. He may be forced to choose between his family and military commitments.

The opportunities for infidelity afforded by frequent separation also often appear as a contributing factor in spouse abuse. Many batterers encountered by the author are extremely jealous and may respond to either actual evidence of unfaithfulness or to unfounded suspicions with violence. Wives, too, may exacerbate marital tensions by accusing their spouses of using "long hours" or forced separations as convenient opportunities for extramarital activity.

Separation from Traditional Support Systems

A couple who have never moved from the town in which they were raised have a network of support persons available. In times of conflict or financial distress they can often turn to mom, dad, school chums, other relatives, church members, or other acquaintances. While family and friends can be a source of marital discord, they are often an invaluable resource for a struggling young couple. And if physical abuse does occur near family and friends the battered wife is likely to have an available refuge and some help in starting over again should she decide to leave her husband. There should be little wonder that we call a soldier's spouse his "dependent." Unless her family is particularly well-off and approachable she must rely on him for her total support.

Nature of the Military. While the differences between military and civilian life are often exaggerated by those quick to stereotype, some aspects of military mission and structure may influence the off-duty life styles of those in the Armed Forces. Certainly the principle that underlies any fighting force is that—in practice, if not in thought—"might equals right." The batterer certainly tends to operate by that same principle. A chaplain at one of the training sessions on spouse abuse held at Fort Campbell pointed to the absurdity of training men to ruthlessly fight and kill during the day, then expecting them to go home at night and settle disputes with tolerance and rational discussion.

The hierarchical and often authoritarian power structure necessary to the military may influence the attitudes of those who work within this structure. In military units one person is in charge. Instant and unquestioning obedience can literally mean life or death in a combat situation. The commander who cannot control his troops is not only a failure but a danger to those around him. A person continually exposed to such an atmosphere might well find the specter of a family not completely within his control so threatening that extreme measures seem necessary to avert such a state. The Army's tradition that "a sponsor is responsible for the actions of his dependents," just as "a commander is responsible'' does not help to counteract such attitudes. The Marine pilot who lines his wife and children up for formations and abuses his wife in the movie, *The Great Santini*,* may be an accurate, if exaggerated, portrayal of some family situations.

A "Military Personality"

While the effects of the previously mentioned factors on the incidence of domestic violence must be left open to speculation, the existence of the factors themselves, is either fairly well-documented or self-evident. However, the theory that a certain personality type is more likely to be attracted to military service is a purely speculative matter and should be treated as such. There may be reason to suspect that more traditional and rigid types would find military life a comfortable existence. Sociologists who postulate that successful fighting units are formed through a process of male-bonding might lead one to believe that a more "macho" male would fit in well in combat units. T-shirts seen on post with mottoes like, "If you ain't Cav,** you ain't shit" tend to support this position. The tendency of young people to join the service to escape unsatisfactory home situations may increase the number of service men and women who had unstable or violent parental models. Judges who in the past offered young offenders the choice of "joining the Army or going to jail" probably did, in a small way, increase the antisocial element in the military community. Those who work with military populations would appropriately be aware of the possibility for such tendencies which might contribute to domestic violence in selected cases, but would commit a grave error in assuming that all or most service members exhibit such personal characteristics.

RESOURCES FOR INTERVENTION

As mentioned earlier, military life has many positive as well as negative aspects. Stressors certainly are present, but they also exist "on the outside." The positive factor in military communities which applies most directly to domestic violence is the unique set of resources available to

---

*Sometimes titled *The Ace*
** The Army's cavalry units no longer ride horses, but may be armored cavalry or air cavalry.

the military family. These resources are noteworthy not only in their individual makeup but in their interrelationship. In the civilian community, women's centers, law-enforcement agencies, civic and religious groups, mental-health and medical clinics all may concern themselves with some aspect of spouse abuse. With luck, tact, and hard work they manage to coordinate services. Military agencies, however, all answer to the same task ("The Mission" in military terms). When in a proposed Directive on Family Advocacy, "The Department of Defense recognizes that child and spouse maltreatment is preventable and requires the application of enlightened attitudes and techniques by command, supervisory and health service personnel," the total system is committed to this philosophy. While some in the helping professions may lament the number of controls necessarily placed on the individual service member, the cohesive, structured and somewhat paternalistic characteristics of the military organization can be an enormous asset in controlling undesirable behavior and protecting the victim of abuse.

The central resource for intervention in military spouse abuse is one unique to the military community. The unit commander and chain-of-command are, as mentioned earlier, considered responsible for the soldier. Army Field Manual 19-20, Law Enforcement Investigation, contains this comment on the Commander's Role in "Domestic Disturbances." "Unit Commanders are normally responsible for the actions of assigned personnel, both on and off duty. This reponsibility normally includes the behavior in military housing areas and in economy housing overseas . . . While the role of the Military Police in domestic disturbance ends with the restoration of order, that of the unit commander should begin." While the commander's scope of responsibility is less well-defined when abuse takes place in an off-post housing area in the United States, the chain-of-command generally maintains an interest in ensuring welfare dependents and in discouraging unit member actions which might result in criminal charges, or negative reflection on the service. Conversely, in the case where an active duty member (male or female) is being abused, the commander would have an interest in protecting that unit member from physical harm or emotional strain resulting in deteriorating job performance. As noted in the draft of the proposed DOD Directive on Family Advocacy, "The quality of military family life affects service members' performance which, in turn, affects the discipline, morale and proficiency of the individual's command; therefore, the growth, social development, health and safety of military families are matters of concern to commanders at all levels.''

Other military helping agencies are considered in many ways to be resources to aid "the commander"—at all levels, from the squad leader to the Commander-in-Chief—in mission accomplishment and dealing with the individual soldier. Military Police, as noted earlier, restore order, investigate, and identify spouse abuse. Each unit is assigned a chaplain to provide guidance and counseling for personal problems and to assist the commander in crisis intervention. Mental-health professionals are available to deal with both family and social problems and with individual psychopathology. Community service organizations such as Army Emergency Relief and The American Red Cross provide financial assistance, while other community service organizations such as the Army-wide Army Community Service or locally developed organizations may sponsor programs to address spouse abuse in their efforts to improve quality of life for military families. Medical treatment for drug and alcohol problems, and legal advice are also available without charge.

MODES OF INTERVENTION

The above-mentioned resource groups may be involved with the violent family at a number of levels.

Identification

The cohesive structure and the central role played by the unit commander facilitate identification of spouse abuse in the military community. The commander may learn of a "problem" in his/her unit through a variety of means. The commander is informed of any on-post domestic disturbance severe enough to warrant a blotter entry and may be informed of those "solved on scene." Anyone taken into custody for assault on post is usually turned over to unit custody. Military Police or Criminal Investigators will investigate and turn their findings over to the commander for disposition. Civilian law-enforcement agencies are less likely to involve the unit unless a warrant or other legal measures are involved, although police familiar with military procedures may turn to the unit or on-post agencies if no resources are available.

Discipline and Censure

In many cases of spouse abuse the offender is initially surprised to find that the Army interests itself in his activities in the privacy of the home. A clear demonstration that such behavior is considered unacceptable and, if continued, could be harmful to a soldier's career, can at times be enough to change the pattern of violence. There are a number of disciplinary/corrective measures available to commanders:

1. Admonition and Reprimand. An admonition is a warning that certain conduct will not be tolerated and that serious consequences can result from repeated misconduct. A reprimand is an act of formal censure which denounces or reproves a soldier for misconduct. Both admonitions and reprimands may be either written or oral and may be placed in the soldier's local personnel file. "The Commander's Guide for Offenses of Rape, Sexaul Assualt and Wife Abuse" published by V corps (Germany) states, "Too often, service members think that what they do to their spouses and dependents is 'none of the Army's business.' Through admonition, the commander can impress upon the soldier that this is far from true . . . A properly administered admonition can have a sobering effect, especially upon a serious career-minded soldier."

2. Move back to post. Directing a soldier to move into the barracks will be discussed later as a means of ensuring victim safety on a short-term basis. This primarily practical measure, however, does serve to indicate the Army's interest and could be seen as a form of punishment since the privilege of off-post lodging is temporary denied. The "Commander's Guide" states "Authorization to live off-post is a matter left to the discretion of the commander, who may determine that in a given case the need to control a soldier's treatment of his spouse or dependents overrides the soldier's to protect a woman they consider endangered. More often a woman familiar with the system or advised by knowledgeable friends will call the commander herself. Chaplains, mental-health workers, or community agencies may suggest and sometimes encourage contacting the commander as one of the alternatives

available to a battered wife. With the victim's permission or sufficient cause, the agency may approach a commander to work together on a problematic situation.

At Fort Campbell Social Work Service becomes aware of battering in a variety of ways. The Military Police send copies of domestic disturbance reports and may directly refer couples. Commanders and chaplains call for advice and to make referrals. The Emergency Room refers all identified cases of spouse abuse to the social worker on call who is available 24 hours a day. Other medical services, the Legal Assistance Office, Army Community Service and other on and off-post helping agencies make referrals. Neighbors call to find out "What can be done about this" and are informed that services are available should any member of the violent family choose to contact the agency. Wives call or walk in for treatment as do, surprisingly, a significant number of batterers—afraid wife will leave or family life be irreparably damaged. Other cases of spouse abuse are discovered during child-abuse investigations or in the course of treating couples, families, and individuals with other presenting complaints.

On other posts, agency involvement may differ somewhat. Army Community Service or a community mental-health activity may play a more central key role in spouse abuse coordination. If civilian agencies dealing with domestic violence are available in the area, military agencies may be more oriented to referral than long-term involvement.

3. Early return of dependents from overseas. Early return of dependents is also often a problem situation rather than a punitive measure. Army Regulations (AR 55-46, Para 5-9) authorize return transportation of dependents when, ".... because of marital difficulties, divorce, or annulment, it is determined that the best interest of the member, his dependents (or former dependents) and the Government will be best served by their return to the United States." While the sponsor normally requests such advance return, the commander or dependents themselves can initiate the request.

4. Bar to reenlistment. Paragraph 1–34c(14) and (15), AR 601–280, cite the failure to manage marital affairs and causing trouble in the civilian community as appropriate factors to consider in not allowing a service member to reenlist.

5. Reduction in Grade. A soldier might be considered for administrative reduction to a lower pay grade either because he has been

convicted by a civil court for assault on his spouse or because acts of violence, along with other evidence of lack of qualities required for a certain pay grade, provide grounds for reduction for inefficiency (AR 600–200, Para 7–64a).

6. Administrative Discharge. Chapter 14, Army Regulation 635–200, provides for the administrative elimination of service members for "acts of misconduct" to include "frequent incidents of discreditable nature with civil or military authorities." Elimination through Chapter 14 is considered a severe measure since it is usually not accompanied by an "Honorable Discharge" certificate. The soldier not only is separated from the service, but may lose some veteran's benefits and may encounter problems in the civilian job market. This administrative measure is generally not utilized unless rehabilitative efforts have failed.

7. Nonjudicial Punishment. The commander is directed to utilize non-punitive, administrative measures to the maximum extent without resorting to non-judicial punishment or court-martial (AR 27–10, Para 3–4). However, when serious measures are indicated and the offense occurred within military jurisdiction either the Article 15 (nonjudicial punishment) or the formal court-martial may be utilized. The Article 15 is imposed by the unit commander and is a less severe form of punishment. Depending on the commander's rank, possible punishments include fines, extra duty, reduction in grade, restriction to the unit area and/or correctional custody not to exceed thirty days. An "Article 15" will also be a permanent blot on a soldier's career.

8. Court-Martial. The court-martial is the most serious form of military criminal sanction. The unit commander can request a solider be court-martialed for misconduct committed within military jurisdiction or a soldier may request a court-martial by refusing Article 15 punishment. (Off-post offenses in the United States are not eligible for court-martial and on some posts such assaults may be tried in U.S. Magistrate Court.) Both simple assault and battery are covered by Article 128 of the Uniform Code of Military Justice, with maximum punishments of 3 months and 6 months confinement respectively. The victim (wife) retains the privilege to refuse to testify against her husband.

Many commanders and investigators become frustrated because most wives change their minds about testifying a few days after an assault. In a local memorandum, "Disciplinary Measures to Deal with

Assaults by Soldiers on Their Spouses,'' prepared by the Fort Campbell Staff Judge Advocate's Office, this phenomenon was explained,
"First, conviction of the husband can be expected to result in fine,
forfeiture, or reduction, any of which would reduce family income.
Second, the inevitable delay in bringing the case to trial provides the
wife with a cooling-off period in which normal spousal affection may
resume. Third, the wife may be intimidated by fear of further harm by
the husband or the fear of further damage to the marriage if she
testifies.'' In short, spouse abuse is one of the few criminal acts where
prosecution and punishment may routinely cause more harm or discomfort to the victim than the offender. In the author's experience,
even those women who wish never to see the husband again don't wish
to "hurt him," further antagonize him, or to have the chance of receiving child support lessened. *Most women desire safety, not punishment.*

Because family involvement is such a delicate issue, the commander
must exercise extreme caution and judgment in choosing any of the
many disciplinary options available. The chance of doing "more harm
than good" in intervening always exists. Generally more severe measures are reserved for severe abuse or a repeated offense, but a firm
stand that such behavior is not acceptable is almost always appropriate.

Separation

Temporarily separating a batterer and the abused spouse can be indicated for several different reasons. Following an assault—or interrupted assault—or when familiar patterns indicate to a woman that an
attack is imminent, ensuring immediate safety is the concern. As mentioned earlier, separation can also serve as a signal that someone is concerned with what goes on in this family and that the wife *does* have access to support systems. The time apart can give all those concerned a
chance to "cool off," bargain, explore options, and make long-term
plans.

One of the ways to effect separation, noted earlier, is to return the
offender to the barracks. A soldier who lives off-post may be temporarily denied that privilege with cause. If disturbances occurred on-
post in quarters, the soldier may be told to stay away from those
quarters until some disposition is made. Many times a soldier may

agree with the commander that a short-term separation will prevent further conflict—especially if he is representing himself as a wronged party. Closer surveillance (confinement to barracks area or checking at predetermined intervals) is more likely in cases where the soldier is pending charges and/or has shown himself to be out-of-control. If the victim is an active duty service member, of course, it is very easy for her to stay in the barracks—as long as no children are involved.

Moving the offender back to the barracks, however, is not always a viable option. On Monday morning a commander can easily call a soldier to his office and make such arrangements. Unfortunately, assaults are more likely to take place on Friday or Saturday night than Monday morning. If the assault took place off-post in the United States and the assailant is still not within military jurisdiction, the commander or police officers cannot go out and drag him to the installation—although a very convincing commander or police officer may persuade him to return to the unit. Even if the assault occurred on a military installation, the assailant may have disappeared by the time authorities appear and may not be contacted until the next duty day. Some batterers may even go AWOL (absent without leave) after an assault, and not return to the unit at all. Sometimes the commander may be unavailable or for some reason reluctant to move a suspected batterer to the barracks.

When removing the batterer from the home is not possible, or when the batterer is so violent and impulsive that safety is still an issue (soldiers have been known to slip out of the unit area and again assault their wives), other arrangements should be made for the safety of wife and any children.

Some military installations are located in or near communities where progressive law-enforcement policies and/or shelters are available. In these cases, on-post helping agencies may need to be involved in assuring safety only on a peripheral basis. However, at more isolated posts no civilian channels may be available for providing victim safety. There are no civilian shelters in the vicinity of Fort Campbell, which straddles the Tennessee-Kentucky state line. In nearby communities in either state it is unlikely that a batterer would be taken into custody by local civilian authorities on an evening or weekend. Even when a warrant can be issued (during weekday working hours) most assailants are immediately released. Because of this lack of civilian resources, the U.S. Army Community Hospital at Fort Campbell has been involved in providing temporary (up to 7 days) shelter for battered wives and children since March 1978. Forty-five women and their children utilized this first-of-its-kind shelter in the first 20 months of operation. More recently, *Army Community Service at Fort Benning, Georgia opened a shelter, and other posts are exploring this possibility.*

Like their civilian counterparts, those operating military shelters must be concerned with personnel, food, space, money, entry system, and security measures. However, such resources may be more easily located in the military environment. The command support necessary to open such a facility ensures cooperation of other agencies and existing resource channels. Buildings belong to the post and may be allocated without exchange of money. Social workers, hospital personnel, police, and even maintenance crews are part of the existing system. At both Fort Campbell and Fort Benning existing dining facilities have been utilized to provide food for battered families—with reimbursement for costs. Incidental costs may have to be covered by more imaginative means. Fort Campbell post wives' clubs have been extremely generous with donations and special projects to aid programs for battered wives. The limited amount of money necessary for shelter operations has never been a major problem. In this author's experience those in positions of authority have been quick to support services for battered wives. The major drawback to implementing a bold new program for abuse victims is that resources must come from somewhere. The system does not provide for new personnel to be hired or new buildings built for shelter operations. Thus every hour a social worker, police officer, or other helping person spends on shelter operation means 1 hour of other services that cannot be rendered. For this reason sheltering operations are best kept as simple as possible or (as at Fort Benning) partially staffed by volunteers. At Fort Campbell, as in most civilian shelters, women are encouraged to view institutional shelter as a last resort. Friends, family, legal, and unit resources are considered first, and only when these prove impractical or unsafe is on-post shelter utilized.

Counseling

Individual, family, and marital counseling are among the services available free of charge to the soldier and his or her dependents. Psychiatric care is always available to the active duty soldier, and is partially paid for under the CHAMPUS insurance program if a nearby military medical facility is unable to provide such care to dependents. The batterer with severe psychiatric problems will often be released from the service. When gross psychopathology is not involved, counseling for violent families is usually provided under medical auspices by a Social Work Service or Community Mental Health Activity—although this arrangement may vary somewhat from installation to installation. On some posts Army Community Service and local civilian agencies may assume more responsibility for counseling and referral. As stated in the section on "Identification," the violent family may come to the attention of a counseling agency through a variety of channels—either directly or through referrals.

A prompt referral can facilitate the course of treatment. Captain Ed James, an Army Social Worker, studied 48 cases of spouse abuse at Fort Carson, Colorado and learned that a rapid engagement technique for treatment (within 24 hours) increased the treatment success probability and decreased the recidivism rate. While a command referral may be less desirable than a self-referral by the batterer, it has some advantages. Since someone else has already pointed out that spouse abuse is unacceptable, the counselor is free to be more empathetic to the stress and learned patterns that may prompt violence. The counselor can help the client realize the maladaptiveness of such behavior while maintaining some of the acceptance and empathy essential to establishing a therapeutic relationship. When the batterer can be convinced that the counselor wishes to and is able to help him improve the quality of his individual and marital life, not to blame and punish him, the stage is set for therapeutic intervention. Dysfunctional marital and individual patterns can be explored and sometimes changed.

In the case where abuse has not reached the attention of the authorities and the wife comes to the agency for assistance, some basic decisions must be made. The counselor can help the battered wife explore her options through a process of information-giving and clarification. Seven options can usually be explored: (1) Leave her husband permanently; (2) Leave her husband temporarily to try to induce change and/or to test her ability to survive on her own; (3) Involve the authorities in the hope that official sanctions will induce change; (4) Try to involve her husband in some sort of counseling; (5) With or without support from the counselor try to "talk to" and/or "stand up" to the husband to induce change; (6) Enter counseling to improve self-esteem, assertiveness, and coping skills until she can choose one of the other options; or (7) Maintain the *status quo*. While women can be encouraged to think of themselves as worthy individuals who do not deserve to live with abuse, the counselor must be aware that some women will choose to maintain the present condition—not because they are masochists who want to be beaten but because alternatives appear more dismal than the present situation. A woman with several young children, no car, no phone, no job, and nowhere to go may choose to stay in a violent marriage until it becomes totally unbearable or other options appear. The counselor can help expand her options and skills, but making decisions for the client can have disastrous consequences. Except in severe or unusual situations, or when the safety of children is involved, the counselor will offer support but refrain from further "helping" until the woman agrees to accept that "help."

In addition to marital, family, and individual counseling, groups for women with poor coping skills and for men who wish to improve self-control have proven helpful.

Commanders and chaplains are also sources of "counseling." The commander is expected to "counsel" miscreant troops. "Counseling" sessions may consist of "chewing out" and clear delineation of future expectations, but they may also include an expression of personal interest and somewhat fatherly guidance that can move a soldier more than the ministrations of a professional counselor. The chaplain is a traditional source of counseling in the Army. "If you've got a problem, see a chaplain," runs an old adage. Many battered wives or batterers seek a chaplain first because they believe their confidentiality will be honored. Chaplains also can at times present moral and ethical issues in a different light than other counselors. They seem to be particularly effective with batterers who defend their actions by quoting scripture. At Fort Campbell, chaplains operate a hot line (798–HELP) 24 hours a day. They will, if requested, go to the scene of a domestic quarrel and begin crisis intervention at this most opportune time.

Concrete Services

Concrete services can be valuable to the violent family in two different ways. Services to the entire family or to the batterer may alleviate stress and indirectly reduce violent incidents. The budget counseling (offered at some Army Community Services); Army Emergency Relief loans; food, clothes or furniture from "loan closets"; help in locating better housing or services; or help in resolving unit problems can "lower the boiling point" in a family.

Concrete services to wife can help eliminate dependent—either changing the balance of power in a relationship or giving her the means to leave. Job placement is probably the most important step in helping a woman become self-sufficient, but other more rudimentary services may be required. Some women do not have ID cards or work permits. A woman may need to learn to speak the English language so that her only source of information is not a husband who tells her that if she makes any complaint about him she will be deported. She may need to find out that there is a commissary, a post exchange, legal-aid service, and a hospital, and to learn how to use them. She may desire medical treatment or birth-control information. In many cases the battering husband has tried to keep her completely ignorant of outside resources and within his control.

Drug and Alcohol Treatment

The Army operates a nonpunitive treatment program for those with drug and alcohol problems which can be very helpful in those cases where substance abuse accompanies spouse abuse. As in any treatment program, the prognosis is better for those who volunteer for help, but a commander may directly refer a soldier to the program. If a batterer is admitted to the residential portion of the program a secondary benefit may be the temporary separation of husband and wife. Those who fail to be rehabilitated by the program can be discharged from the service.

Long-Term Separation

While no one in the Army would recommend long-term or permanent separation as *the* answer to spouse abuse, in certain cases it may be the solution of choice. As mentioned earlier, dependents in overseas areas may be returned to the United States if it is determined that such a move is in the best interest of the soldier, his dependents, and the government. The period of separation until the soldier finishes his tour and returns to the country can allow time for reflection and for the wife to prepare herself for a permanent break if she deems one necessary. In the continental United States resources may be available to send a battered woman and children home to family or friends—if she has someone to go to. This is usually a desperate final move since she will have to leave most of her belongings and physical comforts behind—taking only a few suitcases or boxes. If the husband feels his career is in danger because of repeated altercations, he may agree to find or borrow the money for a ticket home. When the husband is not cooperative and family will not help, it is possible for the wife to get an Army Emergency Relief grant, even though the sponsor is normally required to sign for such grants. The paperwork, documentation, and command support required to get such a grant can seem overwhelming to a woman in crisis with few resources. At some posts, helping agencies are able to aid a battered woman in efficiently completing all the steps in the sometimes lengthy process of grant application. At Fort Campbell the special fund set up to aid in sheltering spouse abuse victims can also provide money for transportation—if family, husband, and Army resources are insufficient or unattainable at a time when an immediate move seems expedient. Since those administering this fund are more familiar with the individual wife abuse case than personnel at Army Emergency Relief, they don't need to rely on so many bureaucratic safeguards. A woman leaving her husband often has many legal questions about support, separation, divorce, abandonment, and child custody. While Army lawyers cannot represent her in civilian courts, they can provide information on civil matters and assist her in understanding and utilizing military law and regulations, i.e., those pertaining to support of dependents.

Several factors can greatly complicate the process of a wife leaving an abusive husband. If she has no supportive friends or family to offer her refuge, she is at a distinct disadvantage. Most battered women have no personal savings and many are unemployed. These women have no financial resources to simply leave the husband's home and set up housekeeping—especially if children are involved. In both states near Fort Campbell, a woman must have been separated from her husband for a period of weeks before she qualifies for financial assistance. Thus the resourceless woman is caught in a classic Catch-22: She can't get money until she leaves, but she can't leave until she gets money. Two solutions traditionally solve this dilemma: She stays until she can find a job and get a first paycheck, or she finds another man willing to support her and the children. Economic factors easily explain a pattern noticed by many military social workers. A woman is more likely to leave an abusive husband if she is, (1) employed, (2) recently married, (3) childless, and/or (4) supported in her resolve by a financially solvent family-of-origin.

For a foreign-born woman, matters may be even more complex. Plane tickets overseas may not be within the budget of husband, family, or helping agencies, although occasionally a combination of resources can be arranged. Biracial children may not be accepted in her home country. If she elects to stay in the United States, language barriers may further hinder the process of finding employment and obtaining services. At Fort Campbell, the best source of homes and jobs for abused Korean women has proven to be a Korean church sponsored by the mission board of a major denomination. But one small church cannot accommodate all the women needing such services.

Military social-service agencies are most likely to be frustrated by lack of available options and resources in aiding women who wish to leave an abusive husband permanently.

Effective Use of Resources

The considerable number or resources available to aid violent families can be most effective if a *coordinated approach to intervention* is adopted. A network of agencies recognizing the serious nature of spouse abuse and working together to assist families caught in this dangerous pattern can be a powerful tool for change. Through agency interplay, identification can be centralized, negative sanctions, can be combined with positive opportunities to develop new behavior patterns, and referral can take place at the time of crisis when therapeutic intervention is most likely to be successful. The dysfunctional family can avail themselves of all existing resources rather than encountering them in some random piecemeal fashion. The impact of abruptly learning, (1) that abusive behavior will not be tolerated, (2) that the victim has some options in dealing with abuse, and (3) that a number of persons and agencies are available to assist the family, can collectively be enough to open a family system to major change. Role perceptions and the balance of power may be radically altered as the family is presented with a number of alternatives to the *status quo.*

Agencies can form such an intervention network through a process of education and communication. First, commanders, chaplains, law enforcement officers, medical personnel, and social workers must begin to understand the nature of spouse abuse. Commonly held myths about wife-beating have been known to prevent families from receiving appropriate assistance. At a minimum, these workers should be aware of five basic concepts:

1. Spouse abuse is a widespread problem throughout the country and it probably occurs in every military unit.
2. Wife abusers do not necessarily look or act differently from other men; they may well be model soldiers and even respected senior service members.
3. Women usually stay with abusive husbands for practical or affectional reasons, not because they are "masochists."
4. While battered wives may exhibit the range of irritating behaviors common to the human race, they do not "deserve" to be beaten.
5. Women tend to drop assault charges, not because they enjoy maltreatment, but because criminal penalties would hurt them as well as their husbands.

The author has found good response to presentations utilizing true and false tests, "What would you do if . . ." situations illustrating the difficult decisions to be made by those involved with a violent family, illustration of major points through case examples, and plenty of opportunity for group discussion.

Next, members of each group must be aware of their own procedures, options, and responsibilities. In-service training in agencies—especially for new workers—can outline possible procedures and resources to use when spouse abuse is encountered. Agency personnel should be aware of their role in the Army-wide or post-wide plan to deal with domestic violence. Large, diffuse groups are the most difficult to reach with such information. Military Police receive information on "domestic disturbances" during training and from training manuals, although they need to be briefed on local policies and procedures. Individual unit commanders are the largest group directly involved in spouse abuse and potentially the group most unaware of its own role. A published commander's guide for dealing with this problem and/or orientation for all those assuming command positions can advise the commander of the Army's interest in this problem, his or her responsibility for dealing with cases identified in the unit, and the various methods, formal and informal, available for intervention.

Finally, agencies must begin to communicate with each other and the community as a whole. Each service provider should be aware of other agency resources and the entry points to each system. As a working relationship develops between various groups, individuals will develop personal points of contact in other agencies and begin to work together to provide a coordinated intervention. The Army already has established an Army Child Advocacy Program with an interagency Child Protection and Case Management Team on each post to deal with cases of child abuse. In Germany a similar Women's Advocacy Board was formed in each community to deal with problems of sexual assault and wife abuse. Posts in the United States have established less formal programs of coordination and community education. The Directive on Family Advocacy currently being prepared by the Department of Defense will further encourage such action.

SUMMARY

The Army and other armed services are vitally concerned with problems of spouse abuse. While some stressors inherent in military life may tend to aggravate problems in violent families, the military is in a unique position to offer a coordinated community response to the abuser, victim, and family.

BIBLIOGRAPHY

Commander's Guide for Offenses of Rape, Sexual Assault and Wife Abuse. Prepared by Headquarters, V Corps, APO 09079

Disciplinary Measures to Deal with Assaults by Soldiers on Their Spouses. Memorandum for Staff Judge Advocate, Headquarters, 101st Airborne Division (Air Assault) and Fort Campbell, February 2, 1978.

Family Advocacy Program. Draft of proposed Department of Defense Directive, unnumbered, undated.*

James, Ed. *Treatment Approach with Abused Spouses in a Military Setting.* Paper presented at Biennial Army Social Work Symposium, San Antonio, Tex., March, 1980.

Martin, Del. *Battered Wives.* San Francisco: Glide Publications, 1976.

Raiha, Nancy. *I can't go home tonight: One hospital's experience in sheltering the battered spouse.* Paper presented at Biennial Army Social Work Symposium, San Antonio, Tex., March, 1980.

Standard Operating Procedures: Battered Wives Shelter. Headquarters, U.S. Army Infantry Center, Fort Benning, Georgia, August, 1980.

Women's Advocacy: Rape, Sexual Assault and Wife Abuse, Crimes of Violence Against Women. Letter distributed by Headquarters, V Corps, APO 09079, July 12, 1978.

USAIC Regulation 40-54: *Medical Service, Spouse Abuse.* Headquarters, U.S. Army Infantry Center, Fort Benning, March, 1979.

---

*Editor's Note: Since receipt of this article, the DOD Directive has been numbered 6400.1 and dated 19 May 1981.

7. From Inmate to Ex-Offender: A Prevention Program For Abusive Partners in Transition

Shelley E. Garnet, ACSW
Executive Director of Abused Women's Aid in Crisis, Inc.,
New York

Irwin L. Lubell, M.S.W.
Consultant at Abused Women's Aid in Crisis, Inc.,
New York

INTRODUCTION

Although the stresses of a highly competitive work world and family role expectations are in themselves overwhelming for most men, the burden of the ex-offender is even greater. Upon leaving prison, he must grapple with the realization that his role in the family has become unclear and that his status as the authority and breadwinner has been greatly diminished. In addition, his ex-offender status greatly reduces his chances for employment in an already tight job market. Other family members often have difficulty adjusting to the change. Resentment and tension are likely to surface, and the family as a whole may have no model for successfully adapting to the required reorganization.

RATIONALE

Abused Women's Aid In Crisis, Inc. (AWAIC) has launched an innovative program for inmates in transition. The AWAIC batterers prevention program operates from the Pre-Release Center of the Arthur Kill Correctional Facility (AKCF) located in Staten Island, New York. The Pre-Release Center, which was founded by inmates, provides both emotional support and practical information to assist volunteer inmates who are eligible for parole in their transition from prison life back to the community. It gives them information about job skills and employment prospects as well as focusing on the psychological stresses awaiting release. Approximately 85% of the population at the facility have histories of violent crime such as murder, rape, robbery, and assault; therefore, it is no wonder that a major concern of the population is domestic violence.

Arthur Kill is a minimum security facility and the average stay is usually two or more years. When a man becomes eligible to go before the parole board, he can opt to join the groups at the PRC about 90 days before review. Since many of the inmates at the PRC had been involved in violent domestic relationships prior to their incarceration, a high percentage feel that this could be a problem upon release.

For this reason, the PRC coordinating committee contacted AWAIC in the spring of 1979 and invited the social service staff to the prison to make a presentation about domestic violence. Both the participating AWAIC staff and the PRC were astounded by the high level of interest on the part of the inmates attending that first meeting. Many of them spoke privately with AWAIC staff members after the presentation requesting counseling. The large number of people attending (between 50–75 inmates) these exploratory sessions, and the continuing positive response since the program's inception, highlighted the need for a bona fide counseling program for this targeted population.

Timing is a significant factor in this model. Since even the most motivated man will have other pressing needs on his mind once a date has been set for his release, discussions about reentry into the family should begin prior to this time.

PROCESS

Inmates are not asked if they have had a history of violence, nor is the reason for incarceration solicited. The point to keep in mind is that motivation is usually high from the beginning, and that most men are willing to give an outside agency a trial run especially when it proposes to make their reentry easier in an area that has hitherto been neglected. At first it may be mere curiosity but it does not take long for this to turn into intense interest.

OBJECTIVES

The following goals are broad and represent an attempt to raise the level of consciousness while providing new models for adapting. All of this must be accomplished in the most benign, unthreatening way possible so as not to discourage participation. The goals are as follows:

1. To explore the alternatives to battering as a means of solving domestic disputes.
2. To inform participants about their legal rights and alternatives.
3. To begin to recognize sex-role patterns and their effects.
4. To begin a process of self-awareness.

These goals are based on the fact that before behavioral changes between spouses can be made, the individuals must have an opportunity to clarify and redefine their own roles, as well as to begin to learn how to articulate their concerns, and so change patterns of communication. According to (Fasteau, 1975; Sutton-Smith, 1966), "sex-role stereotyping does have a confining effect on males; it has restrained the full development of their emotional life."[*]

METHOD

Once the target population was identified, the next step was to establish rapport and to introduce AWAIC as a viable and credentialed agency specializing in the area of domestic violence. Having no formal connection with the correctional institute should have worked in our favor. Surprisingly, the inmates were originally quite guarded and reluctant to believe that we could be interested in their problems and able to accept their experiences and needs without judgment. This was compounded by the fact that originally the presentation was given by

---

[*]Miller, M. *"Masculinity May be Hazardous to Your Health: A Personal Growth Group for Men Only." Specialists in Group Work Journal,* 1980, **5,** (1) 41–45.

an all-female AWAIC team. After consideration, it was decided that this factor contributed to their hesitancy and mistrust, and so thereafter a male worker led the group. Some additional factors which created inmate resistance were their perception of us as white, middle class, and essentially removed from the harsh realities of their lives. These issues most assuredly had to be addressed in order to move beyond the obvious sexual, social, and racial barriers and on to the implementation of the program's goals. Unless the above was successfully accomplished, the presentation could not become anything more than a routine classroom lecture. Indicators such as facial expressions, level of tension in the room, and participation were used to assess the degree of acceptance. In this way we presented a living example of how a person could begin to cope with interpersonal tensions and individual differences without overtly aggressive behavior. It became the first crucial step in changing poor communication patterns. We were also able to win their respect and trust, demonstrating that it is possible to effect change without violence.

The unstructured, open-ended group model was chosen as our mode of intervention, primarily because as social workers we were aware of the fact that in a correctional institute, respect for individual integrity is often violated. The use of such groups helps provide a corrective experience. Elliot Strudt summarized it well in this excerpt from his article on "Correctional Services":

> Groups play an especially significant part in the resocializing process since normal social functioning calls for an ability to relate to appropriate reference groups and to use their resources in a way that is mutually helpful.*

GROUP PROCESS

Each group was composed of two components: the task and the affective. The task aimed to disseminate information about domestic violence through a lecture on the issue and the use of a film. "Violence Behind Closed Doors," is a 24–minute sound/color motion picture

---

* Studt, Elliot. "Correctional Services," In *Encyclopedia of Social Work,* 1965, Harry L. Lurie, (ed.) New York: N.A.S.W., 1965, pp. 690–95.

which was designed to stimulate public awareness of violence in the home by interviewing male batterers and female victims. A major part of the film examines the concrete alternatives such as educational and legal programs, shelters and counseling. While the film is specifically geared for women, it nonetheless fosters a lively discussion. Often it is the film which attracts the largest audience since the men would rather initially observe than risk sharing.

Prior to the start of the film, an announcement is made that those men who would prefer not to participate in a discussion, are free to leave at the film's completion. More than half of the group will leave after the film, leaving about 25 group participants.

The next piece, or the affective, was so called since the focus at this time is on feelings or affects. The film helps to structure this discussion by exposing through the interviews the following precipitants of violence: low self-esteem, financial problems, alcohol abuse, sex-role stereotypes, and the cycle of abuse. All of the above are easily related to by the group members who remain and are anxious to share their ideas and concerns.

No guidelines are set and the atmosphere remains free and unstructured. The result is often spontaneous and dynamic, with expressions ranging from loneliness and anger toward the spouse and/or family to questions around child support and custody. The following are some case examples coming from the group process, to illustrate the potential for growth and the implementation of our expressed objectives.

Case Examples

Case #1. Following the film, there was the usual silence. I asked if there were any reactions or thoughts about the film. Someone in the back said that it only showed the woman's point of view and didn't really bring out what the man has to go through sometimes. I told him that's true and asked him to say more. He said that a lot of times a woman doesn't appreciate what a man does, that he's out all day working, trying to make a buck, support a family and all she can do is nag and complain. A number of other men agreed. The first man then said that sometimes a woman doesn't seem to understand anything but a slap once in a while. I said that there seems, then, to be a problem in getting across to the woman what you're experiencing, or what you're feeling. He said that they just don't listen. I said that even though that might be true, there are alternatives to resolving these kinds of conflicts without physical force, and pointed out that at our agency we see individual men and couples with similar concerns to help them work these issues out. At that point another man asked what we could do for him if, when he gets out of jail, his woman is constantly on his case, saying things she knows will get him angry. Sounds like she's trying to provoke you. Yeah, he said, she knows she's gettin' me upset, but she'll just keep at it. I asked if he tried telling her that when she does that, he becomes really angry. She doesn't care, he said. She'll keep going until I really feel like punching her in the head. He then suggested we do a role play to which I agreed. He would play his wife and I would be him. We arranged the chairs so we were facing each other in the center of the group. He began (to me) Mrs. C (inmate): Uncross your legs! I don't like the way you're sittin'! Mr. C. (worker): Hey, I like sittin' like this. Mrs. C: I don't care what you like. Only faggots sit like that. Mr. C: Hey, you know when you talk like that it gets me angry. Mrs. C: That's too bad. Now why don't you just uncross you're legs. Mr. C: What's bothering you? Why are you acting like this? Mrs. C: Nothin's bothering me, faggot. You're just no good. Now move this chair over, and get outa my way! At this point I stopped the role play and told the inmate that I could really appreciate the frustration he must feel. He said that she'll just back you into a corner until there's no place to go, and then asked, "But what should I do if I really want the relationship to work out?" Another man jumped in saying that it wasn't worth it; that either, "You just keep takin' that kind of abuse or one day you'll just really smack her and end up back in jail. You just gotta be able to walk away." The first man said that that's not easy to do though when emotions are so strong. I told him that he's got a good point and suggested that while walking away was probably a better solution than beating her up and ending up back in jail, it might not be such an easy thing to do. He then said that in the scenario he had in mind, the woman had another man and was actually hoping he would hit her so that she would have grounds to send him back to prison. I then told him that if that's where the woman was at, not at all interested in trying to make the relationship work, then maybe the best way we could help him would be by trying to help him to leave, and by helping him deal with the sense of loss that it would bring about. He said that when you love a woman, it's hard to do what you know is best. I agreed, and told him that was something we could help him deal with, that we know it's not easy. When the group ended, he thanked me and said I had helped him sort some things out. We shook hands.

Among other things, this excerpt illustrates the hope and anxiety often surrounding the inmate's return to his partner and the fearful expectation that he may be confronted with an unsupportive, rejecting woman. The unspoken sense of humiliation, hurt and failure may be great, and this will certainly not increase the chances for a positive reintegration into society.

Case #2. While inmates will frequently want to know how we might help them with anticipated future encounters with their mates—encounters typically fraught with high-level emotional conflict which can easily lead to violence—they will also tell of regreted past experiences which ended in irretrievable loss. In the following excerpt, an inmate recounts events which led to a particularly tragic outcome.

> I said that being ex-offenders, the reality is that their chances of being arrested and imprisoned as a result of a violent fight with their mates were pretty high, but that there were alternatives to violence, and that's where we could be of help. ''We'll advocate for you in court if that's needed and make note of the fact that you sought outside help in a difficult situation; we'll help you work out a strategy so that a violent conflict can be avoided.'' At this point, an older inmate said that he was in prison because of family violence. He said that his wife had been seeing another man and that the two of them got into a fight in her apartment. The other man told him he was going to kill him. The inmate picked up a knife and went for him, just as his wife stepped between them. He inadvertently stabbed his wife and killed her. He said he's been living with that memory for over five years. I said that it must be a pretty sad memory to live with and he agreed. I said that he must be in tune with the issues that I've been discussing. He said that he was and added that situations like his happen more often than most people think. I told him that I thought he was right and then thanked him for sharing his own experiences with the group.

Case #3. For some inmates, the exposure inherent in the group method causes too much anxiety. As a result, we offer brief private meetings for inmates who request to speak to someone privately following the group discussion. In one such meeting, an inmate brings to light the impact of peer expectations inside the prison and the difficulty he had in risking exposure of this true feelings in the group. Nevertheless, the group discussion, coupled with the worker's receptivity, seemed to enable him to explore attitudes and feelings more openly than could otherwise have been the case, and allowed him to begin a process in which novel adaptive responses were examined.

> Inmate: When I get out of here, I'm not even gonna look for her. She knows where I'll be.
>
> Worker: That's not what you said a moment ago.
>
> Inmate: Yeah, I know. But she knows I care about her and that I'll always be there if she needs me. Nobody else will.
>
> Worker: I guess that's a hard thing for you to come right out and say, though.
>
> Inmate: Yeah, that's true. In here, though, you gotta be cool, not let anyone know you got feelings like that.
>
> Worker: What would happen if you did?
>
> Inmate: Well, people will come down on you, try to take advantage of you.
>
> Worker: It's risky to leave yourself vulnerable.
>
> Inmate: Yeah, it is.
>
> Worker: What about what happened in the group today? People seemed fairly open.
>
> Inmate: Yeah, that was OK. But you don't see that too often. Most of the time, you gotta keep an eye out for what people are doin' and thinkin'.
>
> Worker: So when it comes to something like your feelings about your woman friend, it's pretty hard to speak out about it honestly.
>
> Inmate: Well, right. That's the way it is. But like I told you, she means a lot to me and I care about her; it's just hard to reach her sometimes.
>
> Worker: And when you try to reach her, you take the chance that, as you said before, she'll act aloof and sort of disregard what you say.
>
> Inmate: Right.

The discussion continued and other aspects of the relationship which gave rise to tension and conflict, including threats of violence, were touched upon. We explored some of his options and their emotional implications and he said he would contact the agency upon release should he desire more assistance.

The spontaneity and openness of the group members clearly demonstrates the applicability of an unstructured group model for the beginning of a raising of consciousness.

FOLLOW-UP

Our work over the year proved to us that an expanded program was merited at the AKCF. A proposal for a Batterers Rehabilitation Project was submitted to the Department of Social Services, and with the coming of the New Year, AWAIC was awarded funding for the program year March 1980 to February 1981. The Batterers Rehabilitation Project located on-site at the correctional facility offers weekly psychotherapeutic counseling, educational groups, and follow-up counseling at AWAIC headquarters. In addition, AWAIC will engage the family of a man active in the prison program for preliminary family counseling prior to release, as well as provide ongoing family counseling after his release. Extensive documentation is being compiled so that AWAIC can share its findings with the community at large.

IMPLICATIONS FOR FUTURE PLANNING

Once a replicable model of treatment has been developed, it is hoped that the above program will be implemented in other correctional facilities throughout the nation. At present we are beginning the program at female correctional facilities where the focus will be on educating as well as discussing the unique position of female ex-offenders in transition.

The cycle of violence can only be eradicated through education, changes in interpersonal communication, and societal changes. Programs such as AWAIC's are the beginning of this process. This program has shown us that this so-called hard-to-reach population, when provided with a model for change, is eager and willing to participate. No change can come about without solid, clear guidelines.

CONCLUSIONS

Many agencies, even those working with both partners in the field of violence, have expressed their concerns to us in regard to contracting for such a group, and have listed all kinds of potential stumbling blocks. It is just this attitude that certainly is one of the reasons men are unwilling to go to agencies servicing victims of domestic violence. Whether one works on-site or at another facility, the men must be made to feel they are welcome. At AWAIC, special flyers for males were prepared and of course the switch to male counselors is a plus. If we are going to change attitudes and behavior, then we must be the first to set a model.

Interested, concerned, professional male workers are often as sensitive to the issues of wife battering as most female workers. The implication here is that wife beating is a learned behavior which is passed down through family systems. If we do not acknowledge the male, then the work will be one-sided. Just as women have assisted other women, so must men begin to do the same and help other men. This statement, which appears rather simplistic, is quite revolutionary, since many battered women programs were started by women, for women, with little or no help from our male society. Our program shows that change can occur, and must be moved to a level beyond what we started with.

8. Alcohol and Family Violence: Double Trouble

Jerry P. Flanzer, D.S.W.
Graduate School of Social Work,
University of Arkansas at Little Rock

Alcoholism is a disease, a disease for which there is no cure, a disease that we must and can control. Alcoholism is a physiological disease, for people who chronically drink alcohol are: (1) interfering with their bodies' normal ability to adequately synthesize proteins and sugar; (2) destroying brain cells, liver, and other organs; and (3) causing untold damage to their nutritional and electrochemical systems. Alcohol is not only habit forming, but also physiologically and psychologically habit forming. Although thought of as an "upper," alcohol is actually a depressant. Alcoholism also can become a social disease. Society's social lubricant provides the excuse to "get down and really talk" or "act-out" in a way one normally would never dare. Drinking alcohol has become a problem-solving act. Drinking allows one to forget the pain and feel back in control. Certainly this information sheds no new light for this reader. But few realize how similar and overlapping the alcoholism disease problem is with that of family violence.

While there may be some physiological basis, intrafamilial violence is primarily considered a psychological and social disease. As with alcoholism, family violence represents a way for the abuser to gain mastery over his/her own world. Family violence takes many forms:

spouse abuse (primarily wife abuse), sexual abuse and incest, and child abuse and neglect are the most widely known. Sibling abuse and abuse of the elderly (granny bashing) are more hidden quantities. The following focuses for purposes of clarity and brevity only upon the association of problem drinking/alcoholism and domestic violence (spouse abuse), leaving other forms of family violence for other publications.

The presence of alcohol is a frequent component of all forms of family violence—domestic violence (spouse abuse) is no exception. Moderate and problem drinkers are more frequently involved than light drinkers and abstainers! Note that the drinker need not be an alcoholic, but simply a moderate/heavy drinker to be more likely involved with spouse abuse. Certainly spouse abuse exists without alcohol being present, and husbands can drink without hitting their wives. However, the heavier the drinking the worse the physical abuse. The double incident means double trouble.

Repeating, the moderate or heavy drinker is more likely to be the aggressor. Additionally, he or she is more likely to severely neglect his or her spouse. *More often the abuser is the drinker* and not initially the victim. *Most often the batterer is the husband.* This latter point is often debated, for there is a strong contingent who believe that men and women are equally as likely to be the drinker and equally as likely to be the abuser. Their argument is that statistics attributing more abuse to men are a function of the reporting system and societal pressure, and not reality. This contingent often note that women get "hurt more," and show up more frequently in emergency rooms. Furthermore, they note that our society does not allow men to admit their abuse, while male victims show up more frequently in the morgue. The folklore is that the woman must "shore-up" her deficiency in strength with weapons and is more likely to strike when the man does not suspect. This, however, has yet to be proven.

Recent findings by Straus, et al., Flanzer, Spieker, among others, tip the scales in the husband's direction. Where once this author felt that the victim was equally as likely to be the drinker as the aggressor, recent findings have altered this view. This is not to negate the notion of a smaller percentage of retribution by the spouses of the alcoholic mate, and thus, in some cases the victim, indeed, may be the drinker.

Two actual cases which appeared at a mid-south shelter for battered women document this report:

In Case A, *the Virginia Case,* the husband was a moderate drinker. He only drank on the weekends. He often beat his wife, Virginia, age 22—although he never touched the children, ages 4 and 2. However, when he drank, the beatings were severe. Virginia, as a child, often saw her mother beaten by her father.

In Case B, *the Catherine Case,* the husband was an alcoholic, out of work. Catherine's husband beat her only while he was drinking, never when he was sober. Catherine entered the state hospital for depression. Neither Catherine nor her husband came from a nurturing family—both having been abused as children. Alone in the world they found each other.

Three patterns are often seen. In one pattern, the batterer seems to alternate between alcohol and aggression, drinking to avoid hitting, hitting perhaps to avoid drinking. In another pattern, battering appears only when alcohol is imbibed. This style takes three forms: in one the drinker has a few drinks and feels licensed to hit (the Virginia Case). In another (the Catherine Case), the drinking accentuates the act, while in still another, the drinker imbibes until he/she is in a helpless stupor and becomes the easy target/victim for abuse.

Family members look at the drinking father (or mother) in different ways, depending upon which style is operant. For example, the spouse will provide him with a drink if he is a quiet drunk, or if it renders him helpless. (This may even provide a chance for the spouse to get back at her husband.) Mostly though, spouses fear the drinking, as they watch their husband's outward personality change, and they recognize the apparent rage. Two distinct notions persist. One idea is that the drinker loses control of his inhibitions and judgment is impaired and then uses hitting to reassert control. "I just couldn't help myself," or "He didn't know what he was doing," are frequently heard explanations reflecting this position. Another idea is that the drinker drinks to give himself permission to do whatever he really wanted to do and dared not without a drink. Besides, drinking then provides the perfect out. If he is prosecuted his sentence would more than likely be commuted. After all, if alcohol is to blame all he need do is promise to stop drinking. Ironically, the spouse abuse situation which is compounded by alcoholism, is often easier to stop—partly because of the growing number of competent alcohol treatment centers and partly because of the ease of shifting all the blame to the drinking.

The family dynamics involved in battering and alcohol abuse are similar and overlapping. They support each other. Thus the likelihood of battering increases as drinking increases, and vice versa. Alcoholism affects the entire family, but first it affects the alcoholic and then it victimizes the family. The alcoholic must stop drinking in order for the family to be helped further. The family may have contributed to the alcoholic behavior, but first the individual alcoholic must stop drinking, and that's where initial help must focus. Similarly, the batterer must stop his (or her) aggression before the family is to be helped further. The family may have contributed to the aggressive behavior, but first the individual spouse must stop battering, if the family as a whole and the couple as an entity is to "work out" the necessary changes. In both instances, one can help the victimized others (the battered spouse, the alcoholic's spouse) live apart from or learn ways to assert self versus the continuation of the abuse. Without intervention, families become progressively more disorganized, increasing their vulnerability to crisis. Being in a chronic state of crisis becomes a life-style in itself. One must view the response to the crisis as an adaptive mechanism (an attempt to continue functioning and meeting basic needs) while also warding off deep depression and other psychiatric/dysfunctional processes.

These families, these couples, of necessity are faced with meeting their most basic need, that of guaranteeing their own physical safety. If they cannot solve this crisis, they can no longer maintain their family unit. One particular treatment approach, the family management approach, recognizes the meeting of basic individual and family needs as its central concept. The Maslovian building-block hierarchy of basic needs (i.e., physical safety, food and shelter, socioeconomic involvement, social interaction, and family self-actualization) is seen as the "step-ladder" of basics to prioritize intervention. Each need step must be addressed, in the given order, if family functioning is to be restored.

"The family will be able to grow and accept help when its basic needs show signs of being met; when the integrity of each individual family member is safeguarded; when relief from day-to-day crisis decision making gives way to beginning realistic steps in planning for the family and family members; and when the extrafamily resources permit growth and integration into the community. The identified patient will be enabled to accept help when this occurs. He will have been released to take responsibility and his family will have begun to let go emotionally. It means giving up attempts to control the deviant behavior, while providing protection from the consequences. This forces the . . . (abuser) . . . to decide if he wants to be part of the family and places the onus of responsibility where it belongs." (Flanzer, 1978)

Returning to the two cases presented earlier, one notes that:

> They both were housed in shelters to guarantee their own physical and nutritional safety. Virginia's social worker encouraged and supported her in finding a job, as well as completing her high-school requirements. Virginia was working toward meeting her individual needs. The crisis spiral stopped, for Virginia now could "stand on her own" and negotiate with her spouse. When he refused to guarantee her physical safety, she filed for divorce. The family unit was no more.
>
> On the other hand, Catherine was also supported by her social worker to reach a stage of independence and authority to be on her own. Having personal control over her life, she lost her "helplessness" stance and her depression. Shortly afterwards, she confronted her husband toward reestablishing the balance in their marriage. They are proceeding to work on their social interaction needs, including retracting from the victim triangle described next.

Physically abusing and drinking families both may be viewed through the classic psychotherapeutic "triangulation" concept. When both abuses are present, these pathological interchangeable roles are rigidified and intermeshed. (Flanzer, 1981)

Three distinct, but quickly changing roles are noticed: the Abuser, the Victim, and the Rescuer! The Abuser learned this effective response to solving problems, projecting fault on the victim. The Victim,

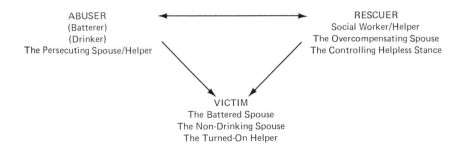

ABUSER
(Batterer)
(Drinker)
The Persecuting Spouse/Helper

RESCUER
Social Worker/Helper
The Overcompensating Spouse
The Controlling Helpless Stance

VICTIM
The Battered Spouse
The Non-Drinking Spouse
The Turned-On Helper

always overly loyal, often is socially isolated and hurt. The Rescuer, well meaning, enjoys controlling others. Each one suddenly finds him/herself in one of the other positions—as the victim uses the one-down position to manipulate new gains; and the overzealous rescuer begins laying down prosecuting rules or finds him/herself accused by the other two of meddling/violating their rights of privacy, etc.

The way out of the "Triangulation" is by: (1) contracting mutual agreements, (2) "taking care of business," (3) watching process, not content, and (4) keeping to the balance of individual and family needs on the hierarchy of needs ladder.

Specifically, mutually agreed upon client-counselor *contracts* focusing upon (1) goals aimed towards meeting individual and family needs, and (2) step-by-step means to reaching said goals, will keep conversations and problem-solving steps/interventions oriented to the "agenda" at hand. Thus the client's being able to "take care of business" has the effect of dropping the "hopeless-helplessness" (Seligman, 1975) model so often taken by the victim. In addition, feelings of success increase self-esteem and counter the exogenous depression felt by the victim and the aggressor.

Content and context are important. The words and interactions of the couple are indeed important. More important, however, is the process—"who says what to whom" and "in what order." What was the content and what are the signals which automatically transfer normal interaction into *all or none, one-up-one-down, win-lose situations.*

Virginia and her husband could not let go of their continuous need to assert control. After a beating, Virginia could count on a "make-up" gift. Giving up the "guilt syndrone" and exploring an equal-cooperative relationship meant facing financial realities. It was easier to dissolve the marriage. Are both Virginia and her husband destined to repeat their disastrous marriage? Statistical probability says yes.

Catherine and her husband are struggling. Years of fighting and bickering, drinking, and accusing are hard to give up, especially in light of an unknown future. Catherine and her husband had to back-track—essentially court again, to learn how to cooperate and not compete. Will they make it? Statistical probability says yes.

In review, regarding alcoholism, first the drinking must stop; regarding spouse abuse, first the hitting must stop, if resolution and change are to occur. Then, careful rethinking of individual and family goals must be made—especially noting the need level of the family. Finally, every effort must be made to get off the dysfunctional triangle. Everyone must be "detriangulated."

When domestic violence is noted—first, stop it, then investigate if alcohol is present or involved (and, of course, vice versa). If one is ignored in favor of the other, neither will cease!

REFERENCES

Berne, Eric. *Principles of Group Treatment.* New York: Oxford University Press, 1966.

Bowen, Murray. *Family Therapy in Clinical Practice.* New York: Jason Aronson, 1978.

Fields, M. D. and Kirchner, R. M., Battered women are still in need: A reply to Steinmetz. *Victimology: An International Journal,* 1978, 3 (1–2): 216–26.

Flanzer, J. P. Family focused management: Treatment of choice for deviant and dependent families, *International Journal of Family Counseling,* 1978, 6, (2): 25–31.

Flanzer J. P. Family management in the treatment of alcoholism. *British Journal on Alcohol and Alcoholism,* 13, Winter Issue, 1977–78.

Flanzer, J. P. The vicious circle of alcoholism and family violence. *Alcoholism,* 1, (3) Jan.–Feb., 1981.

Minuchin, Salvador. *Families and Family Therapy.* Cambridge: Harvard University Press, 1974.

Seligman, Martin. *On Depression, Development and Death.* San Francisco: W. H. Freeman, 1975.

Spieker, Gisela. Family violence and alcohol abuse. *Toxicomanies,* 1980, 13: 13–42.

Star, Barbara, et al., Pyschosocial aspects of wife battering. *Social Casework,* 1979, October, 479–87.

Straus, M., Gelles, R., and Steinmetz, S. *Behind Closed Doors: Violence in the American Family.* Garden City, N.Y.: Doubleday, 1980.

Part V Treatment

"Do give your heart to this, please: human beings are destroying each other through violence, the husband is destroying the wife and the wife is destroying the husband. Though they sleep together, each lives in isolation with his own problems with his own anxieties; and this isolation is violence."

—J. Krishnamurti from *Beyond Violence*

9. The Unmaking of the Abusive Partner

Maria Roy
Founder and President of Abused Women's Aid in Crisis, Inc.
New York

There are close to 2 million reported cases of partner abuse each year, meaning that nearly 2 million abusive partners are known to exist in the United States today. This figure does not reflect the cases that go unreported—one can only speculate about how widespread the problem really is. Of the known cases, there are a growing number of abusive partners who are clearly interested in stopping their violence, and an equally interested professional community intent on assisting them in realizing this goal. Good intentions aside, the greatest single impediment to this achievement could be oversimplification. Oversimplification results in reducing all batterers to one common denominator by lumping them into a unitary clinical category and prescribing treatment strategies for all of them that are likewise singular. Since treatment strategies for this population are still in the developmental stages, the complex etiological factors and their specific treatment implications should be reflected in the final treatment analysis. In other words, a simple single treatment formula applied to all abusive partners—the most common being group discussions/counseling and/or individual psychotherapy—will not always bring about the desired results, *viz.* the cessation of violent behavior. While many abusive partners benefit from such an approach, others do not. The question, then, is why not? Why is it that some batterers do not favorably respond to supportive therapy? Could it be that the etiological picture is different for these batterers, and that a behaviorist approach to un-learning violent patterns of interpersonal communications cannot be applied across the board?

The key word, as I see it, is *differential diagnosis.* Differential diagnosis attempts to uncover the possible cause or causes of the violence by first ruling out certain suspected clinical conditions while being mindful of both the physiological and psychological factors that may be generating the undesirable behavior. By ignoring or being unaware of the possibility of organic problems, the professional reduces the chances of success with each client whose violence stems from a physiological source.

Success depends upon a thorough diagnostic workup—the more thorough, the better are the chances for positive results. When indicated, proper referral for physiological testing may reveal findings that will have significant treatment implications.

There are a number of physical conditions causing a person to be violent—some result from neurological disorders, some from nutritional factors, while others are attributable to environmental toxicity, and still others due to substance abuse.

Below is a partial listing of violence-associated physical conditions.

A. *Neurological Disorders* [*]

1. Disorders of the limbic system
2. Disorders of the neocortex
3. Head trauma or other cerebral insults such as epidemic encephalitis
4. Temporal lobe epilepsy
5. Prenatal, natal, or postnatal histories of birth injury, foetal anoxia, and infantile convulsions
6. Minimal brain dysfunctions and severe cases of cerebral palsy, mental retardation, and arrested hydrocephalus
7. Sequela of viral encephalitis, brain abscess, stroke, subarachnoid hemorrhage, presenile dementia, Huntington's chorea, normal pressure hydrocephalus, arrested internal hydrocephalus

---

[*] See "The Neurology of Explosive Rage: The Dyscontrol Syndrome," by Frank A. Elliot, M.D., FRCP In *Battered Women: A Psychosociological Study of Domestic Violence* Maria Roy (ed.), for additional information.

8. Sequela of cerebral anoxia due to cardiac arrest
9. Removal of tumors of the limbic system

B. *Nutritional and Environmental Factors (Biochemical Imbalances)**

1. Nutritionally induced chronic endocrinopathy (reactive hypoglycemia)
2. Cerebral allergic responses to foods
3. Improper levels of vitamins and minerals
4. Elevated levels of neurotoxins
5. Malnutrition (plain or overconsumptive)
6. Stress induced by certain food additives

C. *Substance Abuse***

1. Depressants: alcohol, barbiturates, nonbarbiturate sedative-hypnotics, tranquilizers
2. Stimulants: cocaine, antidepressants, convulsants, amphetamines (especially in combination with alcohol)
3. Narcotics: heroin, morphine, codeine, demerol, methadone, opium
   NOTE: Depressants and stimulants are highly responsible for violent behavior, while narcotics may indirectly affect levels of violence usually during withdrawal.
4. Hallucinogens: LSD, PCP, marijuana, mescaline, DOM, Psilocybin, and Psilocyn. This drug group, by itself, has little effect on raising levels of violence. However, panic reactions to the drugs could cause adverse reactions.

The above listing represents a skeletal outline of possible physical conditions at the root of partner abuse. It is meant to alert professionals who are in the process of developing therapeutic programs for batterers to the many physiological factors to be considered in diagnostic screening.

---

*See "Effects of Environmental and Nutritional Factors on Potential and Actual Batterers," by Alexander Schauss in this book for more details.
**See "Alcohol, Drugs and partner Abuse," by Robert J. Powers, Ph.D., and Irwin L. Kutash, Ph.D., in this book for more details.

10. Classification of Violent Behavior for Purposes of Treatment Planning: A Three-Pronged Approach

Louis B. Schlesinger, Ph.D.
Coordinator, Violence Treatment and Prevention Program,
V.A. Medical Center, East Orange, N.J., and Clinical Assistant
Professor of Psychiatry and Mental Health Sciences,
College of Medicine and Dentistry of New Jersey.

Mark Benson, M.S.W.
Assistant Coordinator, Violence Treatment and Prevention Program,
V.A. Medical Center, East Orange, N.J.

Michael Zornitzer, M.D.
Chief, Mental Hygiene Clinic,
V.A. Medical Center, East Orange, New Jersey and
Assistant Professor of Psychiatry and Mental Health Sciences,
College of Medicine and Dentistry of New Jersey.

For a great many years, those who acted out in a destructive fashion were typically shunned by the mental health profession and deemed either "psychopathic," untreatable, or relegated to the law-enforcement or correctional sphere. However, since the early to mid-1970s, there has been increased interest in the problem of aggressive behavior because violence has become redefined as a clinical condition (e.g., Lion et al., 1976), and therefore, a legitimate area of study. In 1977, the

Violence Treatment and Prevention Program at the East Orange, N.J., Veterans Administration Hospital was established by the authors. Here, we had the opportunity to study, in depth, various cases of violent behavior that were referred from the local veterans' community. From our work, we developed a three-pronged approach to the classification and evaluation of violent veterans with treatment strategies specific to each category of violence. We also gained some insight into the specific difficulties encountered by veterans who have problems with violence, and the relationship of the military experience to their problems. It is the purpose of this chapter to outline our system of classification in order to facilitate treatment plans that are based on proper differential diagnosis. Our classification systems has three basic dimensions: primary psychiatric condition, episodic dyscontrol, and domestic violence.

Violence, like most psychiatric conditions, is not a unitary concept. There are different clinical pictures, different etiologies, different courses, and different prognoses. There has been a trend in recent years, particularly among those of a purely humanistic orientation, to devalue classification. However, without a structure with which to order events, the world would appear chaotic and without relationships. There has been no generally accepted classification for violence, but there have been various classifications for crime, including violent crime, such as homicide. Clark (1971) divides crime into six specific categories of social offenses while Brancale (1955) believed crime should be classified simply into administrative and psychiatric groupings. Halleck (1971) divided crime into adaptive and maladaptive. Adaptive crime is motivated by some type of logical or purposeful notion while maladaptive crime is a result of psychopathology where the motivations are not always apparent. Tanay (1969) developed a classification system for homicide into (1) dissociative, (2) psychotic, and (3) egosyntonic. The egosyntonic homicide is similar to Halleck's adaptive crime, while the dissociative and psychotic correspond to Halleck's maladaptive crime.

Miller and Looney (1974), in their study of adolescent homicide, argued that the significant common denominator was the degree of dehumanization of the victim by the offender. These authors believed that they could predict violence based on such a degree of dehumanization. The legal profession also has attempted to classify crime, both violent and nonviolent. However, the legal profession deals *only* with the most superficial motivation, and what may seem to be logical phenomena may actually be an irresistable, compelling urge by the offender, who, himself, is not even fully aware of the motivation. The psychiatric diagnosis, per se, cannot be used as a sole basis for classification of violence since only acts that are a direct outgrowth of organic, toxic, or paranoid states are relevant. In search of a common denominator, Revitch and Schlesinger (1978; 1981) have developed a classification of crime—including violent crime and homicide—based on a motivational spectrum of acts stimulated by sociogenic or external factors on one end and acts stimulated by psychogenic or internal factors on the other end of the scale. This latter system's prime purpose is to aid in solving prognostic and dispositional problems.

In our work with violent patients, we have found that the latter methods of classification are not fully helpful for treatment planning, particularly in cases of spouse abuse. Therefore, for purposes of treatment, we have developed, a three-pronged method of classification of violence:

(I)   Violence as a direct outgrowth of a primary psychiatric condition.
(II) Episodic dyscontrol syndromes.
(III) Domestic violence.

It is not always the specific act itself (e.g., wife battering) that forms the basis of our classification; instead, the dynamics and cause of the act are primary. For example, spouse abuse may be the result of psychotic delusions and therefore such a case would be classified in category I rather than III. Additionally, if a patient is battering his spouse and it is uncovered that he is explosive in many other situations outside of the home, he is classified in category II (episodic dyscontrol), since his violence at home is just another incidence of his explosiveness, rather than specific to his wife. Cases of violence that are a direct outgrowth of a psychosis are most commonly paranoid schizophrenia, and various organic and toxic states, typically alcohol and some types of drug abuse. Episodic dyscontrol syndrome covers a wide range of behavior, including the explosive personality and catathymic attacks (Wertham, 1937; Revitch and Schlesinger, 1978, 1981; Schlesinger and Revitch,

1980). *Domestic violence is limited to acts of aggression solely in the home directed toward the spouse or the children, and where primary psychiatric condition and episodic dyscontrol are ruled out.* Such a classification system is not intended to be applied rigidly: it is merely a system of ordering violent patients for the purposes of effective and rational treatment planning.

I. VIOLENCE AND PRIMARY PSYCHIATRIC CONDITIONS

Violence associated with psychiatric conditions most commonly occurs in the organic, toxic, and paranoid states. Regarding the organic conditions, epilepsy stands out, by most, as one of the main explanations of sudden attacks of violence and aggression. The epileptic seizure itself, or violence as a manifestation of postictal confusion, are often cited as causes for unprovoked attacks that are goal-less, chaotic, or have occurred with little provocation. Various encephalopathies have also been cited as the cause of violent or antisocial behavior (Wilson, 1955; Walters, 1977). Bachet (1950, 1951) presented a concept of "criminogenic encephalosis" that is characterized by temper tantrums, violent outbursts, antisocial behavior, and enuresis. Many explosive rages, particularly in children and adolescents, have been thought to be the result of various brain injuries (Bowman and Blau, 1949). Mark and Ervin (1970) reported a case where homicidal violence was linked to tumor in the limbic system, which, after removal, eliminated the amount of overt aggression. The following case is illustrative of the relationship between organic pathology and violence.

Case 1. A 33-year-old male was referred to the violence clinic for repeated outbursts of violence, uncontrolled rages, and explosive attacks that occurred with little provocation and with amnesia for the events. The violence was ongoing for over 10 years beginning after discharge from the military. The patient drifted in and out of various jobs, finished high school and one year of college, and had three marriages, all filled with violence and wife battering. The family history included brutality by his alcoholic father and overprotectiveness by his mother. He reported bedwetting to 10 years of age. During the interview he was spontaneous and easily engaged in conversation; he did not admit to hallucinations but reported "sounds," and feelings of depression with accompanying suicidal thoughts. There was also a paranoid tinge to his thinking. The violent episodes were unprovoked and followed by amnesia. On one occasion, after an episode of violence at home, regarding a younger stepdaughter he stated: "I couldn't believe I did it, I thought it was a dream." Such experiences were also reported after other episodes of wife battering and explosiveness. Neurological evaluation disclosed two abnormal EEGs with spikes in the temporal area. Extensive neuropsychological evaluation supported the diagnosis of temporal lobe epilepsy. The patient was treated with anticonvulsants and supportive psychotherapy with a favorable outcome.

The most common substance associated with violence is alcohol. In Wolfgang's classic 1958 study of homicide, he found that 54% of the offenders and 53% of the victims were under the influence of alcohol at the time of the offense. Mayfield (1976) concluded that most alcoholic murders involve acquaintances and family members, frequently husband and wife. Out of all the drugs, Phencyclidine (PCP or "angel dust") is the most dangerous substance in most provocative, assaultive, or extremely aggressive behavior. Peterson and Stillman (1979) state that patients under the influence of PCP are "dangerous to others because of paranoia and strong tendencies towards violence" (p. 142). Lysergic Acid Diethylamide (LSD) is another agent that may result in violent behavior if the subject develops paranoid delusions and responds to them. Amphetamine abuse often results in paranoia with resultant acts of aggression. Heroin is not directly a cause of violent crime, but it is a major indirect cause since many individuals will engage in aggressive activities to obtain money to buy the drug.* The following case of violence and substance abuse is illustrative.

Case 2.   A 31-year-old male was evaluated in the violence clinic with the presenting problem being domestic violence. The patient had a history of beating his wife, punching a former wife in the stomach during her pregnancy causing a miscarriage, beating his mother and fracturing her ribs resulting in her hospitalization, abusing an 18-year-old younger sister by punching her in the face, and numerous other acts of violence towards women in his home. The patient stated that he did not fight with his father because "he was a golden gloves and would kill me, I'm not crazy." In all

---

* See Powers and Kutash in this book.

relationships the patient had with women, he abused them and would hit them regularly stating "I hit them to keep them on their toes." P.V. recently fathered a child whose mother he also beats and whom he abused while she was pregnant. He plans to live with the woman and child eventually, but is currently afraid he might lose control and abuse both. Violence began after the patient was released from the military. While in Vietnam he became addicted to heroin and his habit persists into the present. Prior to the military, while in high school, P.V. abused some substances such as amphetamines and barbiturates.

At the time of evaluation, P.V. was a patient on a drug detoxification unit. All of this violence and battering, it was dicovered, occurred only when P.V. became "high on drugs and alcohol." He described himself as having a "double personality," inasmuch as he revealed being passive and easy-going when not under the influence of various substances but violent when high. The patient described a childhood and adolescence with much violence in the home, frequent beatings by the father and the like. He now states he would like to "kill" his father but he is afraid to because the father is much stronger. The patient experiences frequent depression of mild to moderate intensity with some suicidal ideas. There is no suicide attempt in his history and this did not seem to present a real threat at present. Psychotic symptomatology was absent both clinically and upon probing in the interview. When his paramour was interviewed separately, she stated the problem as "he drinks too much and gets violent." The same fact was elicited when his former wife was questioned.

Comment.   Initially, this case might appear to fall into category III of domestic violence. However, analysis of the dynamics and causes of his behavior reveals it is only when abusing substances that he becomes violent. Therefore, for therapeutic purpose, he must be classified in category I, and his addiction must be treated as primary. If treated only as a case of domestic violence (i.e., through family therapy), the addiction would not be touched and his aggressive behavior would definitely continue.

Paranoid schizophrenia and the spectrum of the various paranoid states and disorders are frequently the causes of violent, even homicidal, acts. Swanson et al. (1970), in their extensive review of the paranoid conditions, state pathological jealousy and paranoid delusions as a major cause of homicide. Lanzkron (1963) found 37.3% of 150 mental patients charged with murder had paranoid delusions and

20% displayed pathological jealousy and delusions of infidelity as the causes of their crime. Conjugal paranoia, originally described by Revitch (1954), is the condition whereby one spouse develops an ingrained, delusional system that the other spouse is unfaithful. Such a delusion is intractable and frequently results in wife battering, sometimes homicide. The following is a case of a disorganized paranoid psychotic where violence was a direct outgrowth of delusions and his mental condition.

Case 3. A 34-year-old married male initially presented to the hospital complaining of auditory hallucinations, inability to sleep, loss of appetite, and memory disturbances. He reported that he started to feel depressed 4 years previously when his wife deserted him (apparently due to abuse), taking their two children, furniture, and household goods while the patient was at work. Three weeks prior to admission to the hospital, L.R. began to wake up with nightmares in which he saw himself involved with people falling and dying one by one. He would awaken at night believing he heard the hissing of cobras that were supposed to have been brought to him by Black Muslims. Upon examination, his affect was inappropriate, and loose associations and confusion as to his real identity were also striking presenting symptoms. He was hospitalized, successfully treated with antipsychotic medication and supportive psychotherapy, and was discharged with the diagnosis of paranoid schizophrenia.

Four months later, he was readmitted to the hospital because of an urge to jump from a building rooftop along with auditory hallucinations telling him that he was not himself but actually another man. He believed he lost his purpose in life, that he was being persecuted by Black Muslims who were "out to get everyone who is not like them." He also revealed homicidal ideation towards his brother-in-law. He stated that if he did not get help, he would be compelled to kill this individual. While on the hospital psychiatric ward, he threatened to "punch out" other patients whom he felt were picking their noses in an attempt to annoy him. He assaulted two other patients whom he perceived as threatening to him, and on one occasion, he required physical restraint and seclusion. Once again, he was treated with antipsychotic medication; his condition improved and he was discharged. After his discharge, he stopped taking the medication and once again he began hearing voices telling him "don't stop fighting, keep on hitting." The voices also told him he was someone else; he then became extremely delusional, believing he was two different ages, and unsure of which was real. He believed he had two sets of children, and at different times, that he either had two wives or that one of his wives had different identities. He thought he was married at age 12 and that his family was conspiring to abscond with money he made from best-selling songs he had written and the like. While working, he assaulted a co-worker stating that the man had "grabbed his ass." Upon questioning, L.R. revealed that he believed his co-worker, a Black Muslim, was trying to rape him, and this was, he said, part of the group's initiation ritual. The patient's history was replete with family violence between the parents and himself.

Comment. L.R. was seen in the violence clinic for evaluation and recommendations as to treatment. We agreed with the psychiatric finding that L.R. was suffering from paranoid schizophrenia, and his violence was, for the most part, a direct outgrowth of a psychotic process, particularly paranoid delusions. The patient was again treated with antipsychotic medication and once again his condition improved. He was followed for over 2 years in out-patient supportive psychotherapy with a very good result. While L.R., at the time of the evaluation, was not engaged in battering women, he had done so in the past and could do so in the future if women (or his wife) were woven into his paranoid system.

The following case illustrates the relationship of pathological jealousy (conjugal paranoia) to wife battering.

Case 4. A 38-year-old male and his 37-year-old wife were referred to the violence clinic through the courts with the presenting problem being domestic violence. Each partner was interviewed separately and then together. During the interview with Mr. M., he admitted to wife battering for the length of their 3-year marriage. However, he argued that it was in response to constant provocation by his wife. He related his belief that Mrs. M. was "mentally ill" because she was obsessed with his infidelity, a charge he denied completely. He stated that she calls his office "30 to 40 times a day," searches for clues to prove his unfaithfulness, follows him in her car, questions his friends and co-workers, and then becomes violent and hysterical herself when he denies seeing other women. Mr. M. described his wife as "throwing things throughout the house," "faking passing out," hitting him and frequently getting into violent and verbal arguments while in public. Mr. M. was nonpsychotic with no psychiatric history and no history of battering his previous wife or any other woman. He was a retired Army sergeant who currently had a stable job and was, apparently, an adequate provider.

Mrs. M. was interviewed and questioned about her preoccupation with her husband's unfaithfulness. She stated that she never found him with another woman; yet, she could not help but believe, for various and numerous bizarre reasons, that he was "fooling around." She stated that she does get emotional and violent herself at home, and further stated that she cannot control her behavior, particularly when she questions Mr. M. in regard to his fidelity. Mrs. M. impressed the examiners as an hysterical individual suffering from conjugal paranoia. Prior to her marriage, she was a professional flamenco dancer, and she described a history in which she was raped at ages 9 and 13 by her father who was an alcoholic, semiprofessional boxer.

Comment. This is a complex case in that we are dealing with conjugal paranoia which results in suspicion and an intractable belief system that one spouse is unfaithful. Prior research (Revitch, 1960) finding that marital therapy in such cases is impossible recommends separation when conjugal paranoia is diagnosed. Mr. M. is, in part, reacting to his wife's violence, hysteria, and accusations; in part to his frustration and stress at living under such conditions, and also in part to his pent-up hostility and anger towards his wife. Despite the many problems both Mr. and Mrs. M. had, wife battering probably would not have occurred if not for Mrs. M.'s mental condition of pathological jealousy. Both patients were treated for a period of 9 months in individual psychotherapy with little success and no change at all in Mrs. M.'s mental state with regard to her suspicions of infidelity by Mr. M. After 1 year, both partners decided to separate, and at last contact, they were living apart peacefully.

II. EPISODIC DYSCONTROL SYNDROMES

The episodic dyscontrol syndromes can be conceived of as a spectrum of disorders. On one end of the spectrum, organic factors play a role etiologically and on the other end of the scale, psychodynamic factors predominate. In between these two extremes are various dyscontrol syndromes with a mixture of both organic and psychodynamic factors which result in explosive behavior. Menninger and Mayman's (1956) and Menninger's (1964) theory of mental illness is based on a number of possible adaptational stages to life's stress. Their third level of adaptation was labeled episodic dyscontrol. Each stage is defensive in nature in that it prevents a lower level of adaptation such that, in the case of episodic dyscontrol, psychosis or suicide is prevented by the outbursts of rage. Such a theory is essentially psychodynamic in explanation. The following case is illustrative:

Case 5. A 34-year-old male was referred to the violence clinic by the court and probation department. Current charges included three counts of assault and battery which occurred under the following circumstances. In the first incident, while the patient was driving a cab on New Year's Eve, a van accidently hit his vehicle when he cut the van off. There were four men in the van who alighted from it and confronted J.K. J.K. stated "I had to prove something. I had an attitude on." He continued that he felt "they were laughing at me." He grabbed a tire iron which he kept under the car seat and assaulted all four, inflicting serious injury which required hospitalization for three of the men. The second atrocious assault and battery involved the cutting of a fellow motorcycle club member. The patient described the incident as follows: "This guy used to beat up Donna (the patient's paramour), but she deserved it." J.K. indicated the two men had an argument which led to the patient's cutting his opponent with a knife when J.K. began to feel threatened, confronted, and put down. The third assault involved an attack on a polic officer when he arrested J.K. J.K. had been offended by the officer's manner of arrest and so he kicked, hit, and assaulted him.

The patient's history was replete with acts of explosive violence beginning at age 9 when he stabbed a classmate in the eye with an umbrella for no apparent reason other than he "got angry." His violence was indiscriminate, with the victims being girl friends, wives, friends, foes, family members, or just about anyone who "provoked" him. There were numerous other antisocial acts including breaking and entering, stealing cars, selling stolen property, violating parole, and the like. J.K.'s home life was described as very disorganized. He was raised by his mother and step-father whom he "hated" most of his life. An uncle lived in the home and he apparently molested J.K.'s younger sister on one occasion. He reported one homosexual experience at age 14 while incarcerated. He said he engaged in this because "I wanted to see what a chick is experiencing." After extensive interviewing, the patient stated that he is basically passive and tried in prison and in his developmental years to act violently to hide his "passivity." There was no evidence on any of the neuropsychological or neurological evaluations of organic pathology, and there was no significant psychotic process revealed. Diagnostically, he falls within the spectrum of the antisocial personality disorders with obvious episodic dyscontrol syndrome.

Comment. The dynamics of this case clearly involve violence as a compensation or reaction formation against underlying passivity, feelings of weakness, and possibly even homosexual pressures. After 3 months of outpatient psychotherapy, during which time such conflicts were discussed, there was a clear reduction in the patient's violent outbursts. He was lost to followup when he moved to a different state.

Monroe (1970, 1974, 1978) elaborated upon Menninger's original concept and took a middle ground with regard to the etiology of the dyscontrol syndromes. Monroe believes that both organic and psychodynamic factors play a role. He referred to "faulty equipment" as the neurophysiological substrate and "faulty learning" as life experience and psychodynamic factors. A case of murder illustrating episodic dyscontrol was presented by Ratner and Shapiro (1979) and discussed by Revitch and Schlesinger (1981). In this case, a man suddenly stabbed a woman to death after she apparently laughed at him. Once the offender gained control, he called the authorities. Psychological testing, soft neurological signs, and brain damage elicited by a CAT scan were suggestive of organic pathology (faulty equipment), while a history of intrafamilial violence and feelings of inadequacy suggested psychodynamic factors (faulty learning). The following case, seen in our violence clinic, is also illustrative of Monroe's concept of episodic dyscontrol:

Case 6. A 35-year-old male was seen for evaluation through the courts for numerous arrests due to explosive violence, and, as in Case 5, the victims ran the gamut from wives, girl friends, co-workers, and associates. The latest episode involved the stabbing of a police officer when R.J. was told to stop loitering. He had previously served several years in state prison for atrocious assault. Throughout his life he had been arrested over 15 times for various other assaults, but admitted to hundreds more, most of which occurred in the home and almost always went unreported. He cut his friend's throat because "he yelled at me." He "stabbed a guy with a knife because he didn't say 'excuse me.' " There were other offenses including "cutting a friend over a pool game" and "hitting a man with a garbage can and sticks," shooting an acquaintance in the leg, and killing many Vietnamese soldiers while in the service. R.J. stated that his "feelings" are hurt easily and he cannot control his violent rages. He was reared in an inner-city ghetto, being one of 10 children whose father was an alcoholic. His entire upbringing was impoverished and he experienced violence as a way of life to some extent.

R.J. sustained a head injury while in the Army, and he reported being unconscious for 3 days. He was treated with anticonvulsants for almost 10 years but is currently medication free, but under neurological care and follow-up.

Comment. In this case, both the neurophysiological (prior head injury) and the psychodynamic components (traumatic upbringing, feelings of inadequay, low self-esteem, etc.) interact resulting in the episodic dyscontrol syndrome.

Catathymic crisis was originally introduced into the field of criminal psychopathology by Wertham (1937) and used as an explanation for the various unprovoked episodes of severe violence without an organic etiology. Gayral et al. (1956) described emotional outbursts under the name catathymic paroxysms, and Revitch (1964) differentiated severe emotional outbursts in a prison population from psychomotor epilepsy with the former being labeled catathymic attacks. Wertham's original definition of catathymic crisis was as follows: "A catathymic reaction is the transformation of the stream of thought as the result of certain complexes of ideas that are charged with a strong affect, usually a wish, a fear or an ambivalent striving." (Wertham, 1937, p. 975)

Revitch and Schlesinger (1978, 1981) define catathymic crisis not as a diagnostic entity but rather a psychodynamic process frequently accompanied by disorganization and characterized by an accumulation of tension released through the violent act and followed by relief. Two types of catathymic process have been defined: (1) acute and (2) chronic. The acute process is essentially a sudden, unprovoked murder or violent act without obvious motivation. Ruotolo (1968) believed that an injury to the pride system was fundamental in precipitating such rage. Satten, Menninger, and Mayman (1960) described a classic case of acute catathymic attack when a soldier killed a preadolescent girl by drowning her without any obvious provocation and with partial amnesia for the event.

In the chronic catathymic process, depressed mood, loose schizophreniclike thinking, and obsessive preoccupation may precede the violent act for weeks, months, and even up to a year. For some reason, the patient comes to believe that the only solution to his state of distress and tension is through violence. Once the act is accomplished, a sense of relief is felt. In retrospect, the act itself often seems ego-alien and of a dreamlike quality. It is common for such individuals to seek attention through various mental health channels while in the early stages of this condition, and even while toying with the idea of violence, typically towards family members and wives. Frequently, however, such fantasies tend to be dismissed and the patient is treated solely for depression.

Revitch and Schlesinger (1981) have differentiated various important characteristics of the acute and chronic process. For example, the victim in the acute attack is usually a stranger while a family member, spouse, or one with an otherwise close relationship is the victim in the chronic process. The following case of an individual in the incubation phase of the chronic process is illustrative:

Case 7. An 18-year-old male presented himself at the evaluation clinic of our hospital complaining of depression and the inability to sleep. While being examined by an attending psychiatrist, he revealed homocidal ideas and impulses directed toward his immediate family, and was admitted to the hospital. At this point, he was referred to the violence clinic for evaluation and recommendations.

The following information was brought forth: The patient was discharged from the Marines just 7 days prior to having been seen at the V.A. hospital. He had been in the military for 13 months, but was discharged for psychiatric reasons after having spent several months in a military hospital. His ideas of killing began when he entered the Marines, and he even became a rifle expert because "I like shooting so much." He got involved in many fights where "I tried to kill several of my friends—I said that it was an accident that I stabbed them, but it really wasn't. I wanted to kill them." After discharge, he went to his parents' home where he lived with them, his wife, and baby daughter. He reported that he did not leave his room for the 7 days he was at home. He had "constant thoughts of killing." The patient stated: "I felt like I was going to do something. If I had a rifle, I'd go on top of the roof and start sniping. I'd kill 100 people." He also said, "I thought of killing my whole family. I thought of stabbing my father in the back while he was sleeping, and killing my wife and child." A.G. further stated: "I think I'll feel better after I kill someone. It will be one less mouth to feed, one less scum of the earth." He revealed hatred for drug dealers and criminals and furthered expressed rigid moral ideas that, at time, bothered him. Prior to the military, there was no real history of psychiatric treatment. He was seen by a school counselor at age 13 for abusing pills and "drinking a lot." During the interview, he related in an emotionless and detached manner, speaking almost in a monotone. He had little insight into the seriousness of his condition as he expressed a desire to be released to "get a job."

Comment. The patient was evaluated as being very dangerous and was committed to a longer term V.A. hospital. He was essentially in the incubation phase of the chronic catathymic process. He came to realize that the only way he could resolve his dilemma was through killing his family or other passersby. Many mass murders of strangers and family members reported in the literature and through the newspapers are essentially catathymic releases, typical of this case.

III. DOMESTIC VIOLENCE

The incidence of domestic violence has been well documented by many sources (e.g. Gelles, 1973; Roy, 1977; Hilberman, 1980), including other chapters in this volume. The causes of domestic violence are many, but the recent rapid increase, in our opinion, is due in large part to the breakdown in social stability. Rapid social change, strained economic conditions for the lower and, more recently, the middle class, all provide for extreme environmental stress. Durkheim (1897, 1951) felt the concept of anomie, the result of a breakdown in social order, contributes directly to crime (Merton, 1957). There is also a deterioration of interpersonal bonds, as well as a feeling of pessimism and lowered morale. There are numerous historical examples of increases in violence in the home, as well as outside the home, during times of great social change. Wedgwood (1957) describes the wanton killings by the mercenaries during the Hundred Years War when social order fell apart. The atrocities of Nazi Germany provide another classic example of how shifting social values and unrest can not only foster violence but also condone it.

Family violence and child abuse are almost always due, in large measure, to stress (Schlesinger and Revitch, 1980). In child abuse, individuals under the age of five are the most common victims, and the mothers or primary caretakers are the most common offenders. Beatings, burning of the hands, immersion in boiling water, starvation, and murder have all been reported in the literature. Many child abusers themselves have been abused children, and frequently state they love their children (Kemp, 1962). It is clear that psychological factors are also involved in the etiology of domestic violence, but without stress, it is unlikely that violence would occur. Gil (1969, 1970), a leading exponent of the stress theory of domestic violence, finds such violence concentrated mainly in the poor. The reason for this is that the poor are subjected to greater stress than the other social classes and therefore more violence erupts. Gelles (1973) views child abuse and family violence as an adaptation to social stress. Gelles (1975) cites cases where pregnant wives have been assaulted, and concludes that such acts indicate the family's use of physical aggression as a response to such stress. Experimental evidence by such authors as Justice and Duncan (1976), Garbino (1977), and Passman and Mulhern (1977) cite findings supporting the social stress factors in family violence. Stress can be external as described above, with regard to social and environmental conditions, or it may be internal and of a psychogenic nature (Schlesinger and Revitch, 1980). We believe that in cases of domestic violence, either external, internal, or a combination of both may be involved. The following case of domestic violence, specifically wife battering, is classic:

Case 8. A.B., a 35-year-old male, contacted the clinic for help because of his inability to control anger and frequent physical and verbal abuse of his wife. The assaults ranged from throwing objects to brutal beatings that left his wife with a broken nose and several fractured ribs. His rage states and consequent violent behavior were often elicited by what he called "deliberate stupidity" and "inconsiderate behavior" on the part of his wife. Many of his violent episodes occurred over timing and preparation of meals. A.B. held rigid notions of women's roles and expected unquestioned acquiescence to his beliefs. He frequently humiliated and degraded his wife in order to insure her compliance to his "rules." If this was not effective and he was met with resistance, he believed physical coercion was his only option. He exhibited strong needs for control in the relationship. Mrs. B. lived in such fear of his anger and explosive episodes that she was unable to communicate in a straightforward manner. She often rambled and became verbose, further infuriating her husband. A.B. felt that his wife was deliberately being difficult and provocative. Her overall inability to communicate proved to be a frequent source of their confrontations. Mrs. B. separated briefly from her husband on several occasions following particularly brutal attacks. A.B. could not tolerate such periods of separation, and his wife often returned on the condition that he would change and "things would be different." Mrs. B. had a strong fear of failing at this, her second marriage. She felt that she had to make a genuine effort to get the marriage to work.

A.B. had a history of assaulting women with whom he had become romantically involved. Spouse abuse was the primary reason for the break-up of his first marriage. He had physically abused several women he had dated prior to his first marriage. At the time of referral, A.B. was on sick leave from his job, and this was particularly stressful for him as he derived much of his identity and self-worth from his career which included a great deal of responsibility and prestige. He was becoming increasingly depressed and agitated during this period, and conflict and violence became more frequent between his wife and him. A.B. had undergone treatment for alcohol abuse which continued to be an ongoing problem at the time of evaluation. The patient felt several prior efforts at psychotherapy were unsuccessful because the treating professionals were not sensitive to his problems with uncontrollable rage states and violent behavior.

A.B.'s childhood and home life were characterized by tension, chaos, and intrafamily violence. The patient lived with several vivid memories of his father's physical abuse of his mother as well as physical abuse perpetrated by his father under the influence of alcohol. The patient believed that he was often "set up" by his mother for many of his father's brutal beatings. The mother, sensing the father's rage, would deflect attention to A.B., thereby protecting herself but leaving her son at the mercy of her husband. After these "set ups" the patient's mother would attempt to comfort and console him by holding him while she was partially clothed. A.B. was a confused and angry youngster but generally in control of himself. He had no significant problems with violent behavior in his youth. After high school he attended a local college and lived there for 1 year, but he found it impossible to concentrate on his studies. He then quit college and enlisted in the military for the next 4 years. After discharge, he returned to college and received his degree. During his senior year he married his first wife, and after graduation began training in a quasi-military occupation. Their marriage lasted 5 years and was characterized by much conflict and periodic physical abuse. After this marriage ended, he dated several women and abused them all.

Comment. After 2½ years of therapy, we concluded that A.B.'s problems with uncontrollable anger and violent behavior emanated from unresolved conflicts with his parents. He displaced much of his deep-seated anger and aggression on the most convenient targets in his life—his wives and girl friends. These intimate love relationships resurrected many unresolved issues in this individual. His need for nurturing and dependency were frequently played out in these relationships and when these needs were not met he became violent. A.B. found the military experience an escape from the stress he experienced at home. For this patient, the military was a rational, structured existence, free from the chaos and mixed messages he lived with. A.B. developed a rigid belief system which revolved around his basic needs for love and security. His rigid cognitions also revealed the patient's need to identify right and wrong, good and bad, etc. The military's emphasis on formality and depersonalization of people and situations fed into A.B.'s need. The rigorous physical and combat training he received provided him with a legitimate outlet for much of his anger and aggression and bolstered his sense of security via his physical prowess. He internalized the military's basic image of "might makes right."

THERAPEUTIC CONSIDERATIONS

Specific techniques and problems of the various psychotherapies and pharmacotherapies have been reported elsewhere (see Lion, 1972, 1975; Lion et al., 1977; Madden, 1977) and in sufficient detail in other chapters of this volume; therefore, such material will not be repeated here. Moreover, we have found that it is not specific techniques that have given problems to clinicians but rather a basic overall plan of treatment or approach with such cases. Except for certain key issues (e.g. countertransference and dealing with specific patient populations) the treatment of violent patients should not be that different from the treatment of any other case by an experienced and competent clinician. Where to begin, however, has been most problematic.

Without an appropriate system of classification out of which therapy grows, treatment of the violent individual may be haphazard, inconsistent, and most of all inappropriate. Therefore, our therapeutic approach follows directly from our system of classification presented previously in this chapter. When a patient is first seen in our violence clinic, he is evaluated and classified as falling into one of our three divisions: (I) primary psychiatric condition causing violence, (II) episodic dyscontrol, (III) domestic violence. For those individuals in whom a psychosis is the main cause of violence, chemotherapeutic treatment is indicated. Where organic pathology is the cause of the violence, neurological evaluation and treatment is primary. When violence occurs only when the patient is toxic, such as in Case 2, treatment for this condition must be initiated first. Where episodic dyscontrol syndrome is present, we have found individual psychotherapy of a psychodynamic orientation to be most effective. Catathymic attacks, and particularly the chronic catathymic process, need quick diagnosis so family or spouse murder may be prevented. Hospitalization in such cases is necessary as a first step. In cases of domestic violence, family therapy, marital and group therapy are recommended for batterers and victims. As shown in Fig. 1, some cases of episodic dyscontrol are seen not only in individual psychotherapy but in family therapy, and treated with chemotherapy as well. Cases of violence, the result of primary psychiatric condition, is treated mainly with chemotherapy but some individuals also receive supportive psychotherapy in conjunction with this. Domestic violence cases, while primarily requiring a family/marital approach, do also receive individual supportive psychotherapy for one or both partners if needed. It is rare that a purely domestic violence problem be treated primarily or even at all with chemotherapy, except maybe in an adjunctive fashion; and by the same token, it is rare that violence as the result of a psychotic disorder is treated primarily with family or marital therapy, except again, in an adjunctive way.

Since there are no specific "antiviolent" drugs just as there are no specific "antiviolent" psychotherapeutic techniques, all schools and approaches toward treatment may be relevant given the particular case. By employing the three-pronged approach of evaluation and treatment outlined above, we have had excellent results in treating

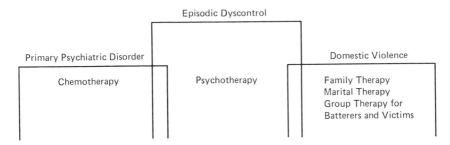

Figure 1. Type of therapy indicated for specific type of violence.

close to 100 cases referred to our clinic in the past 3 years. There have been no suicides, homicides, or any attempts with any of our patients. There also have been no assaults resulting in hospitalization for the victims, and in patients who continue to act out, violence has been considerably less frequent.

DISCUSSION

Since the problem of violence in general, and spouse abuse in particular, often presents itself in a confusing manner, we believe our system of classification and treatment strategies provide order and a method of rationally handling such cases. We presented a three-pronged classification system where we conceive of violence being generated primarily from:

    I. Primary psychiatric condition (including organic and toxic states);
   II. Episodic dyscontrol syndrome; and,
  III. Domestic violence disturbance.

We developed this approach with a population of male veteran patients; therefore, its use, with all types of violent patients, may be limited in some respects.

All of our patients had a military experience and we found this to be important in understanding many of our cases. Military experience seems to have a direct effect on stimulating violence from actual killing or being violent in service, or from various reactions due to the stress of combat. There is also an indirect effect from the overall military experience where one is trained and conditioned to be violent in order to survive. We believe, as do other researchers in this field (Bourne, 1970; Figley and Eisenhart, 1975; Figley, 1978), that the experience of being in combat is crucial in terms of predicting which veterans will have major adjustment problems in which violence and assaultiveness will be found. We further believe that the combat experience, especially if the patient has killed, in some ways upsets his psychic hemeostasis which may never be completely reintegrated. Reactions from combat often have a delayed onset that may not erupt for several years after the actual stressor has been removed. This was noted by Archibald, Long, and Miller (1962) in their review of World War II veteran cases, and it was reconfirmed by Figley's (1978) studies of stress disorders among Vietnam veterans.

The role of the military, specifically with regard to violent behavior, is relevant for all categories but especially for II and III in our classification schema. In category I, where there is a primary psychiatric disorder, it was probably either preexistent to the military or merely exacerbated by the general stress of military life. Substance abuse disorders often begin or increase during military years; in cases of organicity, many are due to head injuries sustained in service. Episodic dyscontrol and generalized explosiveness, however, as well as domestic violence, are two key characteristics that are common and are linked, at least in part, to the veteran's military, especially combat, experience. It is hoped that, with future study and reformulation, more sophisticated approaches to the classification and treatment, as well as to the exact relationship of the military experience to violence, will emerge.

REFERENCES

Archibald, H. C., Long, D. M., and Miller, C. Gross stress reaction in combat: Fifteen-year follow up. *American Journal of Psychiatry,* 1962, **119**, 317–22.

Bachet, M. *Les Encéphaloses Criminogenes.* Paris: Les Editions Foucher, 1950.

Bachet, M. The concept of encéphaloses criminogenes (criminogenic encephalosis). *American Journal of Orthopsychiatry,* 1951, **21**, 794–99.

Bourne, P. G. *Men, Stress and Viet Nam.* Boston: Little, Brown, 1970.

Bowman, K. M. and Blau, A. Psychotic states following head and brain injury in adults and children. In *Injuries of the Brain and Spinal Cord and Their Coverings,* S. Brock (ed.) Baltimore: Williams & Wilkins, 1949.

Brancali, R. Problems of classification. *National Probation and Parole Association Journal,* 1955, **1**, 118–25.

Clark, R. *Crime in America.* New York: Pocket Books, 1971.

Durkheim, E. *Suicide* (1897). New York: Free Press, 1951.

Figley, C. R. *Stress Disorders Among Viet Nam Veterans.* New York: Brunner Mazel Inc., 1978.

Figley, C. R. and Eisenhart, W. Contrasts between combat and non-combat Viet Nam veterans regarding selected indices of interpersonal adjustment. Paper presented at the annual meeting of the American Sociological Assocation, San Francisco, August, 1975.

Garbino, J. The price of privacy in the social dynamics of child abuse. *Child Welfare,* 1977, **56**, 565–75.

Gayral, L., Millet, G., Muron, P., and Turnin, J. Crises et paroxysmes catathymiques. *Annales Medico-Psychologiques,* 1956, **114,** 25-50.

Gelles, R. J. Child abuse as psychopathology: A sociological critique and reformulation. *American Journal of Orthopsychiatry,* 1973, **43,** 611-21.

Gelles, R. J. Violence and pregnancy: A note on the extent of the problem and needed services. *Family Coordinator,* January, 1975, 81-86.

Gil, D. Physical abuse of children: Findings and implications of a nation-wide survey. *Pediatrics,* 1969, **44,** 857-64.

Gil, D. *Violence Against Children.* Cambridge, Mass.: Harvard University Press, 1970.

Halleck, S. *Psychiatry and the Dilemmas of Crime.* Los Angeles: University of California Press, 1971.

Hilberman, E. Overview: The 'wife beater's wife' reconsidered. *American Journal of Psychiatry,* 1980, **137,** 1336-47.

Justice, B. and Duncan, D. F. Life stress as a precursor to child abuse. *Public Health Reports,* 1976, **91,** 110-13.

Kemp, C. H., et al. The battered child syndrome. *Journal of the American Medical Association,* 1962, **181,** 105-11.

Lanzkron, J. Murder and insanity. *American Journal of Psychiatry,* 1963, **119,** 754-58.

Lion, J. R. *Evaluation and Management of the Violent Patient.* Springfield, Ill.: Charles C. Thomas, 1972.

Lion, J. R. Conceptual issues and the use of drugs for the treatment of aggression in man. *Journal of Nervous and Mental Diseases,* 1975, **160,** 76-82.

Lion, J. R., Madden, D. J. and Christopher, R. L. A violence clinic: Three years experience. *American Journal of Psychiatry,* 1976, **133,** 432-34.

Lion, J. R., Christopher, R. L., and Madden, D. J. A group approach with violent out-patients. *International Journal of Group Psychotherapy,* 1977, **27,** 67-74.

Madden, D. J. Voluntary and involuntary treatment of aggressive patients. *American Journal of Psychiatry,* 1977, **134,** 553-55.

Mark, V. M. and Ervin, F. R. *Violence and the Brain.* New York: Harper & Row, 1970.

Mayfield, D. Alcoholism, alcohol intoxication and assaultive behavior. *Diseases of the Nervous System,* 1976, **37,** 288-91.

Menninger, K. and Mayman, M. Episodic dyscontrol: A third order of stress adaptation. *Bulletin of the Menninger Clinic,* 1956, **20,** 153-63.

Menninger, K. *The Vital Balance.* New York: Viking Press, 1964.

Merton, R. K. *Social Theory and Social Structure.* New York: Free Press, 1957.

Miller, D. and Looney, J. A prediction of adolescent homicide: Episodic dyscontrol and dehumanization. *American Journal of Psychoanalysis,* 1974, **34,** 187-98.

Monroe, R. R. *Episodic Behavioral Disorders.* Boston: Harvard University Press, 1970.

Monroe, R. R. Episodic behavioral disorders: An unclassified syndrome. In *American Handbook of Psychiatry Vol. II,* S. Arieti (ed.) New York: Basic Books, 1974.

Monroe, R. R. *Brain Dysfunction in Aggressive Criminals.* Lexington, Mass.: Heater & Co., 1978.

Passman, R. H. and Mulhern, R. K. Maternal punitiveness as affected by situational stress: An experimental analogue of child abuse. *Journal of Abnormal Psychology,* 1977, **86,** 565–69.

Peterson, R. C. and Stillman, R. C. Phencyclidine: A review material. *Journal of the Medical Society of New Jersey,* 1979, **76,** 139–44.

Ratner, R. A. and Shapiro, D. The episodic dyscontrol syndrome and clinical responsibility. *Bulletin of the Academy of Psychiatry and Law,* in press.

Revitch, E. The problem of conjugal paranoia. *Diseases of the Nervous System,* 1954, **15,** 271–77.

Revitch, E. Paroxysmal manifestations of non-epileptic origins: Catathymic attacks. *Diseases of the Nervous System,* 1964, **25,** 662–69.

Revitch, E. Diagnosis and disposition for the paranoid marital partner. *Diseases of the Nervous System* Monograph Supplement 2, 1960, **21,** 117–18.

Revitch, E. and Schlesinger, L. B. Murder: Evaluation, classification and prediction. In *Violence: Perspectives on Murder and Aggression,* I. L. Kutash, S. B. Kutash, L. B. Schlesinger (eds.) San Francisco: Jossey-Bass Publishers, 1978.

Revitch, E. and Schlesinger, L. B. *Psychopathology of Homicide.* Springfield, Ill.: Charles C. Thomas, 1981.

Roy, M. *Battered Women: A Psycho-Sociological Study of Domestic Violence.* New York: Van Nostrand Reinhold, 1977.

Ruotolo, A. Dynamics of sudden murder. *American Journal of Psychoanalysis,* 1968, **28,** 162–76.

Satten, J., Menninger, K. A., and Mayman, M. Murder without apparent motive: A study in personality disorganization. *American Journal of Psychiatry,* 1960, **117,** 48–53.

Schlesinger, L. B. and Revitch, E. Stress, violence and crime. In *Handbook on Stress and Anxiety,* I. L. Kutash and L. B. Schlesinger (eds.) San Francisco: Jossey-Bass Publishers, 1980.

Swanson, D. W., Bonhert, P. J., and Smith, J. A. *The Paranoid.* Boston: Little Brown & Co., 1970.

Tanay, E. Psychiatric study of homicide. *American Journal of Psychiatry,* 1969, **125,** 1252–58.

Walters, J. H. Encephalitis lethargica revisited. *Journal of Operational Psychiatry,* 1977, **8,** 37–46.

Wedgwood, C. V. *The Thirty Years War.* Harmondsworth, Middlesex, England: Penguin Books, 1957.

Wertham, F. The catathymic crisis: A clinical entity. *Archives of Neurology and Psychiatry,* 1937, **37,** 974–77.

Wilson, S. A. K. *Neurology,* Vol I, Baltimore: Williams & Wilkins, 1955.

Wolfgang, M. E. *Patterns of Criminal Homicide.* Philadelphia: University of Pennsylvania Press, 1958.

11. Men Unlearning Violence: A Group Approach Based on the Collective Model

David C. Adams, M.Ed.
Andrew J. McCormick, M.S.W.

David C. Adams and Andrew J. McCormick are both founding members of Emerge. David is currently the Intake and Referral Coordinator for Emerge and also works as a private therapist for New Directions for Men, Boston, Mass. Andrew McCormick is Community Education Coordinator for Emerge and also a Clinical Social Worker in the Domestic Violence Unit of the Roxbury District Court Clinic in Boston, Mass.

INTRODUCTION

In 1977 a group of eight men in Boston joined together to form the Emerge Collective at the request of women working in the Boston area shelters for battered women to begin counseling work with men who are abusive to their mates. At that time the shelter workers felt that they had no place to send a man who was interested in changing his violent behavior. The women who worked in the shelters did not want to work with the men themselves, rather they wanted to concentrate their energy on providing emergency services and support for women who

The authors would like to acknowledge and appreciate the assistance, suggestions, and other editorial input provided by the members of the Emerge Collective in helping us to prepare this article and to develop the theory and approach which this paper presents.

were being battered. However, it was clear that services for men were needed.

The mainstream family-service agencies and mental-health centers at the time did not view woman abuse as a primary problem in family life. Even today, there are many who identify abuse as a symptom of deeper problems in the individual man, or in the relationship between the man and woman, or regrettably in the individual woman, by asserting that *she* somehow asked for the violence. Practice based on any of these theories is bound to relegate the violence to a secondary position of concern in the course of treatment. As we now know from experience, working on woman abuse in this way has not stopped the violence and injuries to women.

Change occurs at both the personal and the institutional levels, and in fact must affect both of these spheres to be lasting. Because this problem is so widespread and so disruptive to family life and child development, it is not enough for men and women to silently disapprove of abuse toward women. It is important to speak to others about it. Men have a particular role to play in educating other men about the nature of abuse and how men can change. Emerge hopes to continue its high visibility as a group of men who take a public stand against wifebeating. We encourage other men to do the same.

Emerge is making one effort to integrate a precise theory and an active practice in work with abusive men. The first section of this article will address theoretical concerns from psychological, sociological, and political formulations of the problem and attempt to extract from them a comprehensive statement of the problem of woman abuse from the male perspective. The second section will demonstrate the application of this theory to group counseling with extensive use of case material to illustrate the report of the progress of a typical Emerge group.

It should be noted that Emerge considers a strong community education program to be equally as important as counseling men in the work of stopping the abuse of women. Community education brings an awareness of the extent and the severity of the problem to people. It functions as the first step in treatment by informing men that abuse will no longer be sanctioned and offers men a supportive environment in which to change their behavior and attitudes. Ultimately our goal is to join with women to change the social norms and structures which spawn and perpetuate violence against women. To this end fully one-half of our time is devoted to providing training to other agencies and education to the general public. This article will not present the specifics of Emerge's Community Education Program but will focus primarily on our work in counseling men.

THEORY: A SOCIAL-POLITICAL PERSPECTIVE ON MEN WHO BATTER

Heritage of Violence

Very early in our history the Emerge Collective made the decisions to work only with men and to be an all-male organization. These decisions were based on several months of study, discussion with battered women and shelter workers, and self-disclosure of violence in our own lives. The importance of a process by which men would help other men to overcome violence toward women in all its forms, but particularly physical abuse within interpersonal relationships, cried out for a statement by men.

Societal acceptance of male violence is strong. We are not shocked by it, except in its more heinous forms, such as brutal killings that are clearly psychopathic. In general, violence by men has become an expected, if not accepted, form of behavior. Much of this violence is directed toward women as sexual harassment, pornographic films and advertising, rape, and battering.

Discussions as to the causality of rape and battering have historically hinged on the folklore that accuses the woman of having provoked the attack and absolves the man of responsibility for it. It is believed that the woman must in some way have caused the man to attack her, either by being seductive in her dress or actions in the case of rape, or provocative with her words or behavior in the case of abuse. By contrast the man is seen as acting out of his natural instincts which are uncontrollable and unchangeable.

These parallels between rape and battering are not coincidental. Both restrict and intimidate women through the use of force. The effects of these attacks reverberate in society to contribute to a climate of fear among women which perpetuates the dominance of men. The acceptance of violence as part of the repertoire of men's lives, even though there are nonviolent men, creates an environment in which women cannot feel safe, because they never really know who will attack them and who will not. The rape of daughters and nieces by men is a perfect example of how trust in men can be betrayed. As Brownmiller has noted violent men serve to control all women, for the benefit of all men.[1]

The widespread nature of violence is in this way peculiar to men. Violence or the urge to be violent is an experience that virtually every man can understand. Emerge views *all men on a continuum of violence* and believes that almost every man is capable of violent behavior at some time in their lives. Because of this it is vital that men speak out against violence towards women and make the choice to be nonviolent. We are convinced that with support and vigilance, *men can learn not to be violent.*

Men in Emerge share a common heritage of violence with other men and it helps us to empathize with them. It also gives us an authority to speak out with the strongest voice possible against violence. In both our counseling and community education programs we offer "supportive confrontation." We will not tolerate violence, but will work with any man who wants to leave violence behind. That men have completed our group-counseling program and are no longer violent, confirms that men can change. There are alternatives for men.

Development of a Strategy

Emerge has its roots in three traditions: Feminism and the Men's Movement, the social change movements of the 1960s, and work in the social services. Our work has borrowed from each area and we will summarize each briefly to demonstrate how.

Several men who organized Emerge worked for many years doing men's consciousness-raising groups. The experience gained in those groups through sharing our emotional lives, and examining what life for us as men was all about, created a strong base from which to reach out to other men who need more support. This made it possible to develop an analysis of the conditions of men's lives and a willingness to become involved in helping them change.

For many of us the narrow range of the consciousness-raising groups and the influence of feminist theory created a desire to deepen our exploration into men's experience to include an examination of sexism and patriarchal social structure in order to find an explanation for the behavior of men. For us, the patriarchal structure, which all societies experience at this time, is characterized by the dominance of men in the social institutions and in personal relationships between men and women. Within this structure women are expected to confrom to behavioral criteria that are decided upon and enforced by men. Abuse is one way that men get women to do what men want them to do.

By examining sexism and our heritage in patriarchal relationships, Emerge has extended the concerns of men from a focus only on feelings and life-style to the pursuit of a strategy for helping men contest the history that binds them into roles that are oppressive to women. The work against violence against women provides a context within which men can confront their own sexism. At the same time we can help free women from the bondage of fear of continued violence at the hands of men.

Many Emerge members also worked in the student and worker struggles of the 1960s in attempts to gain control over their lives and to develop a more egalitarian society for all. A major part of this work is still directed at analyzing and changing the capitalist economy, which is characterized by sudden and inevitable surges and recessions. This erratic economic behavior creates a passivity among working people, who begin to believe that they are powerless to change it. There is, however, a contradictory process occurring at the same time. When the products of our labor go directly to the company owner, who then gains the profits from the sale, employees are immediately alienated from their work and do not receive the fruits of their labors. In addition, the workplace experience of most people of the arbitrary authority of administrators spawns an antagonism toward the boss. The combination of this hierarchical structure of domination, and the alienation from the products of their labor, produces a deep level of frustration which can be channeled into a desire to change the system of production, so that everyone has some measure of control over the process and earns an equal share of the profits.

The lessons learned from these struggles are also applicable to the human services, and have helped Emerge members design a collective organizational structure that is characterized by an equal sharing of responsibility and decision making based on a consensus model. *We have organized ourselves as a collective in order to deal more directly with the competition and hierarchy among ourselves as a model for other men to evaluate their own relationship with authority and to encourage them to establish structures that will nurture them as they work.*

For many Emerge members the experience of working in other human service agencies that advocated an apolitical approach to the delivery of service, left them frustrated at the limitations of such work. This experience has been accumulated in inpatient units of state mental hospitals, drug and alcohol counseling programs, runaway houses for adolescents, and day-care centers. In these settings the structure of the organizations and the values expressed by the administrators reinforced the leadership positions of men and the secondary positions of women—even within the so-called "women's professions." This affirmed the conviction among Emerge members that the problems faced by individuals and families in our society are a reflection of the social order. The problems cannot be isolated from the whole.

If we take a systems view of these problems, we can see them as either closed or open systems. Agencies which establish themselves to work on a single problem often set themselves up as a closed system. This allows them to isolate the problem and develop a specific theory for correcting it. The trade-off for this attempt to find precision in solving the problem is that stimuli from outside the system are discounted when the theory is developed and when outcomes are assessed. In the case of battered women, a closed-system approach limits the gathering of information to that within the family or the personal life of the participants. Techniques for treatment are then directed toward changing individual men and women, or relationships.

On the other hand it is possible to take an open systems approach to solving this problem. This requires the assimilation of much more data as the boundaries of the data field are broadened. What might be lost in focus here is made up for in completeness. Openness to input on a continual basis from every available source requires an ongoing reevaluation of a program's goals and effectiveness. Large bureaucratic agencies have a very difficult time in maintaining the necessary flexibility to adapt to the changing needs of clientele and the new information gained by personnel in the daily contact with clients. A theory and practice of work with battered women and abusive men, which includes attempts to change individuals as well as the social structures which support and encourage the use of violence, is possible when we maintain an open-system perspective in which the effects of the social environment and the history of human relationships are included as pertinent facts.

An Analysis of Patriarchal Attitudes

To develop our analysis of the problem of abusive men Emerge has borrowed from the psychological and sociological constructs and combined them with a political component which integrates all three in an examination of the patriarchal attitudes in our society and their effect on men. This conscious borrowing from psychology, sociology, and politics gives Emerge workers a solid foundation from which to do both counseling and community education.

Emerge's work is predicated on the understanding that woman abuse is a learned behavior of men. The abuse of women is the man's problem; the woman is the victim. The use of violence as a method of solving problems and settling differences is a result of three interrelated forces: (1) the socialization of boys to be aggressive and dominant in their social relations; (2) the reinforcement of these values by parents, teachers, and social forces such as the media, television, films, and the use of violence by the police and military; (3) the social norms of patriarchal society which dictate that men are the dominant gender and are free to exercise this power in family life, social relationships, and in the institutions which direct our lives. The learning continues throughout the life of men and these values are conveyed to future generations as proper for men.

As boys grow they quickly learn around preschool age that certain behaviors and qualities such as gentleness, cooperation, warmth, and expression of emotions are reserved for girls and not for boys.[2] Parents are more likely to reward boys for aggressiveness and exploration in play.[3] Teachers, coaches, and relatives also encourage that learning of toughness, coolness, independence, and control in boys to such an extent that they become almost totally focused on emulating the compulsive masculinity of military generals, police officers, violent cowboys, space men, and sports heroes.[4] Each man and boy monitors the other to screen out any of the "female" characteristics.

Despite the fact that more people recognize the long-term negative effect of the rule that, "Big boys don't cry," the trend to reward boys for being "strong" continues almost unabated in homes and day-care centers. Boys learn that they are different from girls and should not adopt any of the characteristics of girls. They are instructed to model themselves after their fathers.

The boy's father is often a lonely person with few friends of his own. He is a man without the richness of intimacy, because he has never learned to express himself with the openness necessary to develop the deep levels of sharing that build intimacy. He is not really close to his son. He fears this closeness, as he fears it with any man, because it suggests homosexuality. Men are rarely, if at all, affectionate with their sons after they reach the age of three or four. Men are almost never affectionate with each other. The male self-monitoring is very strong here, with reminders in the form of name calling (e.g., queer, faggot, sissy), physical attack, or ostracism.

To compensate for their inability and fear of displaying affection, fathers often project the need to defend against their feelings of love and warmth to their sons, and require them to adopt the same restrictive attitudes toward "ideal" behavior for men and force their sons to repress their needs for emotional expression. Both father and son suffer from the loss of the expression of this love. The father loses because it increases his isolation. The son loses because he inherits his father's pain.

These characteristics of men are clearly part of the etiology of the abuse of women. *It is not without penalty that men repress their needs.* The reality of the feelings and the frustration of not sharing them confront all but the most defended men throughout their lives. Rather than struggle to free themselves by opening themselves to emotions, men transfer the responsibility for this part of their lives to women, thus creating an inordinate dependency on women for fulfillment in the relationship. The woman's role becomes one of second guessing or intuiting the man's needs and meeting them without his having to ask her. One member of an Emerge group put it very well when he said,

> (She was) there to make me feel good. "Why didn't you fix my supper the way I wanted it?" That sort of thing. In any number of ways that was her primary role, I think, feeding me, nourishing me emotionally. And after a period of time, I became very inept at nourishing myself.

Men often describe themselves as being "uncomfortable" before they are abusive, and are rarely conscious of other feelings, such as pain, hurt, sadness, fear, and loneliness. Often the response to this suddenly conscious, festering pain is rage, triggered by an incident that elicited anger at feeling uncomforable. The woman is then blamed for causing the discomfort because she did not act in the way he expected or wanted her to act. When pressed on this point men will admit that what they feel uncomfortable about is not being in control. The reassertion of control restores his level of comfort, even if accomplished at the expense of the woman's comfort, as through a beating.

In a connected way abuse is used as a method to maintain control by preventing the woman from leaving him. Her departure would create a void and force him to confront his dependency on her; a prospect which elicits fear in many men. In this way the psychological dependency of men is served well by the social norm that encourages abuse as a way of keeping control.

Men use the requirement that women fulfill their emotional needs in a manipulative way. When he does not ask for what he needs, either because he feels it is unmanly to need nurturance, or because he cannot admit to the need even if he is aware of it, or because he has repressed the need, he forces the woman to make adaptations in her behavior to please him. By being so unpredictable in his own behavior, he is able to control hers. She must constantly be ready to respond to him.

This manner of relating in the family is directly related to male dominance in the society at large. The problem cannot be limited to that of a certain population of men or to men with a particular psychological problem, because so many men do it. Nevertheless, it is clear that the inability of men to express either their emotions or their needs to be emotional has psychological consequences and needs psychological attention. What this phenomenon does demonstrate is how a social system based on the dominance of men over women contributes to the creation of an aberration in the psyches of men, which is renewed in each succeeding generation. It does so because it is the expected role for men to play. One Emerge group member acknowledged the widespread nature of the problem quite simply when he said, "We're a majority. We're not a minority. There's a lot of us out there."

These attitudes of antagonism toward anything feminine, and the acceptance of them, are reinforced in boys when they observe the behavior of men toward women. This is particularly true of boys who witness their fathers beating their mothers, or who are beaten themselves.[5] This violent behavior serves as an example of how women can be controlled. In short, the boys learn that it is permissible to dominate women and that violence is a way to do it.

What is important here is the desire to dominate. The violence is the tool, which can be used selectively. As illustrated by one Emerge client, violence was used only when it was "necessary."

> Gerry: I think that I always had to feel that I was in control and I got that control through being in charge of everything, taking all the responsibility, by requiring that my wife follow me absolutely. . . . When you talk of physical violence, there wasn't any need for that at the time because I got the same thing through verbal violence as I've come to know it and I told her that if she didn't do something that I would.
>
> Counselor: Would what?
>
> Gerry: Would do whatever was necessary including probably that I would kill her.

The social reinforcement of abuse through the family structure becomes more apparent when we see how many families are exposed to it.

Sociologists have reported that the violence in families is the result of a myriad of influences which include the pressures of work or school; changes in employment status; changes in family make-up through pregnancy, birth, death, or other loss; and the general stress of life in industrial society. Further influences abound through violent entertainment and police and military violence.[6]

Although these are all important triggering mechanisms, none provides a sufficient condition for the abuse of women. The analysis must go deeper. In summary of the arguments in this paper, Emerge offers three basic conditions that lead directly to the abuse of women once the man has been triggered by some incident. He will attack a woman if he believes: (1) that it is permissible to dominate women, (2) that it is permissible to use violence to solve problems, and (3) that it is permissible to beat a woman.

COUNSELING

The Emerge counseling and community-education program deal with these three conditions directly. This two-pronged effort at social change is necessary to ensure that the gains made by men in the groups will be supported by an increasing awareness of the need for change in the community, and to prevent boys and men from abusing women in the future by creating a negative public opinion of battering behavior. Emerge has made a strong effort in this regard and has developed a successful model for group counseling.

After experimenting with individual and occasional couple counseling, Emerge has settled on group counseling as the treatment of choice for abusive men for two principle reasons. First of all, since these men, to a large extent, receive their schooling in compulsive masculinity and violence in groups of peers, it makes sense to create new peer groups to retrain men so that they can learn alternative behavior and develop more flexible understanding of themselves as men. In groups, when there is appropriate modeling and norm setting by group members and counselors, abusive men can get the reinforcement and permission they need in order to change.

Secondly, Emerge hopes to foster the development of self-help skills among batterers, so that changes can be continued and transferred to their relationships at home. In groups men not only have the opportunity to gain insight into their problems, but also gain experience in practicing new behaviors and modes of relating, and thereby help each other's growth.

By contrast, in individual therapy, the client's only source of information is the therapist. The individual therapist's ability to serve as a role model is impaired by the client's conception of him as different (e.g., "He doesn't beat his wife," "He's more educated"). In a group, however, an abusive man is more likely to find role models he can use. As Jerome Frank says about groups, "Each (member) can learn from observing how others handle contingencies arising in the group and learning how they cope with living situations resembling their own. Although seeing other group members improve may make some members discouraged or envious, more typically, it inspires emulation and raises hopes." [7]

Group counseling has already proven to be a very exciting and productive alternative for many men. During the past 3 years Emerge has had approximately 115 men attend the group-counseling program. These men have come to Emerge with a wide range of backgrounds and previous violent behavior. Although the sample is small, some patterns have developed which are helpful in understanding the men who come forward for counseling.

To date Emerge has had no problem finding men to attend group counseling. Their motivation at first is usually due to the crisis that arises in their lives when their wife leaves or threatens to leave. Many men view counseling as a way of putting their marriage back together or of filling the void they feel in their lives when they are alone. However, when a man stays with the group for several sessions his motivation often changes to focus on helping himself.

Reinforcing this experience is our finding that most men (50%) come to Emerge for counseling after they learn about us from the shelters or their wives who are in shelters. Many men refer themselves after seeing Emerge presented in the media (18%). Other counseling programs (14%) and courts (14%) have also referred men to Emerge. In a relatively new development former Emerge clients have also begun referring men to the groups (4%).

The men themselves have ranged in age from 18 to 50 and have been involved in abusive behavior from as short a period as a few weeks to as long as 25 years. Most of the men (63%) have been abusive for 5 years or less (40% between 1 and 5 years). Twenty-three percent have been battering for more than 10 years.

The battering behavior of Emerge counselees extends from verbal abuse only (4%), to the use of weapons (4%) such as darts and guns. Fifty-nine percent of the men have punched, severely beaten, or inflicted injuries such as broken bones and black eyes on women. A third (33%) of the men have participated in slightly less severe violence such as pushing, shoving, or slapping women.

Men who come to Emerge have a very high percentage (77%) of previous exposure to abuse, either by being beaten themselves or by witnessing abuse in the home. Although this appears significant it may not be higher than the exposure to violence in the society at large, when we consider the social acceptance of violence as a form of discipline. As a causal factor it does not explain the behavior of the remaining 23% of the men.

APPLICATION: EMERGE GROUP COUNSELING

We can now turn to a discussion of our group-treatment approach by tracing the life of a typical Emerge counseling group. We will follow a group developmental schema, beginning with early group dynamics and treatment interventions and proceeding to middle and ending group issues. In order to further illuminate these issues, we will use case examples which will give glimpses of group life during each developmental stage.

The group we have chosen to present ran for 24 weeks. Since one member dropped out of the group after the first session, profiles will be given of the remaining eight members only. The seventh and eighth members listed, Hal and Ron, joined the group in its ninth session:

Group Client Profiles

Don, age 33, referred himself to Emerge after being served with a Restraining and Vacate order restraining him from abusing his wife and ordering him to vacate his house for 90 days. Don and Jane have been married for 11 years. They have three children, aged 10, 7, and 5. The last time Don had beaten Jane, she sustained a broken nose. She was 3 months pregnant at the time. Employed as a part-time bartender, Don is very friendly and outgoing, a person who expressed a strong desire to end his abusiveness and save his marriage.

Jack, age 43, has been married for 7 years to his second wife, Judy, age 27. Jack's first wife, Martha, died 8 years ago due to a drug/alcohol overdose. They had five children, aged 14–23. Three of these children presently live at home along with Judy's 8-year-old son from her first marriage. During his intake interview, Jack expressed much sadness and guilt over Martha's death and his previous treatment of her. Jack said he feared that he was repeating the same mistakes by being abusive to Judy. At the time Judy was attending a support group for battered women. Jack, who works as a salesman, has few friends but likes to see himself as a "ladies man."

Jim, age 37, had been separated from Barbara, his wife of 18 years, for 6 months. Barbara had filed for divorce and was awarded custody of the couple's three teen-aged daughters. Jim had been seen individually for 3 months by one of the group counselors, David. A quiet, sober man, Jim is presently unemployed. He had quit his job as a shipping clerk.

Eric, age 30, is an investment counselor. He has been married to his wife, Ann, for 7 years. The couple has two children, aged 6 and 4. Eric had slapped or pushed Ann several times during their marriage. He has seen a private therapist for 2 years. Eric is intelligent, articulate, and has a somewhat boyish manner.

Assa, age 26, was a graduate student who had lived with his woman friend, Linda, for 2 years. Born in Morocco, Assa had lived in this country for 2½ years. He had frequently been abusive to Linda and was intensely jealous of her relationships with others. Linda was seeing a private therapist at the time.

Joe, age 29, was under a Restraining and Vacate Order preventing him from abusing or visiting his wife, Susan. The couple had been married for 5 years. A Vietnam veteran, Joe projects a rigid "tough guy" image. He works as a court advocate for Vietnam vets.

Hal, age 28, works as a carpenter for a private contractor. He had lived with his woman friend, Sara, for 5 years. Hal and Sara lead an alternative life-style and are involved in several political causes. Hal is quiet and soft-spoken. He described himself as a pacifist.

Ron, 31, had been married for 4 years to Joan. Ron referred himself to Emerge following an abuse incident. He had broken several of Joan's ribs by kicking her. Joan had threatened to leave unless Ron sought counseling.

Ron helps to manage a restaurant, and he is on probation for several drug offenses. He is talkative, vague, and manipulative.

Early Group Dynamics and Treatment Interventions (Sessions 1-3)

Abusive men may bring fears and anxieties into group counseling. Group members are often nervous about the idea of talking about their personal problems with strangers; particularly a group of men. This apprehension gives rise to homophobic concerns which tend to have a major effect on early group dynamics. Homophobia, or the fear of intimacy between men, usually surfaces in sporadic and off-handed ways during early group sessions. Members may jokingly comment on the "coziness" of the counseling room, for instance, or suggest that time could be better spent by going bowling or "looking at girls."

As a related dynamic, it is common for early group members to refer to their wives continuously; often in depreciating ways.[8] By focusing on their wives rather than on themselves, group members are able to alleviate homophobic anxiety and avoid a more "here and now" interaction. Their habit of denigrating their wives reveals a high degree of defensiveness which is also unique to early group life.

> Jack: Jack reported a recent abuse incident: I'm not trying to justify my actions or nothing, it's just that sometimes a man can only take so much. My wife just never lets up, I mean she really knows how to get me going. Don't you think sometimes the woman is asking for it? (looking at the group leaders).
>
> Bob (group counselor): Did you have a specific incident in mind, Jack? Maybe the group can help you answer that question.
>
> Jack: Well, this weekend. . . Judy knows I like to go and visit my old man on Sundays. I like to bring him his favorite cigars and we usually go for a walk or something. I been doing that for years but this Sunday Judy thinks I should be spending more time with her and the kids. I guess because she never got along with her folks, she thinks I should neglect my own father, or something. She's kind of screwed up in that way but that's another story. So she gives me all kinds of shit about how I care more about my old man than about her and the kids.

Then, of course, once she gets started, there's no stopping her. On and on she goes about my not doing this and not doing that.

Joe: You sure you and I aren't married to the same woman? Your wife sounds an awful lot like mine. (laughter from the group)

Jack: Yeah, and she knows just how to bust my balls. I mean, she's not big enough to hurt me physically or anything but she's good with words. She can talk circles around me. But what I want to know is, shouldn't she know how to handle me?

Don: Yeah, shouldn't there be help for the women too? I mean, did Emerge ever think of having a woman's auxiliary, or something like that? (laughter from the group) No, seriously, I always figured it takes two to tango, you know what I mean? I admit that I hit my wife and that's wrong but, it's like Jack says, isn't the wife asking for it sometimes?

Jim: I used to think that but my eyes have been opened a lot lately. I can look back and see times when there was just no excuse for what I did. But I didn't think that at the time.

Assa: My girl friend is good, you know, smart. She's always so reasonable. Sometimes it makes me feel like I'm a kid. That's when I get angry; when she makes me feel guilty or wrong about something.

Jack: Judy does that. She's always accusing me of seeing other broads; the minute I'm in the door, she's on me about where I was and who I saw. I get tired of having to answer to her all the time. (Jack had brought this same issue up in the previous group session.)

David (group counselor): Does Judy have any reason to trust you, Jack?

Jack: (looking startled) Well, no, I guess I screw around with the broads from time to time. But she drives me to it; I wouldn't do it if she trusted me. So as long as she's not going to trust me. I might as well have my fun.

David (group counselor): So if your hands are so tied, like you seem to be saying, why are we still talking about this?

Jack: Well, I wouldn't say they're exactly tied. But, you know what they say, a stiff prick has no conscience.

David (group counselor): Oh, I see, first it's your wife and now it's your prick?

Jim: So you're (David) saying he should be responsible for what he wants to do?

Jack: I see what you're saying. I guess that's true. I shouldn't blame Judy for the broads. She's always been a good wife as far as that goes. All right, I confess (throwing his hands up) that's my problem. (laughter from the group)

As this bit of group dialogue illustrates, defensiveness and the projection of blame are much in evidence in early group life. By projecting blame onto their wives, men who batter are able to disclaim responsibility for their violence. By degrading their wives and trivializing their wives' concerns, group members are able to alleviate their homophobic anxieties and consequently feel more comfortable with each other as men.

Talking tough and the putting down of women as methods for making men feel better about themselves are common aspects of male bonding. These phenomena occur not only in groups of male abusers but are common to virtually all types of male groups—whether they be on the street corner, at sporting events, in bars, etc. Complaining about, or mocking "the wife" and "rating" women's bodies are perhaps the most familiar forms of this male social behavior.

It is typical (as the case example shows) for early group members to relate to each other through their wives. In other words, group members tend to talk about their wives rather than themselves, early on. Moreover, members' comments are usually directed at the group leaders rather than to each other.

Group members often direct anger at the group leaders for "making us feel as if we're to blame" or "not telling us what to do." This type of response on the part of group members indicates a transference reaction which subsconsciously attempts to put the group leaders in the role of group members' wives. For example, group members will blame the group leaders, as they do their wives, for "making" them feel guilty, "making" them look bad, or for withholding unlimited approval.

There are three primary group counseling tasks in the early stages of groups.

1. It is important for group counselors to resist overreacting by making premature interpretations to group members or by becoming defensive in the face of anger directed at themselves. The group counselors' primary task is to build linkages among group members in order to enhance member interaction and stimulate a more "here and

now" group focus. Often, group counselors are able to find therapeutic allies (such as Jim) who, through modeling and giving feedback, help other members to pay more attention to themselves and accept more responsibility for their violence.

2. Another early task of group leaders is to encourage group members to verbalize their feelings of nervousness and apprehension about being in the group. These feelings, when divulged, convey the sense that "we are all in the same boat," as group members have observed, and provide a rudimentary basis for group cohesion.

3. A third group-counselor task involves suggesting and soliciting alternatives to the members' violent behavior. Such alternatives include removing oneself from potential abuse situations, yelling to reduce tension, or calling a friend. Group members are encouraged to call each other for support—particularly when abuse seems imminent.

Occasional paradoxical challenges by group counselors (such as the one posed by David to Jack) help group members to see their rationalizing and blaming by mirroring it back to them. By the middle stages of Emerge groups, group members begin to assume more of these leadership tasks and to give each other more direct feedback.

Middle Group Issues (Sessions 4-18)

> Joe: I always had problems trusting other people. I never would show them how I really feel because I always figured they'd use it against me. My wife says I keep things to myself, like that.
>
> Bob (group counselor): How is it for you to be talking about how you feel in the group?
>
> Joe: O.K., I guess because we all have the same problem. I was surprised to hear Jack saying the same thing because I thought I was the only one. (laughter)
>
> Eric: Me too. Anytime Ann would try to find out what was bothering me, I just couldn't talk about it—or I didn't know. Now, I realize that sometimes I don't feel so great about myself like I always thought. It's funny how you fool yourself sometimes. What you really feel is just the opposite of what you think.
>
> Joe: I guess that's what men are supposed to think, you know, you always got to be on top of everything, but it's not right. I've always been a loner and I've never bothered other people with

            my problems, but sometimes you need a shoulder to cry on, not just bullshitting in a bar either.

Jim: The first night I met you, Joe, I thought to myself "Jesus, watch out for this guy; he's one mean-looking bastard." (laughter) Now, I can see you're not that way at all.

Eric: Yeah, I thought that at first too. But you're really a marshmallow underneath.

Joe: Christ, you guys make me sound like some kind of criminal or something. But I guess that's just how I used to always see myself; someone that nobody dared to mess with. That's a good way of keeping people away—just keep them scared of you.

David (group counselor): It sounds like that's changing for you now.

Joe: Well, now I realize it's me that I'm really hurting. I always wanted to hang around with the other kids, it's just that I never thought I was good enough so I said, "Fuck it, I don't need these people." But I did need them, I just never realized it at the time.

Ron: That's just what I thought. Only I used to get around that by conning people: you know, "screw them before they can screw you." I was always small for my age, so I had to learn how to out hustle them, And I was good at it too. But it didn't really make me feel good like I wanted it too. It was just a way of staying alive.

This middle-group exchange illuminates a major shift in group functioning. The group members have become more interactive and self-helping. Content-wise, as they become more introspective, their discussions shift from their wives to themselves. When group members begin to express underlying feelings of inadequacy, fear, and failure, which do not conform to the perceived male norms, a new group concensus emerges which gives men permission to have these feelings and to talk about them with other men. Frequently, group members express relief that they are not "the only ones" to harbor self-doubts. A deeper sense of mutuality develops around the sharing of these feelings.

This development is significant therapeutically because it indicates that these men are learning a new way of feeling comfortable with themselves and each other which does not require the devaluing of women. With this kind of self-affirmation and peer support, abusive men become more able to see and talk about their wives more positively. Beyond showing a more positive regard for their wives, middle-group members also begin to develop an appreciation for the caretaking roles that their wives have served. Caretaking is an alien role for most men. Therefore, men often take for granted the care that they receive from their mothers and wives and fail to recognize how critical caretaking and nurturance is for human sustenance and growth. Typically, men lay claim to seemingly more masculine roles like problem-solving, giving criticism, and being the financial provider.

Before men who batter can become caretakers of others, however, they must be made more aware of their own needs for nurturance and emotional support. In group counseling, learning how to acknowledge and express one's own needs often goes hand in hand with learning how to help others. Group members learn that by helping others, they are helping themselves.

As group members become more interactive and self-helping, the group counselors become less intervening and directive. The group counselor's role shifts from one of building and maintenance to that of supportive resource providers. Thus, group leaders might suggest and facilitate exercises such as the following role play which serve to enhance the development of certain skills or illuminate particular issues:

Don reported on a verbal encounter he had had with his wife: In the previous week, Don had learned (from a friend of Jane's who had volunteered to look after the children) that Jane had been admitted to the hospital following a miscarriage. Don said that he resented having a "complete stranger" taking care of his children and felt hurt that Jane had not informed him of her miscarriage. Don phoned Jane at the hospital and ended up getting into a bitter argument with her. The group leaders suggested that the group role play this telephone conversation. Don played himself and Jack agreed to play Jane's role. The role play went as follows:

Don: Hello, it's me.
Jane: (played by Jack): Hello. (In somewhat resentful tone)
Don: What happened, why didn't you call? (with a light tone of anger rising)
Jane: I don't feel anything for you anymore.

Don: Yeah, what about the kids, do you care about the kids? (angrily)
Jane: What do you mean, the kids?
Don: Leaving them with a stranger, I mean. (in an angry tone)
Jane: She's not a stranger. She's my friend. (hostile tone)
Don: I don't want my kids in the company of no stranger. (loud and angry)
Jane: I don't care what you want. It's about time you felt hurt.
Don: You want the kids to be hurt too? (sarcastically)
Jane: I'm not talking about the kids. All I care about is hurting you. You hurt me and now I'm hurting you, buddy.
Don: Yeah, well that's a sick attitude.
Jane: You're the one who's sick.
Don: We'll see who's sick in court.
Jane: That's fine with me, mister. (hangs up)

The rest of the group session was devoted to processing the role play and discussing ways that Don could have communicated. Jack said to Don, "You didn't give a shit about me" (Jane), pointing out that Don had never asked Jane how she felt. Hal agreed, adding, "Man, you launched right into your attack without even asking her about her condition or how she felt about losing the baby." Jim marveled at "how fast the fight escalated" once Don and Jane devoted themselves to hurting each other rather than to trying to understand and comfort each other. The group agreed that Don had communicated poorly by:

• Not expressing his own feelings of hurt.
• Not checking in on Jane, and by ignoring her pain and loss (of the baby).
• Using his "concern" about the children as a smokescreen for his feelings of hurt and resentment.
• Using inflammatory words like "stranger" and "sick" which caused further hurt and retribution.

This role-play exercise not only proved to be therapeutic for Don but was also a vicarious learning experience for the entire group. Considerable insight and helpful feedback is evidenced by group members.

Receiving feedback from one's peers can be a powerful stimulus for change. Abusive men often seem ignorant about how they come across to others. More specifically, they seem blind to the devastating impact that their violence has on others. This is because batterers tend to focus more on their "good intentions" or their wives' alleged "provocations" than on their own behavior. But through education and feedback from peers in Emerge groups, abusive men are made aware that their violence induces fear, destroys trust, and makes intimacy impossible. Once this information is learned, the abusive man must then decide whether or not these are consequences which he *wishes* to create.

Emerge counseling groups use feedback in a formal way during the group-member evaluation procedure in the eighth session. The purpose of this evaluation is to help each member decide whether or not he should continue attending the group beyond the 8 weeks for which he originally contracted. Therefore, each member evaluates his own progress, or lack of progress, in the group and then hears feedback from other members and the group counselors. In addition, the group counselors report on their telephone contacts with each member's partner (assuming they have been given permission for such contact) and her report on the presence or absence of violence during the period of her partner's attendance in the group. Most group members decide to continue for the duration of the group. This more formal evaluation process helps group members learn about giving and receiving feedback in a nonhostile manner. In addition, each member is able to find out how he has helped and been helped by others. Group members are often surprised to learn how much of a positive impact they have had on others. This evaluation process also provides incentive for group members to state in a more direct way what the group has meant to them. Hearing these acknowledgments helps each member to feel more fully invested in the group.

The middle phase of Emerge counseling groups is characterized by the members accepting more responsibility for their violence, becoming more introspective, and learning alternative behaviors and methods of expression. As group members take more risks, their vulnerability contributes to a more cohesive and dynamic group. The group counselors intervene less but continue to provide support, guidance, and direction, as it is needed.

Later and Ending Group Dynamics
(Sessions 18–24)

By the final stages of Emerge groups, group members have become quite familiar with each other and closeness can be more openly acknowledged. Frequently, members socialize between group sessions and some lasting friendships have been forged. Because it serves to break down feelings of social isolation which many batterers have, this extragroup contact is encouraged by group leaders. To avoid divisive hidden agendas within the group, however, group members are asked to talk about their outside-the-group contacts within the group:

> Jim and Don, who were both separated from their wives, began their socializing by offering each other rides to the group. Gradually, as the friendship developed, Jim and Don spent more time together. In the group, Jim reported: I never had a real male buddy before, you know, someone you can talk about things with like I can with Don here.
>
> Don: My wife and kids were my whole world to me, so when they left, there was nothing. We had friends but they were all other couples too. I used to go bowling with some guys but we never did nothing but drink beers and complain about our wives. I just never realized how much I needed a friend—hell, not just one friend—to talk to. It's really helped me to have Jim to talk to 'cause I know he'll understand 'cause he's going through the same thing I am.
>
> Jim: Barbara and I got married when we were both 20 and then that was it for me. I just completely cut myself off from the rest of the world after that. And then I began to blame Barbara for everything. If the kids were whining, it was her fault. If we couldn't make the car payment, she was to blame. Christ, if I wasn't happy, she was screwing up. Now, when I think about it, I just laugh at myself—except when I think about what I done to Barbara.
>
> Don: Boy, it's fucked up like that, isn't it? The way we shit on other people sometimes just because we don't have our own shit together. I feel so much better about myself now. I used to feel superior in some ways to other people, including Joan. But it was just a cover-up for how bad I really felt about myself underneath. Now, I can feel good and I can feel bad, but at least it's me that's feeling it. I don't blame anyone else for it now.

As can be seen in this group exchange, group members begin to change their attitudes and expectations of their wives when their expectations of themselves begin to change. Developing closer bonds with other men (and women) helps the abuser to become less dependent on his wife's "being there all the time," as one group member put it. By the final stage of Emerge groups, members become aware that their previous expectations of their wives were not only unrealistic, but in some cases, impossible for their wives to fulfill. Jim's past expectations of Barbara are typical for abusive husbands. They tend to sub-consciously hold their wives responsible for their own feelings of inadequacy and failure as men. Hostility and violence towards women is the common result of this underlying dependency and envy. Jim's feelings of self-esteem increased as he was more able to "own" his own feelings and learn to take care of himself. Moreover, his feelings of self-worth no longer came at the expense of his wife or others.

Related to the heightening of self-esteem, is the idea of shaping one's own environment. As has been said earlier, abusive men often seem unaware of their damaging impact on others. Conversely, they also fail to recognize the positive influence they may have on others, such as other group members. Their battering reflects attempts to compensate for feelings of passivity and inconsequentiality by controlling and dominating their partners. Ironically, abusive men are often good candidates for assertiveness training in other areas of their lives. Emerge group members have frequently reported situations in which they felt "pushed around" or failed to "stand up for their rights" at their workplaces, for instance. Middle to later group members usually come to appreciate the connection between their feeling "pushed around" at work and pushing their wives around at home. As one group member stated, "I'd come home from work and I'd just be looking for my wife to look at me the wrong way or say something stupid." By becoming more aware of their feelings and needs, Emerge clients have been able to avoid this carry-over from work to home. Some members have been able, as a result, to press for better working conditions, demand higher salaries, and organize unions, at their workplaces, for example. Some have been able to create wider social networks for themselves. These acts of self-assertion have helped abusers to gain some sense of control and self-determination over their own lives. Just as importantly, group counseling helps them learn to live more cooperatively with their spouses and other peers. Consequently, abusive men come to regard their wives as partners, rather than as objects to be controlled.

As the group nears its end, termination issues of separation and loss surface. Group members are encouraged by group counselors to talk openly about these feelings. At this time, group members reveal varying past styles of ending relationships or separating from groups. These include missing the final meeting, regressing, becoming angry, and minimizing the emotional impact of the impending loss. Talking about these previous styles within the group helps group members to acknowledge the difficulty of separating and to avoid repeating past mistakes. Learning to separate and individuate well helps these men to approach new relationships in less self-defeating ways. It also helps them confront their ambivalence toward intimacy. This is extremely important for abusive men, because as we have shown, battering is one way of avoiding or denying intimacy.

As part of group termination, Emerge groups conduct a final evaluation of group members. The purpose of this final evaluation is to review each member's progress in the group and to help each to set goals for the future. Thus, suggestions are made to each member as to how he should continue beyond the group. The group counselors act as resource people in helping the group brainstorm ideas for continued growth. Some ideas from various Emerge groups are: individual counseling, marital or family counseling, mixed groups, men's consciousness-raising groups, recreational or social clubs, taking classes, job changes, dating, yoga or meditation, and volunteer work for Emerge. As each group member is evaluated, he selects which (if any) of the above ideas might be most appropriate for him and other members give their impressions. The group counselors remain available to help locate specific resources for group members and their families and for periodic follow-up.

One Year Later. . . .

Don: Halfway through the group, Don reconciled with his wife. Both Don and Jane report that their relationship has improved in many ways. Jane says of Don, "He seems so much more loving and considerate of my feelings. He's a lot more flexible when it comes to how we spend our time together. I think he realizes that I'm my own person now and he's not threatened by that like he used to be." Don reports that his relationship with his children has also changed, "We're a lot closer and more like a family now. They are not afraid of me anymore, I guess because I don't have to yell to get them to listen to me. It's more of a two-way communcation now."

Jim: Jim continues to live apart from Barbara and she has filed for divorce. Despite this, Jim has made signficant changes in his life.

For the past 9 months, Jim has done much volunteer work for Emerge. He has completed our 8-week training program for new members and has since attended our regular business and counseling supervision meetings. Jim has also done a number of media interviews and has helped to train professionals who want to work with abusive man. Jim states, "Emerge has really helped me to grow as a person. I lived in a cloud for the first 35 years of my life with no awareness at all of what I was doing or how I was feeling. The counseling opened my eyes to a lot of things I really didn't want to see in myself. It feels so much better to be able to express my emotions now and its made a big difference in my relationship with others. Some people hardly recognize me."

Jack: Judy reports that Jack has made major changes in the way he relates to her and the children; "It's like a miracle! He's much more patient and kind. He doesn't raise his voice as much, and even when he does I feel like I can yell back without being afraid of his losing control." Jack says, "I can talk about what's bugging me without getting hot under the collar. The little things that used to frost my ass just don't bother me anymore. I can laugh at things now."

Eric: Eric continues to live with Ann and their children. Following the group, Ann and Eric sought marital counseling and reported that they had profited greatly from it. Eric says he had learned to be more nurturant towards Ann and the children and he no longer expects Ann "to take care of me." Eric observes, "I used to resent Ann for being so strong and rational, but now we are both strong and we can relate to each other as equals."

Assa: Assa dropped out of the group after seven sessions. He continued to be violent towards Linda until she separated from him. Assa has since returned to Morocco.

Joe: Joe dropped out of the group after eight sessions. He continued to threaten and intimidate Susan and she has filed for divorce. Joe has engaged in several acts of violence toward other people and continues to drink heavily. He is being treated as an out-patient at a Veteran's Administration Hospital.

Hal: Hal attended an additional 16 weeks of group counseling at Emerge after completing his original group. (This 16-week group was offered to clients who had joined their original groups after the first 8-week cycle.) Although his relationship with Sara continues to have problems, Hal has not been abusive. Sara observes that Hal seems more able to express his feelings and "does not brood like he used to." Hal and Sara are presently in couples counseling.

Ron: Ron and Joan separated shortly after Ron joined the group. They have since divorced. Ron says of his counseling experience; "It helped me to see how much I was bullshitting myself. I like myself a whole lot more now. As far as the violence goes, I know I would never let that happen again—no matter how uptight I got. I can be more honest with people now 'cause I'm more honest with myself."

CONCLUSION

As these follow-up reports have shown, group counseling is an effective tool in resocializing abusive men to be nonviolent. The group offers a new social environment in which men are encouraged to reject the restrictive norms of compulsive masculinity and have permission to explore new ways of being men. The results of this work have been most positive in cases where men have completed the full 24-week group cycle, although men who stay for shorter periods also derive benefits. This experience of Emerge has demonstrated the viability of group counseling for abusive men and confirmed the need for these specialized services. However, work on this problem should not be limited to the clinical realm.

Success in ending the abuse of women will ultimately hinge on a reduction in the societal tolerance of abuse. To this end it is vital that we treat the social context as well as individual men. Counseling treats the problem after it occurs; community education seeks to prevent the problem before it happens. By coordinating a community education program with the counseling groups, Emerge treats the disease as well as the symptom.

Within our patriarchal social system, abusive men are functional in maintaining the homeostasis of the dominance of men over women. One way of intervening in this system is to change the rules which support the abuse of women. This will require the cooperation of the police, the courts, and human service personnel in supporting the efforts of women to protect themselves from abuse, and in encouraging men to admit their problem and seek help. Gradually a change in attitudes on the part of the community at large will increase the base of support for addressing the problem of abuse. This change will enable us to reach a level of homeostasis in which men and women function as equal partners in their personal relationships and in the social institutions.

FOOTNOTES

1. Brownmiller, Susan. *Against Our Will: Men, Women and Rape,* Chapter 6, The police blotter rapist, is especially good on explaining the power dynamic behind rape and how rapists function as shocktroopers for all men. New York: Bantam Books, 1976, p. 229.
2. Hartley, Ruth. Sex role pressures and the socialization of the male child. In *Men and Masculinity,* Joseph Pleck and Jack Sawyer (eds.) Provides an excellent discussion of the pressures on the young boy to conform to the stereotyped male role. Englewood Cliffs, N.J.: Prentice-Hall, 1974.
3. Greenleaf, Phyllis Taube. *Liberating Young Children From Sex Roles: Experiences in Day Care Centers, Play Groups, and Free Schools.* For a discussion on how to change this pattern. Somerville, Mass.: New England Free Press, 1972.
4. Parsons, Talcott. Certain primary sources and patterns of aggression in the social structure of the western world. In *Essays in Sociological Theory,* Revised Ed., New York: The Free Press, 1966, as quoted in Murray A. Straus. A sociological perspective on the prevention and treatment of wifebeating. In Maria Roy (ed.) *The Battered Woman,* New York: Van Nostrand Reinhold, 1979.
5. Straus, Murray A., Gelles, Richard J., and Steinmetz, Suzanne K. *Behind Closed Doors: Violence in the American Family,* Garden City, N.Y.: Doubleday/Anchor Books, 1980, pp. 101–104.
6. Straus, Murray A., et al., op cit., p. 182. The authors present a list of 18 stress factors and later correlate them to violent acts in the family.
7. Frank, Jerome D. *Persuasion in Healing.* New York: Schocken Books, 1977, p. 276.
8. For the sake of consistency we are using the word ''wife'' generically here and throughout to indicate a co-habitating partner whether she be a wife or ''girlfriend.''

12. Conjoint Therapy: Staff Training and Treatment of the Abuser and the Abused

Janet Geller, A.C.S.W., C.S.W.
Ms. Geller had been the Clinical Director of Victims Information Bureau of Suffolk (VIBS) for four years where she developed a unique treatment model for spouse abuse. She has lectured and consulted on spouse abuse across the country. She is currently providing private consultation, staff development and program implementation in the area of spouse abuse in addition to her employment at Columbia University Graduate School of Social Work where she holds an Assistant Professor position.

INTRODUCTION

Recently, a great deal has been written about why women stay in abusive relationships (Gelles, 1976). Of the abusive marriages* that terminate, some of the women get involved in another abusive relationship, and some of their partners continue to abuse their wives when they remarry. Aside from the socioeconomic factors which heavily account for remaining with an abusive partner, there are the psychological factors as well. Leaving means facing an unknown. Often, it is easier to remain with the known because of the comfort experienced

---

* The terms "marriage," "husband," and "wife" are used to refer to the relationship between a couple cohabitating together and are not limited to a legal marital relationship.

from familiarity. Many people experience feelings of isolation, helplessness, and abandonment upon separation from a significant other (Bowlby; 1973, p. 143). Another important psychological factor as to why women stay is based on what behaviorists have termed the theory of "intermittent reinforcement" (Skinner; 1953, p. 74). Abusers do not exhibit violent behavior all of the time. Couples reported that when partners are not violent, they behave normally in the relationship. Based on my experience, the restoring of normalcy to the marital relationship renews the hope in the women that violence will not resume. Coupled with the cessation of violence is the husbands' promises and vows that they will never abuse their wives again, which the women eagerly and desperately latch onto because of the desire to have things as they were (familiar). Both partners want to believe that the abuse will not resume. However, it does occur again only to confuse and upset the couple. Commonly, upon the resumption of violent behavior, the husband employs all of the defense mechanisms available to human beings and most frequently blames his wife. Over time his wife incorporates the blame (Symonds, 1974), eventually isolating herself from others. She begins to feel more and more powerless in the relationship, and her feelings of self-worth decrease. The unpredictability of her situation may leave her nervous, agitated, emotionally labile and meek. One woman commented that she does not know what happened to her. She had always been a "happy-go-lucky" person. Her attitude had always been that things would work out. After 5 years of marriage to an abusive husband, she found herself plagued by vague worries, a general pessimism, and easily irritated.

Typically, the woman is home taking care of children. With the feelings engendered as a result of the violence inflicted upon her, the mother usually loses her effectiveness in taking care of her children. This often leads to a pervasive sense of failure. In addition, the children begin to show signs of emotional turmoil which frequently manifests itself in acting out and misbehavior. Further, as a result of the continued abuse that she had suffered, if she has visible signs of injury, she will remain out of sight, thereby denying herself contact with friends and family who are potential helpers. The possibility of realistic feedback often lies in the contact with the outside world where she might learn that the battering is not her fault. In short, a battered woman is often alone, isolated, and friendless. Her home is a battleground rather than a haven, her children are a toil rather than a pleasure, and her husband is her enemy rather than her friend.

In working with abusers at Victims Information Bureau of Suffolk, batterers report feelings of depression and loss of self-worth as a result of wife battering. Abusers often experience guilt over how they have hurt their wives and families. Some men secretly believe that there is something seriously wrong with them because of their uncontrollable aggression. One husband told me that he used to think that men who hit women deserved to be "spit on" and now he is "spitting on himself." Another husband was obsessed with going to a neurologist to find out why he hit his wife.

In order for abusive behavior to stop, treatment is necessary. Abusers who articulate their feelings about their violent behavior are generally amenable to verbal therapy. There are certain types of abusers who could not benefit from counseling or psychotherapy (Geller and Walsh; 1977–1978, pp. 627–32). The abusers who can be worked with within a psychotherapeutic model typically lead normal lives, and aside from the abuse inflicted upon their wives, show no other signs of deviant behavior. They conform to society's mores and values and they are usually good citizens. When they are not being abusive, they relate to their wives normally and most of these men are often good fathers.* They reflect society's values and their goals conform to the norm (Rosenbaum and O'Leary, Unpublished). These men are disturbed by their behavior but they often feel a sense of hopelessness concerning their ability to control their violent behavior. As a result, they defend their behavior through rationalizations, externalizations, denials, etc. The use of defense mechanisms is a normal psychological function (Freud, Anna, 1966). Eventually the abuser incorporates the rationalizations, believes they are the truth, and views his wife as the triggering mechanism. It is also not uncommon for the abuser to feel victimized by his wife. The question, "Why did you make me hit you?" is a familiar one to battered women. While the husband sees himself as the culprit who is behaving violently, he also blames the victim because he feels that she made him do it.

---

* Derived from author's experience counseling approximately one hundred couples in conjoint therapy.

Case Example. After a phone call initiated by the wife, she and her abusive husband came in for conjoint therapy. Initially, he was very guarded and suspicious. He asked if I was one of those "women libbers" who always think the woman is a "saint" and the man is an "animal." Before I could respond, he said that he was really glad that his wife called up because he had his side of the story to tell and he was glad to get a chance to do so because "no one wants to listen to the man's side." He told me that I can be easily fooled by his wife who "always acts like she's the good one." He stated that he bet she was hoping he wouldn't agree to come to see me so that she could paint him as the "bad guy." He turned to his wife and said, "Fooled you, didn't I? I did come." Before anyone could respond, he continued in the same vein, telling me that his wife always acts like he's "Mr. Macho" and she tells people that he "runs the show." In a blaming tone, he said to her, "You know that's not true. You make me act a certain way. You make me get mad at you and then when I start to yell, you twist the knife in deeper and make me yell until I'm so mad, I smack you." He then turned to me and pleadingly asked me to tell him why she does that to him. He said that he had no other "problems." His boss likes him; he has friends he goes bowling with. They all think he is a "good guy."

TREATMENT

What has been described above is a system that develops long before the abusing couple comes to the attention of a helping person. When the choice is to terminate the marriage, individual therapy is prescribed. However, if a battered woman chooses to remain in the marriage, then the treatment of choice is conjoint therapy. Viewed from a systems perspective (Satir, Stachowiak, and Taschman, 1975), there is a locked pattern of behavior based on an interaction between both partners. The woman is the victim and the man is the assailant. One cannot be without the other. This is not to say that the abuse is the woman's fault. It cannot be emphasized enough that the violent behavior is the *sole responsibility* of the violent partner. From a systems orientation, however, the most effective method of treatment is to work with the system, and thereby change the environment in which a person lives. All husbands and wives experience conflict; sometimes the wife initiates a conflict situation, sometimes the husband does. However, not all wives who initiate an argument are abused. Those who are abused are involved with a partner who has a problem controlling his aggressive impulses for a variety of reasons. It is now recognized that *abusers must be treated for their violent impulses.* Some services treat the abuser in isolation (such as Emerge in Boston). While this approach rightfully is targeted at the abusive behavior, it does not take into account the context of an abusive relationship which includes another person. Even though the responsibility for controlling the violence rests with the violent person, this approach does not take into account the effect of battering on the wife. How the husband has treated her over all the abusive years of the relationship, has shaped her view of herself and the world in which she lives. If treated conjointly, the husband's abusive behavior in conjunction with the effects of the abuse on the wife are dealt with. This approach can be more advisable than dealing with each partner or one partner singularly. Moreover, the way the couple relates to each other needs to be improved. As a result of the violence, each partner views the other with suspicion and mistrust. They have to learn how to live together compatibly, with mutual understanding. In addition to the cessation of the abuse, there needs to develop a mature love relationship. In other words, in addition to treating the violence, the couple is in need of marital therapy. By conjointly working with the identified problem of violence, other overall marital problems can be treated as well (Geller and Walsh).

Case Examples

1. For one couple seen conjointly, after a year of counseling, the violence did not stop. In my experience, when the abusing partner agrees to therapy, the violence gets under control relatively quickly (about 2 months). Since this was an atypical case, I saw the couple together with the worker in an attempt to diagnose the problem of continued abuse and to make recommendations for effective treatment. During the session, the husband said that when he gets mad he needs some time to cool off but that his wife continues the argument. His wife readily agreed and said that when she's in the middle of an argument, she can't just "stop" until her husband cools off. She went on to say that she needs to get "off her chest" what is bothering her. The couple acknowledged that the argument does stop, however, when he hits her. In spite of her need to finish the argument, she was asked which of the two alternatives was better at the moment—getting

things off her chest or not getting hit. She, of course, said she prefers to not get hit. It was explained to her that, in this case, it's possible that she would have to give up what she needed immediately because her husband could not continue to argue without hitting her when he needed a cooling off period. He was asked what he could do to cool off and how much time he needed. He said that he would like to go into a room just by himself, close the door, and calm down. He thought that it wouldn't take more than 15 minutes for him to cool off. He was asked whether he could resume the argument after the 15 minutes because his wife needed to "finish." He felt that he could, and similarly his wife agreed she could wait provided they continued the argument after that. The couple said that they did try this before but that it didn't work. In questioning them further, the husband said to his wife, "It's because you follow me into the room and continue the fight." The wife acknowledged that this was true. She was told that she would have to stick to the agreement and that it was a contract between them. It meant that she could not follow him into the room. It was emphasized that the two of them had to cooperate in this plan. Both agreed and the battering stopped with no resumption. This couple spent another year working on marital issues. Follow-up a year later showed no resumption of abuse.

2. After two sessions which were dominated by the abusive partner's monologue on his wife's victimization of him, and where both she and I were relatively silent, I asked him how he felt when he hit her, regardless of the reasons. He did not seem to understand what I meant, acting bewildered. Finally, he said that he doesn't feel anything. He tried to again convey that it was all her fault. I interrupted him and asked the wife how she felt when he yelled at her and eventually hit her. She said that she felt afraid. I encouraged her to elaborate on her feelings. He tried to interrupt several times to explain how she "made" him respond as he did. Each time, I cut him off and asked him to listen to what his wife was saying. I told him that he would have his chance to respond, but I thought that we should let her finish first. With my encouragement and probing, the wife was able to add that in addition to the fear, she also felt angry and hurt. She said that she lost her "self-confidence," and that she's nervous all the time, and that she gets "sick" a lot. He seemed concerned about her health and said that he didn't know that she was getting "sick all the time." For the first time since they started therapy, Dick did not seem self-absorbed. I commented that he seemed concerned about his wife's health, to which he agreed. He went on to say that he would be very upset if his wife got sick and began to dote on her. He became very demonstrative and asked what "hurts" her and what could he do, taking her hand gently. His wife was silent but looked forlorn.

At this point, the session ended. They left with the husband fussing over the wife telling her to button her coat and the like.

In the next session, I focused in on the wife's state of health. She said that she was never sick "before" but she didn't explain (what my hunch was) that she meant her husband's abuse. I attempted to increase the husband's concern about her health. I asked him what he would do if she got very sick. He responded in earnest that he would "wait on her hand and foot." I commented that it sounded to me that he was quite devoted to her, which he acknowledged. I asked him what lengths would he go to get her well and keep her well. He responded immediately, "Any length." I then asked him why he thought she was getting sick a lot. He said he did not know and suggested several possibilities from bearing the children, taking care of the children, to not eating right or taking enough vitamins. She was asked to respond to each of his suggestions. She denied that anything her husand said was the reason. I asked them both to tell me how she used to be physically and when did each of them think it changed. Both of them described her as having a lot of energy. He used the word "bubbly," and that she used to be "athletic." Both said that now she's tired all the time, "jumpy" and that she frequently suffers from severe headaches and a "nervous stomach." Her doctor told her it was "just nerves" and prescribed Valium.

In subsequent sessions, she was finally able to tell me in front of her husband that she gets sick the day after he's violent with her. But this time, he was open to hearing this and was no longer avoiding responsibility for the abuse. He had come to understand that part of being a married couple means that there are fights and sometimes one partner starts a fight and at other times the fight is initiated by the other partner. Both he and Susan had begun to accept that getting angry was "normal" and that each of them had anger in them. He began to see that how the anger got expressed was the important issue and that he could no longer blame his wife for his abusive behavior. He also got in touch with how he didn't like himself when he hit her saying, "Guys aren't supposed to hit girls." They both understood that her illnesses were related to and a result of his violence. He admitted that he needed help in controlling his violent behavior and the couple was able to work together on ways to get the violence under control. When he said that he would go to "any length" to help his wife get well, I was now able to remind him of this, telling him the length he had to go to was to overcome his violent temper. Eventually, the wife was able to stop taking medication for her "nerves." The old personality of the wife was able to emerge again bringing physical health. In time, the violence stopped and the couple was able to work together on other issues affecting their marriage.

THE INITIAL CONTACT

Most commonly, it is the woman who initially make the contact requesting help (Chesler, 1972). In view of the deterioration of her self-image and her psychological victimization, it would not be unusual for the woman to appear helpless and dependent. If conjoint treatment is indicated, then the first appointment must be with both partners together and not either individually. When a woman requests treatment because she is in a violent relationship, she often feels a need to come in alone and for good reason. With a damaged self-image and an assailant for a partner, the thought of coming for help together with her husband probably seems an impossibility. At face value he abuses her and she's afraid of him. It would mean overcoming her fear of her husband to suggest conjoint treatment to him. Further, she and her husband have a pattern of behavior; she is the victim and he is the attacker. By that definition she can never get her needs met and he would never do anything that she desires. Coming for treatment because she asks him to means a change in their pattern, because coming for help is his acknowledgment of her needs and his problem. In and of itself, the act of coming for help as a couple results in a dent in their "bad guy-victim" system as it requires a cooperative action as well as a mutual admission of the existence of the problem (Miller, 1976). Therefore, postponing treatment until both partners agree to come in has already had therapeutic value. If the wife is successful in getting her husband to come in, she is no longer just the victim. Similarly, he is no longer just the abuser. *The initial session, therefore, is one of the most critical points in the treatment of abusing couples because of its impact on the system.* But it is often very difficult to achieve a conjoint first session. There is usually resistance by the couple because of the very nature of the effect on the system. Since the couple is in a locked but familiar pattern of behavior, the familiarity defies change. The issue of resistance in therapy is common knowledge to therapists. In the case of a couple or system, two parties join in collusion to avoid changes (Sager, 1976), and resist the worker's attempts to see them together conjointly. This can be manifested in a number of ways, the wife may claim that under no circumstances can she convince her husband to come in, or that there may be more battering as a result. If the determination is made that conjoint therapy is the treatment of choice, the therapist must then overcome the couple's resistance. In my experience, the key to overcoming resistance lies in tapping into mobilizing anxiety. It is well known that battering is a chronic problem. (Women report that onset is usually within the first year of marriage.) In general, people often seek help for a long-standing problem, rather than a sudden event.* What mobilizes the person to seek help at a particular moment is extremely significant and should be noted. In the case of abuse, there is usually a precipitating event which creates a motivation for change. For example, one wife stated that she took all the years of abuse until her husband went after one of the children. When he did that, she made up her mind to go for help. The momentary mobilizing of resources must be tapped into and sustained until both partners come in together for therapy. This can be done by keeping the anxiety or motivation at a high enough level in order to overcome the resistance. Said another way, the therapist must draw on the mobilizing anxiety to break through the pull of maintaining homeostatis (Satir, Stackowiak, and Taschman, 1975). If at first the woman is seen individually, then the contact with the therapist (the session) only serves to sabotage the treatment. Individual therapy can be counterproductive; the risk run is that her anxiety may be alleviated and drop down to a neutral or immobilized state. The problem becomes further compounded if the other partner in the system (the abuser) views seeing his wife individually as perpetuating his rationalization that it is all her fault (she needs the help), or that he is "the bad guy" and the therapist and his wife have developed an alliance and are colluding against him. A case example of how treatment can be sabotaged, and the system can defeat the therapist when individual treatment is given initially, is as follows:

Mary had been abused for many years. She was quite familiar with the options available to her. In the past, she had taken legal action through obtaining an Order for Protection (The Family Court Act, "State of New York," 1969, S.6617-A.8842) against her husband. She had also been in counseling through women's groups and individual counseling. She called (the Victim's Information Bureau of Suffolk) for help, conveying the above information. She wanted to come in and see me alone. In questioning

---

* There are times that a sudden event is the precipitant for help as in sudden loss, rape, discovery of a serious illness, etc.

her further she stated that, as a result of the last violent episode, she and her husband were separated but she eventually wanted to return to him. She saw the separation as "teaching him a lesson" so that he knew that she wouldn't take his abuse. I reinforced that she should not take his abuse but since her interest was in reconciliation, I thought that they should come in as a couple. She agreed that she would want to do this eventually, but that right now, she wanted to come in alone. When I held firmly to the fact that they should come in together, she insisted that Jim (her husband) would refuse. She said that he came to a session with her on a previous occasion. They had an argument in the session and the worker thought that they should be seen separately. Jim thought that the argument was Mary's fault as she started it, and he didn't see any reason to continue. He told the worker that the problem was Mary's as she started most of the arguments. He felt that Mary needed the help, not he. Jim dropped out of treatment, but the worker continued to work with Mary. Eventually, Mary dropped out too as she felt there was nothing more she could work on. Everything that Mary told me convinced me that she and Jim needed to be seen together. She finally agreed and the case was assigned to one of my workers who was fairly new to the agency although an experienced worker. Before the first appointment, Mary called the worker telling her that Jim wouldn't come. The worker reinforced that the couple needed to come in together, at which point Mary accused the worker of not wanting to help her. Mary slammed the phone down and proceeded to call me as the worker's supervisor. She complained about not being able to get help from the agency. After she and I talked for a while, I referred her back to the worker to work things out. Mary had become quite volatile on the phone and manipulated the worker into seeing her alone. I advised the worker against this, but the worker acquiesced to the client's wishes. After one session with Mary alone, the worker and I discussed the case. The worker said that Mary felt a need to be seen alone in order to develop the confidence to get her husband to come in. The worker didn't see how she could refuse service to the client. After several individual sessions where Mary often reported that Jim was convinced that the problem was Mary's, both Mary and the worker realized that seeing Mary alone was counterproductive. The next session was set up as a couple session. Between the week that elapsed until the couple's appointment, Mary called the worker several times, telling the worker that Jim was refusing to come in. Jim finally agreed to keep the couple appointment two days before the appointment time. There had been another battering in the interim. Mary called the police who suggested an Order of Protection. Mary told the police that she had had one in the past, but she didn't want one now because she was trying to convince Jim to go for help with her. The police reinforced that to Jim and he said he would. Although Jim and Mary came to the session together, things did not go well. Mary began to accuse him of not being satisfied until she "was dead" at his hands. Although Jim denied this, Mary persisted in her beliefs, which led to an escalating argument. When the worker attempted to intervene, Jim accused the worker of being on Mary's "side" and that there was "no use" in coming for help. With that, Jim walked out. Succeeding attempts to get Jim to come in failed.

One cannot say for sure if the outcome for Mary and Jim would have been different if the worker was able to hold firm in her conviction that this couple should be seen together. However, by insisting on a conjoint approach from the onset, there might have been one less obstacle to overcome.

Selection of the appropriate course of treatment determined at the initial contact can reduce the woman's venting or spilling and redirect her energies into getting her husband to accompany her. The following case material from my own practice will illustrate a different outcome:

Amy called for help because she heard that I worked with spouse abuse. I asked Amy how long the abuse had been going on. Amy said that George (her husband) has been hitting her for the 7 years that they have been married. I suggested that 7 years was a long time to live with violence. Amy readily agreed with me and began to relay the details and frequency of the beatings. I interrupted and asked her if she wanted to leave the relationship, explaining her options, or did she want to remain in the marriage? Emphatically and then apologetically, Amy told me that she wanted to stay married to George. I asked if she wanted her husband to stop hitting her to which she replied "of course." I suggested that Amy ask George to come in with her. Amy stated that George would never come for help or even admit that he needed help. Amy went on to say that George said it was all her fault anyway. Amy attempted to vent, telling me what was "wrong" with George. I again interrupted her saying I could hear that she had a need to tell me about how abusing George was, but I thought that right now we should talk about George coming in with her. I asked if she wanted George to go for help. She again replied "of course." Before she could tell me that he would not, I asked Amy how she could get George to come in with her. Amy insisted that she couldn't get him to do "anything." I thought that we'd better figure out a way to get him to do this because I didn't know any way that he would stop beating her unless he came in. I asked Amy if she'd been able to get him to stop hitting her, to which she replied "no." I wondered then how she thought that if she came in alone that would get him to stop hitting her. Amy could see the logic in that, but she again said that she couldn't convince him. She asked me if she could come in alone a few times and I could try to help her get him in. I didn't think that this would work. I, therefore, told Amy that in my experience, if the husband doesn't come in right away, then he never comes in; that her coming in alone would only appear to George to support his view that she's the one with the problem and that she knew him better than I did. She was better equipped than I to figure out how to convince him to come in. I said that once she convinced him to come, I would help in keeping him coming. Amy said, "but how?" I turned the question back to her. I said that sometime in their relationship she must have gotten him to do what she wanted. When she again said no, I asked if they ever went where she wanted to go socially even if George didn't want to? She said that she did and told me about it. I thought then that she knew how to get George to do what she wanted. She tentatively said that maybe that was true. I asked Amy to try this approach. She said that she would try. I asked Amy if I could call her back the next day to find out what happened. She said that she would try to talk to George that evening and agreed to have me call her back the next day.

The resistance to change was very strong in this case. Amy was a dependent person by nature and she attempted to switch her dependence from George to me. It was only through my firm stand and consistent message that she must appeal to George on her own, that she agreed to try. Even before the first treatment session, changing the system had begun in the telephone contact. Amy was asked to act, to initiate, and to be effective. It was hoped that her mobilizing anxiety or desire for change would motivate her to get her husband in. By not eliciting the details of the batterings, she had no opportunity to vent and thereby alleviate her anxiety, or portray her husband as the "bad guy" and herself as the "victim." From the very first contact, there was an expectation for a change in the system. As it happened, Amy did come in with George. I was asking her to take action and be effective as well as influence her life. Sometimes people are not able to respond to the idea of change the first time it is presented to them, but when the notion of change is discussed, it might be acted upon at a later date.

THE THERAPIST

Amy really pulled on my rescue fantasies. She presented herself as helpless and in need of a protector. The part of me that identifies with the character of Wonder Woman wanted to take care of her and right her life. She worked very hard at attempting to induct me into her system. Based on my strong need to rescue, I had to work harder than she to remain free of the seduction. If I was going to be of help to Amy I could not allow myself to get sucked into this couple's system. (Satir, et al., 1975)

The issues concerning self-awareness, professional discipline and countertransference are familiar to the helping professions (Satir, et al., 1975). The underlying principle it speaks to is the need for professionals to be *acutely* aware of their own feelings which are being triggered by their clients throughout the therapy process. (Sager, 1976) Since the central tool that the therapist has at her/his disposal is use of self, how that self is used becomes a pivotal point of the treatment process. If I rescued Amy in any of the number of ways that she asked me to, then the message given to her would have been that I agreed that she was dependent and helpless. The result would have been that I infantalized her and helped to maintain the homeostasis. At the moment of the phone call, the treatment could have been sabotaged by the collaboration between herself and I to keep her childlike and ineffective and thus, keep the system the same. Seduction into the system is easy to slip into because of the great strength of the pull. In order to prevent this from occurring, the therapist must be aware of her/his own responses, feelings, and emotional issues. (Sager, 1976)

A given part of any therapist's work is continual self-examination. Working with abuse requires extra effort in self-awareness because of the nature of the issues. Violence is abhorrent to us all. Abuse taking place in the intimacy and sanctity of the family is devastating to comprehend. As therapists, we are in intimate contact with the people that we help. Working with abusive partners brings the nature of the violence to the forefront of our consciousness and it is often difficult to bear. Why then would anyone want to work with violence? When would anyone who has a choice about being in a violent environment move toward it rather than away? Since this is not a commonly researched question, only assumptions can be made to shed light on the issue. Possibly, therapists who choose to work with violence may be dealing with their own unresolved conflicts. Perhaps they may have experienced violence in their own backgrounds which they were helpless to deal with at the time. Working as a helper may be the therapists' way of working through their own violent experiences. As for myself, I grew up with violence. There was violence in my home and I spent most of my playtime with boys rather than girls; routinely engaging in physical fights was expected and accepted behavior. Additionally, the show of overt power was modus operandi. During my professional career, I most often worked with acting-out problems. Based on my background, violence was familiar to me. I felt I understood violent behavior. Having experienced violence, I knew it as abhorrent. I became committed to helping others to become nonviolent.

Another assumption concerning therapists who choose to work with violence might be related to the therapists' own unresolved aggressive impulses. The therapist might draw vicarious pleasure from working with abusing couples and thus safely act out her/his own aggression. There may be unresolved anger toward a parent that gets projected and displaced onto clients. For example, the therapist might experience the abuser as being like her/his father who always picked on the woman in the family. In supervision, one worker told me that she could not feel sympathy for the abuser because she believed that men need to dominate women and physical violence was the way men maintained their position of power. Another possibility is that the therapist may have deeprooted hostility toward a particular sex and may perceive all women as victims and all men as abusers, for example. In this case, working with abusive couples confirmed the therapist's own projection and distortions. Another salient issue for self-examination is what have been the therapist's own experiences with violence.

RESCUE FANTASIES

Many people who enter the helping professions are plagued with the need to rescue (Masterson, 1972). Therapists must wrestle with their own rescue fantasies. Battered women are particularly tempting. The issue of power gets triggered when working with abuse. There is no question that the abuser is physically stronger than the victim. The word "abuse" is defined in the dictionary as "to misuse." Another word might be "mistreat." Helpers strongly respond to someone who has been mistreated. Because abused women become helpless in the abusive relationship (Walker; 1977, 1978 pp. 525–533), it would not be surprising that therapists would feel a need to be powerful for the victim. I described the gradual erosion of self and environment that battered women experience. I also mentioned their sense of entrapment with nowhere to turn. In light of their victimization, they convey a need to be rescued. Our society has acknowledged that need for rescuing a child from an abusive situation (Social Services Law; 1973; Ch. 1039). While we have not extended this law to abused wives, victims of child abuse and victims of spouse abuse share many of the same characteristics. The pull from the client to rescue her is strong. How a therapist deals with that pull relates to the therapist's own psychological development. Some issues that come into play center around countertransference and magical thinking. Does the therapist interpret the victim's wish to be rescued as positive or negative? Will the information be used constructively or counterproductively in the treatment? Does either the client or the therapist believe that rescuing is possible? And what is the fantasy concerning the outcome of the rescue? Another question to be answered is, who is the therapist really rescuing? These are just a few of the questions requiring self-examination when working with abusive couples.

How then do therapists keep their own feelings, conflicts, and confusions from emerging? What prevents any of the above from happening or a numbing out and loss of sensitivity? Work with battered women and their abusers can have a battering effect on the therapist. It is my belief that the answer lies not in the blotting out of the emotions that the therapist experiences, but a totally conscious confrontation of the experiences. The therapist must take in the depth of the assault to her/his own consciousness and fully wrestle with her/his own unresolved conflicts concerning violence.

STAFF TRAINING

While there now has developed specific techniques and models for working with abusive couples there must also be the opportunity for therapists to be open to an exploration of their own feelings. Whether as a private practitioner or a therapist in an agency, an atmosphere must be created where a therapist has ample opportunity to explore her/his own feelings and reactions to abusing couples. It is my belief that creating this atmosphere must be formalized and structured. In my experience, the structure for staff training was imposed on the staff through both individual and group sessions which were scheduled by myself as their Clinical Director.

Although it is fairly common for staff to share with their colleagues, it is important to build in the opportunity to share with staffs' supervisors or superiors. Sharing with peers has more of a flavor or ventilation and mutual aid. Because of the devastation experienced by workers in spouse-abuse centers, it is essential for staff to feel that there is access to those people in the agency who formulate policy and procedures. It is important for staff morale that superiors know what working with violence is like on the direct services level, not just at the policy-making level. If not directly experienced, supervisory staff can understand the experience by participating in the staff-training process. Further, staff might try to cope with the assault to their own senses by denial if staff training is not a structured part of the agency work. My staff put in a request for a punching bag for staff. They said that they needed a release for their frustrations. I refused this request and instead started a staff sensitivity group. When supervisory staff builds in staff training with a specific scheduled time, it creates the opportunity for the staff to confront their own feelings. In agencies, it is recommended that training consist of didactic teaching, experiental learning, and group process or sensitivity training. Staff needs to attend conferences to synthesize their own learning and be apprised of relevant new techniques to enhance their skills. Cognitive learning should be supplemented by experiential training. One excellent technique is supervision with a one-way mirror. The need for group process should not be minimized. Working with abusive couples is draining and can easily lead to burn-out. An important way to extend the life of workers is to allow for ventilation, working through feelings and peer support. The group process should focus on the work experience, with an inviolate rule that whatever is expressed is accepted and not judged. Workers need the help of a facilitator who is in the position to affect policy and set the tone for the group experience as being agency sanctioned. Since work with violent couples is very difficult, it is very important for staff to feel supported by their colleagues. Worker differences left undiscussed lead to backbiting, mistrust, and stress.

Energy should not be wasted on staff rivalries and alliances but rather, the energy should be directed toward the work itself. The group process is a good forum for working out staff differences and the developing of a cohesive unit. In addition to the scheduled time for staff training, there should be some flexibility for calling a group at any time that poor worker relations affect productivity. Any member of my staff could call a group any time the need was felt. There were occasions when the staff called a group to discuss differences with me and to point out patterns that I was unaware of which were affecting their ability to work with me. While this model for staff training can be very time consuming in the short run, it allows for a freeing up of energy. The result is that workers more fully devote themselves to the work with clients, as there is no "excess baggage" or preoccupations lurking in the background. This approach also aids in job satisfaction thereby lessening staff turnover. Another aspect of the training relates to the model recommended for working with the couples. Part of the effort with couples is to help them to become a cooperative team rather than rivalrous enemies. Workers in an agency form a family of a sort. It is important for workers to be able to put into practice what they are asking of their clients. If staff cannot relate to each other, how well are they able to teach these skills to their clients? If staff does not experience what it means to work through differences, how will they recognize whether or not their clients are doing this effectively? To "practice what you preach" or ask your clients to do what you yourself have done has a greater import and can be transferred to clients more readily.

When working with abusive couples as a private practitioner, the same needs for staff training pertain. In particular, therapists in private practice should obtain supervision either with peers or by buying supervision. It is crucial to be able to look at one's own responses to violent couples. Therapists are in need of continued introspection and increasing self-awareness in order to avoid the pitfalls spoken of earlier. Since inflicting violence can end in murder, therapists working with abusive couples need to be particularly careful in treatment planning. *Feed-back from other professionals is one safeguard and is vigorously recommended.* In addition to the benefits clients receive from workers obtaining supervision, it is a comfort to a therapist to know that there is a second opinion available.

CONCLUSION

Working with abusing couples requires a cogent theory of practice based upon an understanding of sound therapeutic techniques. However, theory alone may not make for effective treatment as the worker's own psychological makeup can affect the outcome. Self-awareness is essential to all practitioners in the helping professions. Because working with violence can be potentially life threatening and the issue of violence between intimates is a jar to our senses, it is essential that a treatment model for abusing couples include staff development and a sensitizing to the totality of a worker's feelings through an opportunity for continual self-examination.

REFERENCES

Bowlby, John. *Attachment and Loss, Vol. II, Separation Anxiety and Anger.* London: The Hogarth Press and the Institute of Psychoanalysis, 1973.

Chesler, P. *Women and Madness.* New York: Avon Books, 1972.

Freud, Anna. *The Ego and the Mechanism of Defense.* New York: International Universities Press, Inc., 1966.

Geller, Janet A. and Walsh, James C. A treatment model for the abused spouse. *Victimology,* 1977–78, **2**, (3–4): 627–32.

Gelles, Richard. Abused wives: Why do they stay? *Journal of Marriage and Family,* 1976, 659–68, 664.

Masterson, James. *Treatment of the Borderline Adolescent: A Developmental Approach.* New York: Wiley Inter-Science, Division of Wiley & Sons, 1972.

Miller, Jean Baker. *Toward a New Psychology of Women.* Boston: Beacon Press, 1976.

Rosenbaum, Alan, and O'Leary, Daniel. Marital violence: Characteristics of abusive couples. Unpublished paper, State University of New York at Stony Brook.

Sager, Clifford J. *Marriage Contracts and Couple Therapy.* New York: Brunner/Mazel, 1976.

Satir, Virginia, Stachowiak, James, and Taschman, Harvey A. *Helping Families to Change.* New York: Jason Aronson, 1975.

Skinner, B. F. *Science and Human Behavior,* New York: The Free Press, 1953.

Symonds, Martin. Victims of violence. Psychological effects and after effects. Paper presented at the meeting of the Association for the Advancement of Psychoanalysis, Karen Horney Clinic, New York, April, 1974.

Walker, Lenore E. Battered women and learned helplessness. *Victimology,* 1977–78, **2** (3–4).

13. Treating Family Abuse Using a Police Crisis Team Approach

John J. Carr, ACSW, AAMFT
Executive Director, Family Service Society of Pawtucket, R.I.
Project Director, Pawtucket Police Crisis Teams
Project Coordinator, Domestic Violence Training Cadre, R.I.,
Department of the Attorney General
Clinical Coordinator,
Providence Police Departmental Stress Unit

INTRODUCTION

No matter how well developed a community's service network may be, it is patently useless if individuals or families in pain are not assisted, encouraged, and supported in making use of it. The combined talents of two major human service providers, law enforcement and social work, offer the best initial community response. The burden for total care—medical, mental health, legal, shelter, etc.—is the responsibility of the entire community involving citizens, professionals, and the political structure.

However, until recently, human service providers have delegated the critical first response function to the law-enforcement profession. As representatives of the total community, often alone, without other agency backup, police officers have found themselves making "house calls" in reponse to requests for assistance. Under the guise of Family Disturbance Calls, law enforcement officers have found themselves responding to situations which often require the skills or services of-

216

fered by other "community helpers," outside the structure of the police department. What remains to be accomplished appears monumental, given national and local economic pressures which tax both families and human service providers to the limit.

MENTAL HEALTH: PRECEDENTS AND PROBLEMS

Life crises related to developmental issues such as marriage, child rearing, employment, illness, retirement, and death, as well as situational crises impacting on the family, e.g., financial stresses related to inflation, underemployment, and layoff, generate stress and pressure. Stress is inherent in our lives and is not by itself necessarily harmful nor a sign of weakness, but rather is part of the human condition. Yet, for any individual or family there is a limit to what they can cope with at any point in their lives. Pushed to this limit the ability to function breaks down. It is often at this point that the dysfunction may lead to inappropriate behaviors with subsequent law-enforcement response. Golan, in her text relating crisis intervention theory to practice,[1] has highlighted our Pawtucket Police Teams operations as a delivery system of crisis intervention skills. She identifies the "current state of the art" in crisis theory summarized in the following points:

Crises do occur within families, often triggered by some hazardous event or series of events. The individual's or family's state of balance is upset as a result of the crisis and becomes vulnerable. Continued states of stress, and failure to resolve the issue at hand, result in a state defined as "active crisis." *Crisis* is a very individualized state. What one perceives as critical, another may not; what is critical is that the person, couple, family be able to perceive that they are in the midst of a crisis. A crisis may be perceived as a realistic struggle for survival. Golan calls attention to the propensity of a crisis to reactivate prior issues and concerns which heighten the current problem. A major issue in crisis response is the ability of the helper to help the client distinguish between problem and symptom. The helper needs to assess the severity of the situation objectively and must learn to empathize and pick up cues from the troubled client or family. Crises are oftentimes limited to a span of 6 to 8 weeks. This is a major factor affecting the ability of structured programs to adequately respond to issues of crises in Domestic Violence Situations, and a leading theoretical justification for the unique ability of a police crisis team to be on the scene at the moment when they can be most effective. In a state of active crisis, the client is most positively disposed toward the acceptance of help. Traditional intervention methods ignore the underlying problem by concentrating on symptomatology. This tends to make the crisis recur and to escalate in both intensity and violence. From the perspective of mental health, what is "criminal" is that a major opportunity to help to utilize both the authority of the officer and the skills of the counselor, could be lost to that family. The charge for mental-health professionals has been to develop models of intervention or delivery vehicles based on the knowledge base already in existence. Bard, in his contribution to *Battered Women*[2] notes the need for the academic community and crisis theorists to put into actual practice the preexisting theory. For far too long social agencies have overlooked the local police department as a viable human service provider within the community. It is incongruous that mental-health professionals who have developed crisis theory, have often not taken the next steps to develop the delivery system. While crisis response units such as the Pawtucket Police Teams may at best be described as providing early intervention in a preexisting problem related to adult family members, they may be preventive in the context that children, future adults, may be salvaged by this bridge to a future life less characterized by violence and victimization of a loved one.

LAW ENFORCEMENT: PRECEDENTS AND PROBLEMS

Historically law enforcement has recognized the issues involved in dealing with family crisis. Whether described as family disturbance calls, domestic violence, family quarrels, or "garbage calls," any prolonged discussion with police officers will be replete with "war stories" describing intervention tactics as frustrating, complicated, and dangerous. Traditionally, police officers have been forced to respond to these situations without the benefit of formal training, relying on their own personal experiences, a great deal of common sense, and little if any, community or departmental support. Mackinlay Kantor, demonstrates this point in his fictional work, *Signal Thirty Two.*[3]

"Get the crap games; watch the pimps; carry the payrolls; . . . . climb with the futile notifications; walk along with the frightened guy who has the summons to serve. . . ."

"You'll call in Aaronson, and the guy on the box will be bored and say, "All I've got for you is a little family trouble at sixteen-thirteen Madison."

"He'll tell you which floor and thank God it isn't the top, and so you'll climb, climb, climb, and all the time you'll be preparing to say,

"listen. What's the matter with you folks? Pipe down, can't you?

"Oh, shet ep, sister."

"Look—people are complaining; you're waking up folks in the building."

"O.K.,—so you can't get along. O.K.—so you're drunk too. Now, look. I want you out of here! Get down the street until you sober up.

"Stay out of here, and quit socking your wife, and if I see you around here again before morning—before you're sober and ready to behave—I'll break your head wide open!"

That's the little speech, the succession of disciplinary directions that you'll be composing as you trudge upstairs; and then you hear that shuddering gasp and somehow you're through the door before they've opened it for you, and he's standing there all alone.

The woman is on the floor with her skirts up around her middle . . . . her tights are extending themselves into a big oval patch on the floor.

But beyond her he is there.

He's very large; he looks colossal to you now . . . . He keeps watching you. He has the bloody bread knife in his hand, and you keep saying "Put it down, put it down—let go that knife," as he comes toward you a step at a time . . . . you've got to decide, and all in an instant: do you shoot or do you try to use your stick? Do you try to take the knife away from him? . . . . You don't like to be alone. Nobody would like to be alone.

In recent years law enforcement and other human service professionals have recognized the role of law enforcement in family crises. In 1967 the President's Commission on Law Enforcement and Administration of Justice found:[4]

The organization of police departments and the training of policemen are focused almost entirely on the apprehension and prosecution of criminals.

What a policeman does, or should do, instead of making an arrest, or in a situation in which he may not make an arrest, is rarely discussed. The peacemaking and service activities, which consume the majority of police time, receive too little attention.

In 1976 the concerns regarding protection for officer and citizen in domestic situations were highlighted by the Police Foundation study[5] reporting a high correlation between domestic calls and officer injury.

In order to survive, the law enforcement profession has been developing response procedures to family disturbances, such as sending a backup car to the unit initially responding, and has further developed control tactics within the household which come under the heading of "Officer Survival" tactics, as have been taught at the Providence Police Academy.

Officers are taught to employ basic interviewing skills while breaking the eye contact of the disputants. Yet, if we consider the disturbance as not simply a problem of behavior, but also a symptom of underlying causes, where does the officer proceed to once control has been established? Until recent years, he or she proceeded to the next call, leaving the family with the same precipitating problems which escalated to the next crises and a subsequent police response.

PROBLEM DEFINED

The problem is to attempt to develop an understanding that will improve the response of law enforcement to family violence. The United States Justice Department Report of January 1980[6] for the period 1973–76 identified 3.8 million incidents of violence among intimates. Of nighttime incidents more than three-quarters occurred prior to midnight. Thirty-one percent of attacks by intimates took place at home and 13% close to home. Two-fifths of intimate attacks resulted in injury, and in three out of five cases, an actual attack took place. Clearly the home is not the safe place our romantic ideas make it out to be. The issue is further compounded by the fact that this is the most unreported of crimes with an estimated 55 of every 100 incidents not reported. Some reasons for this are lack of support by family and friends, shame, embarrassment, and fear. The report omits another important reason which pertains to the victim's perception of how the police will respond to the incident. Most often the victim assumes that the response will be inadequate or judgmental. The most difficult first step in the helping process is to ask for help. If a community develops a positive response system in conjunction with its police department; if it is highly visible and has community, political, human service agency, and citizen support, one wonders if victims might be more willing to request assistance.

SOLUTIONS

In the past decade, law enforcement programs have evolved which focus on both training and skills building as well as the development of tactical units to respond to family violence calls. Training for line officers has ranged from identification and empathy towards issues of mental illness,[7] to training of specialized units within juvenile bureaus related to child abuse issues.[8] Teams of trained patrol officers with intensive consultation and support have been described in the literature by Bard.[9] The establishment of social work programs within a police department, supportive of and available to line personnel, were developed by Michaels and Treger of Illinois.[10] From these writers' perspectives no one program can claim to have developed a foolproof approach to responding to domestic violence calls. Community attitudes, funding restrictions, departmental size, the political climate, and what Bard aptly describes as the dichotomy between police functions of law enforcement, traditional police business, and behavior management, all affect the decisions as to what constitutes "appropriate" law enforcement response. However, after 6½ years of operating multidisciplinary crisis teams, established to train social workers and police officers in conjunction with both training and consultation to police agencies and specialized units, my impression remains that the team approach offers more collaboratively than any one discipline can offer alone. At a minimum, basic understanding of human behavior will assist an officer in developing a knowledge base which will help the officer to understand behaviors presented under stress. Additionally, this knowledge base may also be personally helpful to the officer in that it lessens his/her use of personal family experience as a frame of reference, which in many instances tends to be very authoritarian. For police, the problem at hand is the resolution of the dual roles of law enforcement and community service. Up until now the emphasis has been on the former. The service component, therefore, needs to be developed and incorporated into police practice.

MULTIDISCIPLINARY POLICE CRISIS TEAMS: THEORETICAL BASE

In approaching violence within the family we need to deal with both behaviors and the associated feelings or affects. We are addressing dysfunctional (assaultive) behaviors existing in a state of active crises. Affectively we must address relationship issues of rage, frustration, depression, and anxiety often brought on by unmet expectations of family or community life. The dysfunctional behaviors may be perceived in a state of crisis as a loss of control by the party or parties involved in the disturbance. It is not enough simply to "take control" or restore order, e.g., to suppress the disturbance. Feelings must be allowed to surface, clarified, and often redirected in a crisis situation. The bridge from affective crisis to the beginning of resolution is the helping relationship. In frustration a police officer might assume that it would take Aristotle's "Philosopher King" to manage such a situation. Yet, in a team approach the above components of control and affect become manageable. The bridge between the disciplines of law enforcement and social work in Pawtucket's Crisis Teams has evolved around the operant term "peace keeping." By the use of the team approach each discipline operates within its own role and from a position of professional strength. Hollis[11] develops the concept of the helping relationship; as the vehicle through which change and growth become possible. This special relationship and its importance to people in pain is described aptly as a "gift of love," the ability of the counselor, from a position of strength and commitment, to mobilize the strengths of the individual or family to ultimately help themselves.

For the professional police officer, the term "Peace Officer" has a long and honored tradition. The officer, by virtue of training and experience, is capable of assertively taking control of a dysfunctional family situation. In taking control or restoring order, the police officer can offer a "gift of peace" to a family in crisis and provide its members with a setting for exploring resources with the counselor's assistance. One focus control, while not dealing with feelings, is short sighted; one discipline without the other possesses limited skills; one gift without the other is impossible. Together with respect for each discipline's strengths, the teams develop the capability to take control, explore appropriate concerns and pain, to consider use of legal, clinical, or other community supports and not to simply restore order but to return both control and peace to a disorganized family unit. In this shared process, the potential for growth is increased while the potential for continued escalation of violence is lessened. Choices, alternatives, and resources available in the community can substitute for the less functional coping mechanisms of assaultive behavior.

OPERATIONAL HISTORY

Pawtucket Police Crisis Teams have now been operational in conjunction with the Police Department since January 1974, having handled in excess of 5000 calls. A team of a social worker and a police officer is on duty from 6 P.M. to 11 P.M. five nights a week. Teams operate in civilian clothing, have access to an unmarked police vehicle, are radio equipped, and the officer is armed. Services were originally offered in three basic situations.

1. Teams were to back up uniformed patrol officers on a disturbance call occurring while on duty.
2. Teams were to be available for receipt of followup referrals from patrol or specialized units of the department on other shifts.
3. Teams were to be available for followup with a family previously seen in order to continue support or encourage follow-through on a referral to another community agency.

TEAM STRENGTHS: UNIQUE TRAITS OF THE TEAM APPROACH

1. Roles are clearly defined; control and counseling services are rendered by a team consisting of a police officer and a trained counselor. Minimal role confusion takes place between staff, and both counselor and officer support each other's professional expertise.
2. The presence of the counselor, supported by the officer, enables the team to explore issues in depth, *in the home,* without the need to depend on outside resources.

3. Followup is encouraged, and referrals, when offered, tend to take place based on the trust established by team members.
4. Together officer and counselor have greater combined awareness of other community resources.
5. The two disciplines with consultation support tend to debrief after a call in a positive and supportive manner.
6. Although presently operating on a part-time basis due to funding shortages, the part-time concept does have advantages:

   a. Officers on the teams at night perform regular duties during regular shift hours. The officer's discussion with his peers on other shifts has encouraged referrals. Additionally, the officer's role as "police officer" is reinforced.
   b. Counselors utilized on teams at night function on a full-time basis in a number of satellite agencies often utilized for referrals. Counselors retain peer contact within the larger human service community and are not isolated in the host setting (police department).
   c. The above duality reduces burnout of staff on the crisis team which further reduces staff turnover.

SCHEDULING AND COST FACTORS

For efficiency and coverage within financial limitations which may preclude a 24-hour-a-day program, the peak coverage hours (identified by the study of the United States Justice Department) are six o'clock at night to two o'clock in the morning. Our crisis teams have always functioned on a part-time basis, often finding themselves active beyond midnight, and have managed to justify their cost effectiveness and continued existence to five distinct funding sources in the past 6½ years.

FUNCTIONAL FLEXIBILITY

For the period of June 1977 through June 1978 our Crisis Teams were operational in three Rhode Island communities. Subsequently we have maintained our core program in Pawtucket as well as having trained teams in three additional communities which remain operational to date. A functional hallmark of the program, is its inherent flexibility (as noted in our article of July 1979;[12]).

In 4½ years of operation, crisis teams have responded to over 1000 disturbance calls per year within a three-community area. A total of 1402 calls for assistance were answered for the 12-month period that ended May 31, 1978.

A categorical review of the 12-month period reflects the diversity of calls received. More importantly, it highlights the inherent flexibility of the team model and its ability to address issues relevant to its particular community. The categories of service were related to issues of family violence and included program areas of concern to all human service professionals.

The area of marital disputes, including alcohol-related interfamilial disturbances, accounted for 6% of the volume. Shelters for women and children, legal resources, and marital counseling services were used for referral in addition to the substance abuse unit at the local family service society.

Families in densely populated neighborhoods or housing projects often developed interfamilial arguments, and teams functioned as negotiators in these disturbances. One incident involved a meeting of 37 members of four families and was held in a vacant courtroom above the police station. This mini "town meeting" enabled issues to be resolved verbally rather than physically. Previously, police officers had been repeatedly called upon to respond to reports of fights and vandalism among these four families; however, teams were able to assist in a resolution that has been maintained to date.

TEAM RECEPTION

1. Departmental

Teams are viewed as a valuable asset by patrol officers, who may be burdened with pressures of time and who have seen a reduction in repeat calls to the same family. Specialized units (such as domestic) increasingly consult with the team, and utilize them for interviewing and referral to other human service agencies outside the criminal justice system.

2. Clientele

As previously noted, a survey was undertaken by the Pawtucket Mayor's Office of Community Affairs in 1975, independant of teams. Seventy-nine percent of the families who responded felt the teams had been a catalyst for positive growth. Eighty-three percent of families felt that they had been treated in a humane manner by team members, and 92% indicated they would call the teams directly if problems arose in the future. A close review of the responses of families reporting no change in their situation indicated that the teams provided only one type of service information, such as counseling, or calming the situation following a uniformed patrol response to a disturbance. Forty percent of the families who reported that the teams' intervention was helpful indicated that the team performed *multiple* tasks, and often followed up with a supportive postcrisis visit. Thus, it appears that the effectiveness of the teams is directly related to the provision of *multiple services* to families in crisis situations.

Related to team composition, 62% of the respondents identified a preference for all-male teams, 4% for a male/female team and 16% gave no preference. Given the number of women assisted during family crises, the expectation had been that a male/female team might be perceived by clientele as more supportive, but the responses did not validate this. It appears that the approach and services offered were more significant than the gender composition of the teams.

3. Community

Recognition, collaboration, and support from the total community is vital to the functioning of any program. Although the team was designed as a service vehicle and was not intended to be a "community relations/public awareness organ," the response to the Crisis Teams has brought recognition to the implementing agency, the participating department and the Pawtucket community. In the past, the police department functioned as a community service agency isolated from other human service providers. In the past, officers normally perceived in the narrow focus of reinforcement-control were called to deal with violent or potentially violent situations which they often viewed as counselors' "therapeutic failures." Originally designed to receive referrals from within the police department's structure, the Crisis Teams now routinely receive and honor requests from other human service agencies and private practitioners. Teams have occasionally called a family's private therapist from the client's home at night to reinforce the therapeutic relationship and encourage follow-through.

In the critical area of child abuse within a family, patrol officers formerly received a call from the state protective agency only when a worker felt the need for police presence, or control, on an emergency call. Now, the Crisis Teams are often requested to evaluate situations for the Protective Unit in the evening, and are utilized by other units of the agency for support of families in the state. The national development of Comprehensive Community Mental Health Centers with their evening emergency units has provided another setting in which law enforcement and mental health professionals often meet in crisis situations. The Pawtucket Police Crisis Teams met with administrative and line staff of our local clinic even prior to the formal opening of their emergency service. The teams now have immediate clinical backup via this service, as well as access to inpatient facilities; conversely the teams have the capability to outreach for the clinic's staff in situations where family involvement may be of assistance to a patient presenting himself in the emergency room. Maintenance of this relationship has developed to the point where the teams check into the emergency room each evening so that each knows who is on duty on that shift. This process has avoided some of the problems that can develop when rotating patrol officers and emergency room staff have only brief contact, usually in a crisis situation, and seldom with enough time to develop an understanding of each other's role. As our local Mental Health Center developed its comprehensive capabilities, the Crisis Teams were contractually recognized in the clinic's grant as "providers of acute psychiatric care," with the clinic providing financial and administrative support for the teams' continued tactical operations.

4. Sharing

Averaging between 15 and 20 calls per week, the cadre of our crisis team has developed skills and techniques in responding to crisis and domestic violence situations. By a consistent pairing of disciplines, they have an inherent flexibility to respond to a number of issues which a community may identify as significant. As a result, our program, beginning in 1976, received funding from the Rhode Island Governor's Justice Commission to provide statewide training, education, and consultation to other law enforcement agencies. Over 40 such training events have been completed at three levels: content at the recruit academy level, on an in-service basis to individual and combined departmental line staff, and at the college level for officers enrolled in Criminal Justice programs. With the receipt of funds from the Domestic Violence Unit of the Rhode Island Department of the Attorney General this year, we have expanded our training cadre to include representatives of the Attorney General's staff, women's shelters, and medical providers to offer community-based content to human service agencies who together with law enforcement, have the concern to address the critical issue of family violence.

CONCLUSIONS

Issues presented in family violence are complex and do not easily lend themselves to resolution. Often, and occasionally by default, the first response to incidents of family violence is via the community's law enforcement agency. The ability or willingness of the family to develop alternative methods of coping, with the support of other more traditional helpers, is to a large extent dependent on the police department's inherent flexibility to address issues of family violence, as the first visible representative of the total community, in a positive and effective manner, nonduplicative of any other service the community has to offer. The Pawtucket Crisis Team experience has shown that collaborative efforts have brought our disciplines closer together in a shared concern for community residents. In an era of multiple concerns and limited resources, community service agencies have to recognize the vital role and immediate accessibility provided by a community's police department. Together they must consider alternative approaches to issues of family violence and community mental health.

BIBLIOGRAPHY

1. Golan, Naomi, *Treatment in Crisis Situation*. New York: Free Press, 1978. pp. 7–15.
2. Roy, Maria (ed.) *Battered Women: A Psychosocial Study of Domestic Violence*. New York: Van Nostrand Reinhold, 1977.
3. Kantor, Mackinlay. *Signal Thirty-Two*. New York: Random House, 1950. pp. 10–11.

4. President's Commission on Law Enforcement and Administration of Justice. *The Challenge of Crime in A Free Society*. Washington, D.C.: Government Printing Office, 1967. p. 92.

5. Domestic violence and the police, studies in Detroit and Kansas City. Washington, D.C.: Police Foundation, 1976.

6. Intimate victims: A study of violence among friends and relatives. United States Department of Justice, Bureau of Justice Statistics, January 1980. A National Crime Survey Report, U.S. G.P.O., Washington, D.C. SO–NCS–N–14, NCJ–62319.

7. Janus, Samuel S., Bess, Barbara E., Cadden, James J., and Greenwald, Harold. Training police officers to distinguish mental illness. *American Journal of Psychiatry*, February 1980, **137**:2. pp. 228–229.

8. The role of law enforcement in the prevention and treatment of child abuse and neglect. National Center on Child Abuse and Neglect, Department of Health, Education, and Welfare. August 1979, Office of Human Development Services, Admin. for Children, Youth, and Families, Children's Bureau, National Center on Child Abuse. Gov. Printing Office, 1979.

9. Bard, Morton, The role of law enforcement in the helping system. *Community Mental Health Journal,* 1971, **7**. pp. 151-160.

10. Michaels, Rhoda A. and Tregor, Harvey, *"Social Work in Police Departments,"* Social Work, (*Journal of the National Association of Social Workers*), New York, **18**, no. 5, (1973). pp. 67–75.

11. Hollis, Florence. *Casework: A Psychosocial Therapy*. Second Edition, New York: Random House.

12. Carr, John J. An administrative retrospective on police crisis teams. *Social Casework,* 1979. July 1979, V. 60, No. 7. pp. 416–22.

13. Burnett, Bruce, Carr, John J., Sinapi, John, and Taylor, Roy. Police and social workers in a community outreach program. *Social Casework,* January, V. 57, no. 1. pp. 41–49.

14. A National Survey of Services for Batterers

Albert R. Roberts, D.S.W.

It is 9:00 P.M. Charlie and his wife Joan have another argument. Unlike their previous arguments in which he would slap her two or three times and push her to the floor, this one ends with Charlie punching Joan repeatedly in the face and stomach. While Charlie is taking a shower, Joan, trembling and dazed, with a bloody nose and severe abdominal pain, grabs her 4-year-old son from his bed and goes to her neighbor's house where she telephones the local shelter for battered women. The shelter provides emergency refuge, crisis intervention, a supportive environment, legal advocacy (including information on initiating divorce proceedings), and welfare advocacy. She remains at the shelter for 4 weeks, thinking about her situation. During her stay, her son's behavior is more aggressive and uncontrollable than usual. He has asked for his Daddy again and again, and has been told that Daddy is away on a business trip. Charlie buys Joan a large box of her favorite chocolates and a dozen long-stemmed red roses and asks Joan's sister to bring them to the shelter. Joan contemplates her future. If she were to divorce Charlie, how would she manage when she has no money, no job skills, and no job prospects? She reminds herself that she is still very much in love with him and that their relationship has been a very satisfying one except for the times he has hit her. Upon leaving the shelter, Joan and her son return home.

What will happen to this family, and to thousands of other families who find themselves in a similar situation? There are three options: The first is that the wife become the habitual victim of her husband's assaults, and that her son grow up in an environment where wife abuse is commonplace. The second option is that the wife file for a divorce, join the labor market, and make a new life her herself and her son. And the third option is for the husband to participate in a treatment program for batterers where he can learn to handle stress, frustration, and anger in nonviolent ways. This last option is now starting to become recognized as a viable means for stopping domestic violence.

Most batterers are not psychopaths. Their violence against wife or girl friend is a learned behavior and, sadly, one which has traditionally been sanctioned by society. Batterers resort to violence because they have learned to deal with anger in this way. In all likelihood, their early socialization has included much exposure to family violence. For example, during his childhood, a boy witnesses his father beating his mother again and again; this same youngster is whipped by his father for misbehavior; as he grows up, he adopts the views of his father that the function of a wife is to obey her husband's commands and if she does not, she is severely chastised. Thus, as an adult he resorts to violence against his wife when he has difficulty coping with the stresses of everyday life.

Helping the batterer is a complex and difficult task. By means of education and therapy, abusers can learn to deal with stress and anger in nonviolent ways.

Since 1975 (when there were only two specially designed treatment programs for batterers in the nation), the number of programs for men who have physically abused their wives or girl friends has increased dramatically to about 80 programs as of January, 1981. Throughout the United States, we are beginning to see a surge of interest in treating abusive men. This chapter reports on my national survey of treatment programs for batterers.

The study was undertaken in an effort to collect aggregate data and develop basic information about programs for perpetrators of domestic violence. Although wife abuse has become recognized as a prevalent and increasingly common social problem, surprisingly little is known about the abuser and services which have the potential for changing the abusive behavior pattern. In general, these programs focus on teaching batterers anger control techniques, behavioral approaches to stress management, and alternative communication skills. The overriding goal of most of the respondents to this survey is to help the individual to understand the dynamics of his out-of-control behavior and to take responsibility for his actions.

METHODOLOGY

During the summer of 1980, the author developed and mailed a 29-item questionnaire and a stamped, self-addressed envelope to the 84 programs for abusive men listed in the Directory published in two installments in the *Response Newsletter* (Center for Women Policy Studies, April and June, 1980). Four of the 84 programs responded with a note indicating that they are not currently providing any direct services for batterers. The result was a listing of 80 programs for abusive partners.

Eight weeks after the initial mailing, a follow-up letter with an additional copy of the questionnaire was sent to the nonrespondents. As of January, 1981, responses had been received from 44* of the 80 programs (55%) which offer intervention services to violent men. It is conceivable that the overall response rate is even higher than it appears because there may be others listed in the Directory which did not respond because they are not currently operational.

Survey researchers are often faced with the following dilemma: either constructing a one-page questionnaire (that explores the topic only superficially), which has been found to yield the highest response rates, or preparing a more detailed questionnaire (designed to obtain the most useful information), and risk losing respondents who do not have the interest or time to answer a lengthy questionnaire. Considering that my questionnaire was detailed and four pages long, the overall return rate of 55 percent is considered high.

Most of the nonrespondents were services for battered women which have developed an assailant counseling component, and a few were counselors with private practices. It is conjectured that the non-

---

*A complete listing of the respondents is in the Appendix.

respondents' reasons for not answering the questionnaire may be one or more of the following: They may be insensitive to the potential of research; they may be too overwhelmed by the demands and pressures of the job; or they may be tired of responding to numerous questionnaires sent to them from which they have never benefited. Nevertheless, the majority of programs contacted did respond, and the responses were representative of a cross-section of urban, suburban, and rural programs from all regions of the United States. It seems that the follow-up letter further demonstrated to some of the programs the author's commitment to this research. The second mailing (which was sent during the first week in October, 1980) resulted in responses from 16 additional programs.

In reviewing the data, the researcher examined the following aspects of batterers' counseling programs: referral sources, telephone hot lines, services provided, staffing patterns, problems encountered, and community education. The findings are discussed below.

REFERRAL SOURCES

Referral sources appeared to be a significant factor in linking batterers to a treatment program. Referrals came from many sources, including courts and district attorneys, the staff at shelters for battered women, police officers, lawyers, relatives and friends, physicians, clergymen, social workers, and alcoholism counselors. However, merely listing the various referral sources can be misleading because, for example, a referral source such as the court might provide a program with as little as 2% of its clients or as much as 95%.

The two most frequent sources of referral were the court and battered women's programs, while the least frequent referral sources were clergymen and child protection agencies. Two-thirds (29) of the programs reported receiving referrals from the courts. Eleven of the 29 programs that receive court referrals stated that between 40 and 95% of their clients are referred in this way. A number of states have developed a deferred sentencing program for first-time offenders, which is what batterers generally are. The number of court referrals would be greater if more judges and district attorneys were aware of batterers' counseling programs in their area.

Twenty-four of the 44 programs indicated that men had been referred by local battered women's programs. Half of these programs indicated that from 30 to 80% of their clients were referred from battered women's shelters; 7 did not indicate the percentage of referrals from each source identified; and the other 5 programs reported that less than 30% of their referrals are made in this way.

Although over three-quarters of the programs receive self-referrals, this source constitutes only a very small percentage of the overall number of clients referred for services.

TELEPHONE HOTLINES

The telephone hotline can be utilized to help abusers in two ways: the first is as one component of the treatment program for men who have already joined a batterers' counseling program. While a man is participating in the treatment program, it is likely that he will have an argument with his wife and that the argument could escalate to the extent that he is about to lose control and abuse her. The hotline functions as a "safety valve" which can provide immediate intervention between counseling sessions. Ideally the hotline should be available 24 hours a day, and the telephone workers should be knowledgeable about the educational and counseling techniques which are being utilized during treatment sessions.

The second purpose of the hotline is to provide crisis intervention for men who are batterers but who have not yet come to the attention of a treatment program. An example of this type of hotline is located in Minneapolis, Minnesota. It is operated in cooperation with the Men's Center's Men in Violent Relationships Project. This hotline is operational daily (except Tuesdays) from 6:00 P.M. to 2:00 A.M., and is staffed by 25 volunteers who have completed a 25-hour training course. In addition to the obvious goal of defusing the man's anger, the purpose of this type of hotline is to provide an appropriate referral to a treatment program.

Unfortunately, the potential of hotlines for preventing violence by providing the perpetrator with timely crisis intervention is being only partially realized. Of the 44 programs in this survey, only half (23) reported having a telephone hotline service. Of these 23 programs, 18 had a 24-hour, 7-day-a-week service. The remaining 5 programs indicated that their hotline was available for a large part of the day and evening, but not around the clock.

An abusive male may be so resistant to therapy that a hotline may provide an acceptable and anonymous way for him to seek help. While the crisis is unfolding, the man is often overwhelmed by the fear that he is out of control, and the hotline worker has the best chance for encouraging the caller to begin a treatment program. But too often, once the crisis has passed and the man has calmed down, his desire to attend the program is diminished. While the hotline can provide timely crisis intervention and psychological support at critical moments, it should not be viewed as a substitute for face-to-face therapy. Rather, the hotline should be viewed as a facilitator for moving the caller into treatment and as an auxiliary source of assistance for bolstering a man's problem-solving and anger control techniques once he has joined a program.

SERVICES PROVIDED

The services provided by programs for abusive partners are aimed at eliminating violence in the home. The goal for most services is not only to stop/prevent wife abuse at a particular moment, but to provide education and treatment which has the potential to change the assailant's violent and destructive behavior patterns. Thus, violent men are taught about rational and irrational belief systems, cultural stereotypes, sexism, anger control techniques, behavioral approaches to stress management, and communication skills.

No one treatment approach was uniformly selected by the respondents as the most appropriate. Instead, treatment for batterers takes several different forms. Slightly over one-third (15) of the programs use a combination of individual counseling (particularly at the beginning of treatment), group counseling, and couples counseling as needed. Thirteen (30%) programs listed group counseling as the preferred method of treatment, although most of those programs reported that they do an individual intake interview. Five of the 13 programs use couples counseling in addition to the group approach. Another quarter of the respondents (11) have no group component, using instead a combination of individual counseling and couples counseling, as needed. Of these, one program responded that they would like to begin group counseling but have not been able to organize a group yet. Of the remaining five programs, three begin treatment by utilizing a formal educational approach which may then be followed by participation in a men's support group, individual counseling, or couples counseling. The final two programs use only individual counseling.

Treatment for violent men is being provided primarily by three different types of programs. The first type has been established for the specific purpose of treating violent men, and their clientele consists solely of this population. Examples are: Abusive Men Exploring New Directions (AMEND), in Denver, Colorado; Rape and Violence End Now (RAVEN), in St. Louis, Missouri; Men in Violent Relationships Project, in Minneapolis; and Batterers Anonymous, in Redlands, California.

The second type of program is part of an established social service agency which treats batterers in addition to persons with other emotional problems. These include the Lansdowne Mental Health Center, Ashland, Kentucky; Family and Children Services, Minneapolis; Catholic Social Services of Wayne County, Michigan; and the Family Service Association, Lubbock, Texas.

Finally, there are established crisis intervention services for battered women which have developed a treatment component for the assailant, such as: the YWCA Women's Shelter—Men's Program, Long Beach, California; the Assailant Counseling Program of Every-Woman's Place, Inc., Muskegon, Michigan; the Victims Information Bureau of Suffolk (VIBS), Smithtown, N.Y.; and Sojourn Women's Center—Men's Program, Springfield, Illinois.

The following are brief descriptions of four programs which illustrate the ways in which programs with different orientations and staffing capabilities are working to help violent men.

There is a program called Stop Abuse by Males (SAM) in Champaign, Illinois, which was developed by Steve Everett in 1978. The unique aspect of the SAM Project is that the program organizer and all the counselors are themselves former batterers who work on a volunteer basis. Treatment includes an individual intake session, group counseling, and men's consciousness-raising groups. There is also a hotline which is operational 7 days a week from 8:00 A.M. to 10:00 P.M. The SAM Project is affiliated with the Men's Program Unit of the

University YMCA, and although the project has no funding, the YMCA provides office space, secretarial services, and telephones. The project publishes a monthly newsletter, *Machomania,* which has the motto: "Written by people involved with violent behavior. For people who want to understand."[*]

The Violent Partner Program, a component of Family Service of Duluth, Minnesota, began in the Fall of 1977. The approach utilized by this program is a combination of individual, couples, and family counseling. The preferred modality "is conjoint therapy with a primary focus of ending violence in the relationship."[**] Individual counseling is used when the abused wife refuses to participate in conjoint therapy; when the batterer requests it; or when the abused woman has moved with no forwarding address. Approximately 80% of their referrals come from the local battered women's shelter; 15% come from individuals who learn about the program from Duluth's 24-hour Information and Referral Hotline; and the remaining 5% are court-mandated referrals. The Violent Partner program employs one full-time social worker who has extensive experience in marital and family therapy. His caseload consisted of 45 batterers during 1980. He also works closely with drug and alcoholism programs, and social workers and psychiatrists in the community.

The Volunteer Counseling Service (VCS) of Rockland County, Inc., in New City, New York provides a variety of educational and counseling services for families. In 1979, the VCS initiated its Spouse Abuse Educational Workshop—for men only—which consists of six weekly 1 ½ hour sessions on family violence and its consequences. A male and a female counselor co-lead the sessions. "The goal is to turn hostile men into voluntary clients."[***] Approximately 90% of the referrals to this program are mandated by the family court. Following the completion of the six educational sessions, further services are provided, including individual counseling, family therapy, and a men's support group called Men's Ongoing Voluntary Exchange (MOVE). The support group is not solely for batterers, but violent men are invited to join

---

[*] Subscriptions to this newsletter are available for $6.00 per year from: Steve Everett, Volunteer Organizer, SAM Project, University YMCA, 1001 South Wright Street, Champaign, Illinois 61820
[**] Herron, Norm. *Personal Communication,* Duluth, Minnesota (September 8, 1980).
[***] Houghton, Beverly D. *Personal Communication,* New City, New York (September 3, 1980).

as long as they have first completed the Spouse Abuse Educational Workshop. Marital counseling is also available, but only if the batterer has taken the educational workshop, and he and his wife both request it. The SAEW has a full-time project coordinator and a staff which consists of a combination of mental health professionals and trained volunteers. Leaders of the SAEW receive eight training sessions and weekly supervision by the coordinator. In addition, the program employs a half-time researcher (with a Ph.D.) who conducts research on domestic violence in the community and on the men who participate in the program.

The Rape/Spouse Assault Crisis Center of Every Woman's Place, Inc., in Muskegon, Michigan is an example of a comprehensive service for battered women and their children (including an emergency shelter), which has also developed a treatment component for the batterer, called the Assailant Counseling Program. State endorsement for the Assailant Counseling Program is evident by the fact that the Michigan Domestic Violence Prevention and Treatment Board has provided it with full funding. Begun in July, 1979, the assailant program is directed by Anthony Senna and staffed mainly by volunteers who complete a 46-hour training program. During the first 5 months of 1980, 29 men received counseling. Since the program is an adjunct of a crisis center serving abused women, it is not surprising that almost half of its referrals come from the women's program. An additional 18% of the referrals are court-mandated, and the remainder of the clients are either self-referred or referred by relatives.* The predominant methods of treatment are individual and couples counseling.

STAFFING PATTERN

The overwhelming majority of programs (82%) reported having at least one professional counselor or therapist on staff. These professionals frequently had backgrounds in either clinical social work, guidance and counseling, or clinical psychology. Most staff members saw the men on a weekly basis for individual counseling, group coun-

---

*Ashby, Sue A. *Personal Communications,* Muskegon, Michigan, (August 11, and September 15, 1980).

seling, and/or couples counseling. Several programs conducted group counseling sessions twice a week.

Because of limited funding, programs which have been established specifically to help violent men are often run by volunteers and staff who are paid part-time. Programs which are affiliated with an established social service agency were more likely to have sufficient funding to employ therapists on a full-time basis. As was mentioned previously, professional staff at social service agencies usually had a caseload that was not restricted to batterers alone. However, there were a few notable exceptions such as the Violent Partner Program (of Family Service of Duluth, Minnesota) where Norm Herron, a marriage and family therapist, is working full-time with batterers and their families.

Clinical Staff

Because of the batterers' complex problems, including low impulse control, resistance to treatment, and guilt feelings, it is important to have trained clinicians on staff. Fifty percent of the programs reported having social workers (most of these with M.S.W.s) on staff; 20% (9) had a clinical psychologist on staff; and 34% (15) of the programs had counselors with bachelors degrees in a human service field and/or masters degrees in counseling or human development. Some of the programs which had professional staff employed counselors from more than one discipline, for instance, the YWCA Domestic Crisis Center—Assailant Program (in Grand Rapids, Michigan) has a staff which consists of two M.S.W. therapists, a therapist with an M.A., and a coordinator who has a bachelors degree. For the most part, those programs which utilized couples counseling or family therapy in treating abusive partners had at least one social worker or clinical psychologist on staff; those programs which had neither a social worker nor a clinical psychologist on staff usually used group counseling as their primary method of helping violent men.

Volunteer Staff

Because of limited funds, 17 (39%) of the programs relied on volunteers, the majority of whom were lay people, but there were some professional counselors who volunteered as well. The volunteers were heavily involved in crisis intervention and community education activities. In several instances, they led men's groups and anger control workshops. When a program utilizes lay volunteers, it is important that they receive adequate training and ongoing supervision by a mental health professional (preferably by licensed social workers or clinical psychologists).

It is conjectured that many of the nonresponding programs may be staffed primarily by lay volunteers who are skeptical about the importance of a research effort such as this. Therefore, the survey results may reflect an overrepresentation of batterers' programs which are staffed by mental health professionals.

PROBLEMS

The most frequently mentioned problem was attrition, which was noted by one-third of the programs (15 or 34%). This was followed by a lack of funding (9 or 21%). The two general categories in which most of the problems are found was a lack of motivation among abusive clients and a lack of resources. Thirty-one programs identified a major problem which as indicative of the batterers' lack of motivation. The problems cited were:

    attrition (15)
    resistance to the program (6)
    batterers' denial (5)
    erratic attendance (3)
    getting man to start program (2)

Twenty-one programs identified a major problem which was indicative of inadequate program resources. The problems cited were:

    funding (9)
    limited staff (5)
    no staff to conduct couples counseling (3)
    insufficient staff training (2)
    no follow-up of clients (2)

Several respondents also identified other problems such as the need for linkages with alcohol and drug abuse programs (4), lack of public awareness (5), and arbitrary referrals from judge (1). (Most of the programs listed more than one problem area.)

COMMUNITY EDUCATION

Almost all of the programs (42) stated that they provide some form of community education. However, the respondents' involvement in community education varied widely from minimal involvement to those which seemed to make a concerted effort to educate the public about domestic violence and their role in treating the assailants.

The type of educational activity cited most frequently was speaking engagements and guest lectures (32 or 73%), followed by in-service training workshops and lectures to local human service agencies and police officers (21 or 48%), and radio public service announcements and appearances on radio talk shows (14 or 32%). At the lower end of the frequency scale, only eight (18%) cited the use of brochures and business cards and/or posters in subways and buses; three programs mentioned that they present and rent videotapes describing their counseling program.

The following is a list of the different types of community education efforts which respondents cited:

radio and TV talk shows
in-service training for human service providers
public service announcements on radio and TV
speaking jointly with staff from the battered women's shelter
civic organizations
church and synagogue groups
newspaper interviews
placing ads in the newspaper
preparing a court advocacy videotape to present at speaking engagements
guest lecturing to college classes
presentations to police officers
speaking to judges

The type of presentation may vary. For example, the Community Crisis Center in Elgin, Illinois mentioned that they can provide the following: a seminar or workshop on family violence, rape, or incest; specific information on their Center's services; or technical assistance on developing a program. One of the more comprehensive responses to this question was provided by the Batterers' Counseling Project of Ann Arbor, Michigan, which reported spending an average of 10 hours per month on community education. Their activities in this area are as follows:

"Community education involves increasing public awareness of the problem of domestic violence, and informing the public of the available resources for victims and perpetrators of domestic violence."*

Staff of the Batterers' Counseling Project participate in a variety of speaking engagements before such groups as civic and professional organizations, volunteers at the battered women's shelter, and college students, and in addition, they designed a brochure explaining the program's services and sent it to over 50 local agencies.

Public education is crucial if these programs are to be visible and accessible to the many people who need their services. Obviously, batterers will not be using a new program if they never learn of its existence. Likewise, community agencies will not be able to make referrals to assailant counseling agencies if the community services know nothing about them.

CONCLUSION

In previous research on intervention services for battered women, this researcher documented the necessity for developing treatment programs for batterers:

> ... service delivery for batterers is beginning to emerge as an urgently needed form of treatment. Since the majority of beaten women who seek refuge at an emergency shelter ultimately return to their husbands, it is vital that abusive men become aware that: (1) hitting a woman is unacceptable

---

*Okun, Lewis. *Report of a Batterers' Counselor.* Ann Arbor, Michigan: Domestic Violence Project, Inc., May 22, 1980, p. 5.

behavior and there is no defense, excuse, or explanation which can make it justifiable; and (2) they can learn alternative ways of coping with stress and anger. It is hoped that programs for wife abusers will be developed at an accelerated pace to help the thousands of men who are capable of learning nonviolent methods of problem solving.*

What is the future of treatment for abusive men? It seems likely that the established family counseling agencies, mental health centers, shelters for battered women, and out-patient psychiatric clinics will be devoting increased attention to developing programs for violent men. Because of the nature of domestic violence, professional therapists will need to recruit more community volunteers for outreach and hotline crisis intervention work. As mentioned earlier in this article, many existing programs for assailants have overlooked the need for telephone hotlines. These hotlines can be an effective means of early casefinding and crisis intervention, and should be utilized to the fullest extent possible.

This study has laid the groundwork for further research on a significant type of family violence intervention—working with the abusive partner. This descriptive survey examined the similarities and differences between programs for batterers nationwide. By providing an overview of the programs which are currently working with abusive partners, program planners and researchers may be better prepared to develop intervention programs for this population.

It remains for further research to build on the study findings and increase our understanding of services for batterers. There is little doubt that violent men can benefit from specially designed treatment programs. Further research can help us to answer the crucial question: Which methods of service delivery are most effective in eliminating assaultive behavior patterns, with which types of abusers?

---

*Roberts, Albert R. *Sheltering Battered Women: A National Study and Service Guide.* New York: Springer Publishing Co., 1981, p. 166.

Part V   Materials and Methods

"There are two ways of ending a dispute—discussion and force; the latter manner is simply that of the rude beasts; the former is proper to beings gifted with reason."

—Cicero

15. "Time Out": Description of a Film Series Dramatizing the Conflicts and Consequences Faced by Men Who Batter

Oralee Wachter
President of O.D.N. Productions, Inc.

Thomas Boyd

Oralee Wachter was the Project Director for "Time Out". Other film programs for conflict resolution created by O.D.N. Productions include "Acquaintance Rape Prevention," "Teenage Pregnancy Prevention," and "No More Secrets" (intrafamily sexual abuse of children).

Thomas Boyd is the script writer of one of the films in "Time Out", and co-author of the film guide that accompanies the program. He is a trainer and group leader of adult education programs throughout the country.

"Time Out"   Produced and Distributed by O. D. N. Productions, Inc.
74 Varick Street, New York, N.Y. 10013
1454 Sixth Street, Berkeley, Cal. 94710

All materials copyright O. D. N. Productions, Inc. 1981

Films   Executive Producer—Oralee Wachter
"Deck the Halls"—Written and Produced by Nancy Graham
Directed by Christina Crowley

"Up the Creek" —Written by Thomas Boyd
                Directed by Edward Moore

"Shifting Gears" —Written by Stephen Wachter and Oralee Roberts
                 Directed by Edward Moore

Discussion Guide: Written by Oralee Wachter and Thomas Boyd
                   Edited by Ellen Schecter

O. D. N. Productions, Inc. is a nonprofit corporation.
"Time Out" was produced with grants from LEAA, Office on Domestic
Violence, and private foundations.

I. INTRODUCTION TO "TIME OUT"

"Time Out" uses three short films and a discussion guide to help group
leaders work in short-term counseling for men with a history of
domestic violence. Not a substitute but a complement to comprehensive therapeutic treatment, "Time Out" suggests a sequence of events,
questions, and activities that will put the men at ease; help them focus
on key issues; and open channels for discussion.

Each session is designed to come to rest with some sense of closure
and resolution about the issues raised—at least until the subjects are
broached again in individual therapy or group counseling sessions.
A model session (lasting about two hours) usually includes:

Screening a film. Shown in order, the three films each offer one important
aspect of the spouse abuse syndrome: *the attack* (pressures that trigger or
contribute to the fight); *the aftermath* (consequences for everyone in the
family); and *the alternatives* (helping the man who hits explore other
choices and sources of help available to him). Separately, the films explore
important aspects of the spouse abuse syndrome; together, they can lead
viewers to see the process and cycle of domestic violence as a whole—and
thus begin to change it.

The films (16 mm, color) offer universal, recognizable aspects of spouse
abuse situations, using characters from a range of social classes and
geographical locations. The characters and events are so real that most men
with experiences of domestic violence have no difficulty identifying with
them and finding parallels within their own lives. This provides an essential
pool of experiences that male viewers can draw on to begin their discussions.

The Films

1. Al Greensboro, a midwestern business executive with a perfect family and beautiful home, batters his wife following a Christmas party. "Deck the Halls" reveals both the underlying tension building up in Al, and his violent outburst.
2. Tommy Howell's story begins the morning after a violent Saturday night attack. In his rural home, he picks up the pieces after his wife and children have left—perhaps for good. "Up the Creek" explores the isolation, loss, and confusion of one man as he confronts this possibility.
3. In a working-class suburb, Buddy and P. K. enjoy a close friendship. One of them risks it all with a personal confrontation over the violence in both their lives. "Shifting Gears" proposes another dimension to their relationship, and suggests an alternative to male-approved violence.

The Guidebook

- *Trigger questions* about the characters and situations in the films help men open up and begin to talk to each other. Deliberately nonthreatening and generalized, these questions make it easier to get the conversational ball rolling by focusing attention on the characters in the film.
- *Springboards for introspection.* Once trust begins and develop within the group, leaders can use more probing questions to guide the men to ask themselves more personal questions. These questions invite men to share their own stories and feelings, and to find out about the experiences of others. These essential steps—breaking down a sense of isolation, seeing how widespread the factors are which make violence appear to be the only alternative, and feeling safe exploring these issues in a nonjudgmental group of peers—prepare the men for considering how they might change their behavior and make new choices about hitting or not hitting.
- *Individual or group activities* give the men a chance to explore new ways of behaving; new ways of perceiving themselves; new ways of reaching out for support and asking for help. These exercises

give them an active opportunity to reconsider the kinds of options that are open to them.

Throughout the manual, leaders are encouraged to modify questions and activities whenever necessary to suit their personal styles and methods, and to best address the needs of men in their groups.

Recommendations

The social and psychological issues underlying spouse abuse are critical and complex. This film series is not intended to substitute for a treatment program when used with men who batter. It is designed to be included in a consistent and therapeutic treatment model rather than as a method or approach to treatment in itself. With this in mind, "Time Out" is recommended for use in short-term counseling and treatment programs, and for:

- training in the mental health, social service, and law enforcement systems: public education presentations to increase the awareness of legislators, judges, community groups, and others who determine public policy.

A. APPROACH

"Time Out" is based on three assumptions drawn from current research and established treatment programs around the country. They are: (1) Violence is a learned reaction to stress; (2) alternatives to violence can be learned; and (3) the abuser is responsible for taking the steps necessary to stop his violent behavior.

Change as significant as stopping physical attacks will be difficult to carry out. Change itself may be threatening to some men. Major reasons for resisting change include: not knowing why change is needed . . . change produces anxiety as habits are shed . . . it upsets perceptions of what's "normal" . . . it violates patterns that are learned very early . . . it might be seen as an admission of failure . . . it feels like a challenge to one's own authority. With all these obstacles to change, what roles can be played by outside pressure (such as legal intervention) and outside influence (such as this program)? Though necessary, external pressures are not sufficient. Nobody changes *just because* of pressure from the outside, but nobody changes *without* it either. A combination of internal decision with external suggestions and support seems most likely to produce desired change. Therefore, "Time Out" is designed with this combination approach in mind. Three films dramatize normal people experiencing the rupture that violence creates in their lives. A discussion guide accompanying the films contains pointed questions that will help group leaders generate the external pressure to consider behavior change. Support and reinforcement are initiated by a series of suggested activities for group members to share. Through these activities, men can come to terms with their own violent actions and can learn to help each other in three ways:

1. *By learning to talk about it.* Pressures and fears about violence often become worse because some men mistakenly think of spouse abuse as a "secret" act that goes on in the privacy of homes and families. Many men try to maintain this secrecy because they don't want their friends or community to know. But the truth is that the pressure will build until the secret explodes. As taboos about family violence are broken, and as the courts become more involved, confidential group settings are emerging where men confront this issue directly. Such groups encourage the exchange of confidences that can reduce tension and heighten awareness, relieving men of the tremendous burden of secrecy.

2. *By learning to ask for help.* Nobody expects men to resolve the problems of domestic violence by themselves. It has been shown that the most effective kinds of change take place when people help each other, ask questions, talk about feelings, and come to terms with the *need for change.* In a group, there's a chance to find out that one is not alone, that other men are grappling with the same problem, and that they will support others who try to change.

3. *By recognizing the difference between feelings and actions.* One key to change is to identify the difference between the emotions that set up the behavior, and the action itself. Men can help themselves prevent the hitting by practicing ways to put some distance between their emotions and actions. By naming the emotions

that pressure, men can recognize intense feelings and learn not to act violently when they feel them coming on.

B. GOALS

This program is addressed primarily to men who batter women. The goal at its most basic level is to help these men stop the hitting, stop the violence, and stop the abuse.

"Time Out" can assist group leaders and counselors attain this goal by helping men to:

1. Perceive battering and violence as learned behavior that can be changed;
2. Accept the fact that spouse abuse is illegal, never justified, and has serious consequences;
3. Identify alternatives to hitting and be responsible for learning how to apply them.

C. FIVE KEY ISSUES

The following critical factors in spouse abuse prevention were identified from the work currently being done by counselors, men's group leaders, and others in the field. Although it is unwise to generalize about men who abuse their partners, most men who do so need help with some or all of these issues; all are usually weak in at least one of them.

1. Overcoming denial of beating
2. Understanding the consequences of battering
3. Naming the emotions that set it up
4. Taking control of self (behavior)
5. Recognizing alternatives to violence

Addressing these *immediate* issues is a way to reach the short-term goal of stopping abuse. There are social and life-style questions that will also have to be addressed before there can be an end to battering: changes in workplace pressure; improvements in male-female interaction; portrayal of male violence in the media; equalizing male-female relationships. While the work on these pressing social issues goes on, the films and exercises in "Time Out" concentrate on what can be done *today,* and what practical steps to take *now.*

1. Overcoming Denial of Beating

Breaking through denial is the first urgent task for men who want to stop hitting. Denial involves a man's attempt to mask his victim's pain, terror, and injury from himself. It's not simply lying about what happens; denial is an inability to see and deal with the plain facts of physical abuse. As long as a man denies the suffering of his victims, he will not seriously consider the consequences of physical and psychological abuse. Smokers deny the recognition of damage to their own lungs, so they don't respond to the very real threat of cancer. So, too, men deny (to themselves) the injury and pain they cause; as long as they continue to deny, they cannot hear persuasive arguments to stop.

One of the ways to break down denial is to deal with *isolation.* Isolation supports denial, and makes it a useful defense for the man who batters. Violent men are often solitary men, without the social and emotional skills to share themselves with other people—even the people close to them. Studies show that they and their families are often isolated from the community and generally lack connection with support systems and helpful neighbors. If a man gets no input, no version of his life other than his own, it's relatively easy to continue denying the battering behavior.

A basic purpose of men's groups is to give men outside impressions from other men who can cut through isolation. The way to reduce isolation is to bring men into interaction with other men, other voices, and to use these encounters to let them hear that the secret is known. Using this contact, it's possible to get men to give up some of the denial and confront the cost of violence.

2. Understanding the Consequences of Beating

Because men may deny what they are doing, and may isolate themselves from information that would shatter the denial, it often is not enough to say, "Stop it or else". But once a man's denial is reduced, once he is *listening,* the issue of consequences becomes critical.

Powerful deterrents to hitting exist in the candid truth about what can happen if it continues. For instance:

a. Assault is a crime in all 50 states and men may be surprised to learn that the consequences may well be arrest, prosecution, and jail. More and more women are pressing charges against the men who beat them. Some courts and district attorneys are aggressively pressing charges in cases where the woman does not. Once the law is involved, there are not many avenues left open to the man who batters. He will have to face the charges and probably pay the penalty. Legal action means other potential consequences: loss of status in the community ... termination at work ... alienation from family and friends.

b. The other most important consequence is the loss of the very person the man attempts to keep—his wife or mate. While a man might believe that physical abuse and "punishment" guarantee that a woman will stay with him, the fact is that beating drives the woman away in many cases. And since so many men who batter are very dependent on their relationship with the woman, the potential loss may be one of the most effective blocks to continued violence. Women *do* leave the men who beat them—not always, of course, but often enough to make it a serious factor. Men need to realize that women are not without resources, that they are not powerless, and that more and more women are leaving home if they are abused.

c. The third serious consequence of domestic violence is what it does to the children in the family. Violence is learned behavior; kids who see their fathers hit their mothers take those cues as instructions for their own behavior. Boys learn to be brutal and domineering and physically violent; girls learn to be victims and to expect to be hit. It's a paradox—men and women fight over what kind of example to set for the kids. But by the act of hitting the woman, the man *is* setting an example and perpetuating the cycle of violence whether he knows it or not.

In summary, men should be aware that the battering probably will get them into trouble with the law, it most likely will drive away the woman they are trying to dominate, and it will teach violence as a way of life to the children in the family.

3. Naming the Emotions That Set Up Violence

It's essential for men to learn to distinguish between *who* they are and *how* they've been socialized. Violence is a learned reaction—and it can be unlearned. How are men taught to paint themselves into tight emotional corners from which they think there is only a violent release? The answer lies in understanding a variety of attitudes—fears, values, expectations—that make men ready to be angry and ready to lash out when they feel that anger.

It is hard for men to admit *fear* when they are conditioned to think of themselves as strong, brave, and managerial. This sex-role stereotype leaves no room for fear. History is full of tales to reinforce the stereotype—from slaying dragons to charging enemy-held positions. But men *do* have fears, and not just of dragons or enemy soldiers. Men who learn to see behind their anger often discover fears and uncertainties at the core. Fears of what? Of being left by a woman, maybe for another man . . . of losing ground at work to younger, smarter, stronger men . . . of being relied on by wife and kids, but not being able to come up with everything the family needs. Unnamed and unaddressed, these fears can grow and get out of control. "What am I afraid of?" is a healthy and helpful question for men because it allows them to acknowledge that they do, in fact, have fears. Naming the fears brings them back into perspective, and cuts them down to manageable dimensions.

Another emotional set-up lies in the set of *values* each person possesses. Most values are implicit, never spelled out or declared, but nevertheless influence what we do and how we do it. Values are learned from parents, teachers, friends; from peers who reinforce values (and that's probably how we choose our friends—if they agree with our values, they qualify); and from the community—media, organizations, institutions. One of the issues for a man in treatment is to identify what his values are, how he got them, and whether or not he wants to consider reexamining and maybe rejecting some.

Both fears and values condition men to expect things to work out their way. When "things" fail to materialize according to their expectations, tension and frustration build. Often these expectations are inconsistent with reality. One of the characteristics of some men who batter women is their view that life is shortchanging them. They look for and expect perfection and satisfaction in everything they do and from the people closest to them. Sometimes these expectations, coupled with a man's own interpretation and inference about what he has a "right" to expect, push him into a no-win situation. Because his expectations are so high, he's always on the lookout for failures—always sure that people and events are not going to measure up to his demands. Of course, he doesn't have to look very hard, or find very significant failures, to justify his worst suspicions: he's certain he's never going to get things the way he wants them . . . his expectations are never going to be fully met.

Whether he insists things be perfect, or is sure they won't be, a man's expectations grow out of values and fears and the network of emotional signals we all grow up with. A man who batters needs help with untangling this network and naming, plainly and specifically, the things that make up his view of the world and his place in it.

4. Taking Charge of Self (Not Others)

In the face of these expectations, men often attempt to overpower others and try to force the people close to them to conform to their expectations. They may use violence to maintain a sense of "being in control" of things. But there is a critical distinction to be made between internal and external control.

Men may try to overpower their women by making demands, by "laying down the law," by monitoring their daily routine. They may try to exert power over their children in the same way. They may guard what they say in front of their friends so they "control" the image their friends have of them. All of this constructs a house of cards, a false sense of being powerful or effective; as soon as the house gets too complicated, it collapses. The harder a man works to bend and shape other people, the more problems he creates for himself.

It is important to point out that what a man does control is his own conduct. When he feels ineffective or powerless in the face of job pressures and family demands, there is always one place he has control—his actions, his choices. He can and does manage, control, and direct his own behavior. When the behavior includes hitting or psychological abuse, it is a choice he has made—a bad one, with negative consequences—but a choice. Men who become violent often report feeling "out of control" and certainly they may feel overcome by raging impulses or provoked beyond control. Yet most violent attacks demonstrate some degree of control. A slap is not a punch is not a shove is not throwing a person out the window.

It may be essential to help men get in touch with whatever degree of control they do have. This can be the first step to realizing that they can take further steps to stop the hitting, and that they can take actions and make choices they determine, ones they can take responsibility for and control.

Anger control techniques and walk-away strategies are some examples of men taking control of their own minds and bodies. Men can be helped to see that when they hit a woman they are not *out of control*—not simply reacting to outside forces. They are making choices and handling their own behavior in an unacceptable manner.

5. Recognizing Options to Violence

If a man stops denying that he hits, pays attention to what it can cost him, understands the emotional forces that make him feel angry, and is willing to take charge of himself instead of pretending that he is in charge of others—*then* he may be ready to consider the options to violence and physical attack. Considering options doesn't mean that men won't feel pressured, anxious, fearful, or angry. It does mean that they will have learned to identify those feelings in themselves and do something about them besides letting them spill over into a physical attack.

Finding the alternatives means connecting with other men who are looking for ways to stop the hitting. It means exploring new levels of self-revelation, new risks in terms of asking for help and being willing to give it. There's resistance to anything new in our beliefs, values, interactions with other people. Some men will find it hard to accept the alternatives—until their own "tried and true" methods of handling domestic pressures let them down. Then, it is to be hoped that there will be other men around who will support the struggle for an alternative by showing and sharing their own struggle.

At its most basic, the option to hitting is simple—*not hitting*. But this is not done easily, and men are helped most when they are aware of the component parts of choice:

- admitting the impulse to hit
- thinking about the consequences
- naming the emotions
- practicing alternatives to violence

Then men can try talking through a tough moment, walking away from confrontations when they feel the pressure rise, calling a friend for help, or any action that helps them past the impulse to lash out.

D. SUGGESTIONS FOR GROUP LEADERS

For optimum results, it is helpful for group leaders to:

1. Become familiar with the five key issues that characterize most violent relationships: know what the issues are, how they look in the lives of men, and how they relate to battering.
2. Begin by selecting some trigger questions to start off the discussion. The film scenarios and discussion guide highlight key issues with realistic characters and situations. These provide a baseline to get discussions going.
3. Relate the suggestions and strategies in "Time Out" to the larger picture of your own treatment plan. The films and discussion guide are tools to be used to reinforce and complement your goals.
4. Make sure each man in the group achieves a sense of closure at the end of the session. This will be easiest if you identify a goal before the session, then select sections of "Time Out" that will help you achieve it.

In addition to this suggested format, there are some points to keep in mind:

- Focus discussion on the men and their lives. The film scenarios can serve as illustrations, models, and examples. But the substance of the program is the lives of the men in the group, not theoretical discussions about films or someone else's problems.

* Keep the work focused on *him,* not her. This program is to help men talk about *their* feelings and choices. There may be struggles to put feelings and reactions into words. Encourage the struggle. Naming the feelings is a first important step to being able to manage them.

THE WAY IT IS: A CHECKLIST OF FACTS ABOUT DOMESTIC VIOLENCE

Before using "Time Out," you might want to invite men to decide privately whether they agree or disagree with each item on this list.

After the film and discussion sessions, you can use the checklist as a wrap-up, asking men (again, privately) to see whether their attitudes have changed.

- ☐ Battering happens in all kinds of homes, in all kinds of neighborhoods, among all kinds of people.
- ☐ There may be as many as 4 million women beaten every year by the men they live with.
- ☐ There will be violence at least once in two out of every three marriages.
- ☐ One-third of the murders committed in the U.S. happen in the family—and half of these murders are between spouses.
- ☐ Couples learn patterns of violence—when it happens once, it's likely to happen again and again.
- ☐ Pregnant women are often the target of abuse by men.
- ☐ Although victims of abuse are usually women, both men and women commit homicide as a result of spouse abuse.
- ☐ Children learn violence at home, and often grow up to pass it on as violent adults.
- ☐ Many spouse abusers are also child abusers.
- ☐ Most men who batter are psychologically "normal" people.
- ☐ It is not acceptable to use anger, alcohol, frustration, or stress as excuses to hit another person.
- ☐ Spouse abuse is against the law in all 50 states. It is a crime.

PART II. "TIME OUT" SAMPLER

A. Synopsis of Films and Examples of Discussion Materials

1. "Deck the Halls": the Anatomy of a Fight. *Synopsis.* It's the day before Christmas at the Greensboro home in an upper-class Michigan suburb. Upstairs, AL worries in his mirror about his weight, his health, his job, his son. Downstairs, his wife SUSAN prepares for a big Christmas Eve party—the first the Greensboros have thrown in many years.

In the kitchen, AL and his son DAVID eat breakfast while SUSAN continues party preparations. AL gives lots of directions without offering any help. And while he's looking forward to the party, AL is annoyed that he has to make his own breakfast; he resents the fact that SUSAN is too busy to serve him.

At the party that evening, AL's house is full of friends singing carols, drinking and eating, mingling and enjoying themselves. SUSAN seems to be the perfect hostess. AL talks to several guests. But the conversation seems to focus on competition—on the job or the racquetball court. AL insists that DAVID "play for the people" on his new guitar. It's a good party, but AL insists on managing and directing everything.

The last couple is leaving. As AL glares, SUSAN gives a holiday hug and kiss to TED, a friend who's just been promoted. When they're alone, AL begins sniping at SUSAN: he complains about her behavior, makes nasty cracks about her dress and goodbye kiss to TED, berates her for not serving the food in the right order. He yells, demanding to know why she didn't wear the necklace he gave her. Then he throws the present at her violently. SUSAN defends herself, then turns on him. "You're a hothead," she snarls, "Nobody would promise you Number One of anything!"

AL attacks her, smacking her across the face. He explodes in a rage, smashing presents, tearing at the Christmas tree, knocking SUSAN around. Blood running from her mouth, she stumbles from the living room.

SUSAN retreats to their bedroom, sobbing. AL stands outside the locked door, crying his apology and begging her to forgive him and let him in. She simply turns away in sorrow and resignation.

AL is sitting in the living room, surrounded by the ruins of his violent outburst when DAVID returns home. AL demands to know where he's been. "You're not supposed to go to other people's families at Christmas," he insists. But DAVID wants to know what's happened. When he tries to go upstairs to see his mother, AL blocks the way. DAVID pushes and shoves, AL nearly hits his son, and DAVID runs out, yelling his hatred for his father and kicking his new guitar in the process. SUSAN, in her robe, watches silently as AL sags against the fireplace mantel.

Trigger Questions ask men to consider the ways AL tries to control his family and his status; what he expects from other people around him (and whether these expectations are realistic); what values AL demonstrates in his behavior, including speculation about where he got them. Once men begin to share ideas about the film, group leaders can pose questions inviting more personal responses, such as what viewers guess about AL's father; similarities between AL's values and expectations, and those of their own friends; what they speculate about the expectations members of AL's family have of him (financial, social status, physical, and so on).

Springboards for Introspection. After discussing AL GREENSBORO'S situation, the group can move to more personal issues. Questions in the user's manual ask men to discuss personality factors and expectations they share with Al; what similarities and differences they see in their problems and in their outbursts when compared with AL's.

Group Activities encourage further introspection and clarification of these issues. For example:

THERE'S NO DENYING IT

Men begin to see how denying something to themselves and to the outside world can lead to the mistaken notion that they've "chased it away". By using a *Self-Diagnosis Checklist,* men are encouraged to head off possibilities of violence by understanding some of the serious problems that cause stress in their homes—the kind of stress that can become a set-up for more violence. Men are encouraged to be honest in their "self-diagnosis" and to realize that the man who checks five or more items probably will need some outside help in dealing with stress. Items on the checklist include:

troubles with boss
troubles with co-workers
getting laid-off or fired
death of a close person
pregnancy
serious health problem of family member
sexual difficulty
financial difficulties
moving to a new place
child caught doing something illegal
serious accident or injury

"Up the Creek": the Aftermath. *Synopsis.* This film is about the inner life of a solitary man; what he goes through in his daily life after his wife and children leave him. It opens as TOMMY HOWELL, 33, wanders dazed and depressed through his empty house, picking up the pieces from a fight the night before. He and his wife, DONNA LEE, have fought before, but last night was a bad one. TOMMY'S face registers confusion, despair, and the beginning of panic as he stares at the mess.

TOMMY goes to the shooting range with his pal, RUSS—a cop on the local force. RUSS teases because TOMMY can't shoot straight. Finally, TOMMY blurts out the news that Donna ran out on him. RUSS offers sympathy, then help—but TOMMY tightens up and shuts him off, denying the seriousness of the situation.

Next morning at work, TOMMY calls the boss asking for time off to look for DONNA. He's told to ask his supervisor, ELDON—who happens to be Donna's father. When ELDON barges in, TOMMY asks for the time off. ELDON not only refuses, but offers TOMMY his own macho opinion on how to "handle" women.

Back at home, TOMMY lies to a neighbor who calls to talk to DONNA. But he knows it won't be long before "people know". In desperation, he follows his own blind hope to the bus station where he watches till the last bus leaves without bringing DONNA. TOMMY stays up all that night, calling anybody he can think of in a futile effort to find her.

Early the next morning, RUSS calls. TOMMY reads him a letter from the District Attorney's office telling him to come for a meeting.

Donna has gone to a shelter and filed a complaint: assault and battery. TOMMY presses RUSS to suggest a way around the meeting, but RUSS tells him the law's the law. TOMMY explodes in frustration, still insisting DONNA is the cause of all this and questioning why the law should be interfering in his personal life.

TOMMY storms into the Assistant DA's office, where WILLIAMS forces him to sit and listen to the facts. DONNA was injured; she's asking for a restraining order. WILLIAMS asks for TOMMY'S side. But TOMMY can only repeat the same old thing, insisting it was nothing serious. WILLIAMS finally closes the meeting by telling TOMMY he's "used up all his chances".

Alone in his truck, TOMMY tosses the wilted bouquet he'd bought for Donna's homecoming into the gutter.

Trigger Questions following the film help viewers speculate about Tommy: his feelings, his choices, and his world. They focus on his denial; his sense of loneliness and isolation; and the stresses in his daily life. These discussion questions are designed to help viewers pinpoint where and why Tommy missed out on chances for finding help; how his denial and minimizing his problems—trying to make it so people "never know"—are working against him; how extra pressure built up because Tommy tried to convince himself he could handle everything alone.

Springboard Questions to Introspection help members of the group use their observations about Tommy's life and way of handling his problems as a means of making the discussion more personal. Questions will help the men explore similarities between their lives and Tommy's, leading them to consider what might happen if their spouse or partner left; people they could turn to in times of trouble; what their beliefs and expectations are each time they engage in a fight (and whether these expectations and beliefs are realistic).

Group Activities encourage men to develop some insight and understanding of how it feels to be isolated; what it means to deny the obvious; and the role law enforcement plays in resolving domestic violence.

3. "Shifting Gears": Alternatives. *Synopsis.* Late at night, P. K. and his wife, LYNN, fight violently when he finds a pack of matches from a local tavern in her purse. P.K. hits her hard, several times. It's noisy enough to be heard in the apartment next door, where BUDDY DE FRANCO and his wife, MARY KAY, are trying to sleep.

MARY KAY begs BUDDY to go next door and do something to stop it. BUDDY remarks that "P. K.'s just had a few beers," then angrily rejects her request. There's no way he'll butt in on his friend's fight. MARY KAY reminds him that he knows how it feels; he used to hit her. But BUDDY still doesn't want anyone to know he ever hit his wife. BUDDY's temper flares, but he cools himself out with a moment of silence and some deep breathing. "You don't have to worry," he adds, "it's not contagious".

Early the following morning, BUDDY and P. K. meet in the carport. BUDDY asks P. K. to help him fix a fanbelt. P. K.'s the expert, and BUDDY learns from him. BUDDY cuts his hand when MARY KAY yells at him to come do a household chore. In his anger, he pantomimes a punch he'd like to deliver. P. K. looks at him closely, and BUDDY reveals that he's "trying to get away from that". The two men come close to sharing the truth they both know: that P. K. hits his wife. BUDDY takes a chance and reveals a little about himself, but P. K. refuses to follow the lead. He still seems to value silence and privacy; the myth that "a real man" is one who's always in charge.

Next morning as LYNN gets dressed for work, P. K. watches with obvious hostility. She's got a bad bruise on her cheek, but covering it with makeup doesn't hide the tension between them. P. K. wants to know why she's "all dressed up" with perfume and earrings. And when he runs out of shaving cream mid-shave, he barks about her failure to take care of his needs because of her new job.

The tension mounts in the car as P. K. and BUDDY drive LYNN to her job at an auto dealership. BUDDY kids P. K. because "shop guys" are going to work on his car. P. K. keeps fuming as LYNN needles him about how much money they'll save now that she's working.

At the shop, LYNN's boss extends a hand, but P. K. snarls when the guy uses his real name. BUDDY and P. K. squeal out of the driveway. By this time, it's clear that nearly everything bugs P.K. When BUDDY reminds him about softball practice, P. K. grumbles that he's not coming. BUDDY takes a risk and confronts him, asking for an explanation. P. K. yells at BUDDY to get out of the car.

BUDDY shows strength and refuses. P. K. drags him out and belts him. BUDDY resists the impulse to hit back. Instead, he shows some pleasure at the freedom he feels *not* to hit.

BUDDY challenges P. K. to think about what he's doing when he tries punching out the world to solve his problems. P. K. collapses in a sob. "What am I supposed to do?" he asks, over and over again, clearly in despair.

BUDDY'S nonviolent response isn't easy—but he climbs back in behind the wheel, suggesting that P. K. is not alone; that rage can be overcome; that maybe they'll be able to figure something out—together.

Trigger Questions relating to the characters and situations in "Shifting Gears" are used to generate discussions about anxiety, changes, and alternatives to violence. Questions invite men to talk about:

- why Buddy initially didn't "do something" when he heard P. K. and Lynn fighting . . . and why he changed his mind.
- what kinds of anxieties P. K. might be feeling as a result of Lynn's job and the changes (real or imagined) created in their lives.
- methods Buddy uses to get his violent impulses under control—why they work for him; whether they might work for P. K.; whether they'd work for *you*.
- ways of offering, and asking for, help.

Springboards for Introspection. As members of the group react to Buddy and P. K.'s story, they'll be revealing values *they* subscribe to and fears *they* feel. Discussion levels probe deeper as men in the group are invited to explore differences and similarities they see between themselves and the film characters.

Group Activities will help men explore their own feelings about violence by examining their personal values, acknowledging their fears, and trying to consider alternatives to physical violence.

This list offers men a summary of ideas explored in the films and discussion groups. The users' guide suggests that it be reproduced and given to each man to keep and use as needed.

1. As a man, I have the right to show my feelings and express my fears.

2. As a man, I have the right to change and the right to choose the direction of my changes.
3. As a man, I can ask for help when I need it and offer help when I think it is needed.
4. As a man, I have the right to ask for what I want and the wisdom to know that I cannot always get it.
5. As a man, I have the right to tell people when I cannot fulfill their expectations of me.
6. As a man, I have the right to consider new ways of thinking, acting, and relating to people.
7. As a man, I am not obliged to live up to the stereotypes of how I am "supposed" to be.
8. As a man, I have the right to acknowledge my frustrations, disappointments, and anxieties.
9. As a man, I can choose to take responsibility for my actions and not allow other people's behavior to push me into choices I do not want to make.
10. As a man, I have the right to show my strength by choosing not to hit someone who angers me.

16. How to Set up a Counseling Program for Self-Referred Batterers: The AWAIC Model

Shelley E. Garnet, ACSW
Executive Director, Abused Women's Aid In Crisis, Inc.,
New York

Doris Moss, Ed.D.

INTRODUCTION

This paper will describe the AWAIC (Abused Women's Aid In Crisis) model of a counseling program for men who batter their mates. It will address the following topics:

- Why the program was started by the agency
- How the program works: outreach strategies, results of the outreach, and treatment approach
- Replicability of the model: three "how-to" steps
- Implications for future directions

This model is geared to self-referred abusive men. The literature notes that there has been difficulty in getting abusive men to seek counseling. Del Martin states, "The only way to get him (the abusive man) into therapy or counseling would be for a judge to order it as a condition of release.''* However, the AWAIC model demonstrates that there is an effective approach to reach abusive men and to facilitate their voluntary commitment to counseling.

WHY THE PROGRAM WAS STARTED

AWAIC has been engaged in the provision of a full range of counseling services to women who are physically abused by their mates since it was founded in 1975 by Maria Roy.**

In the course of its delivery of service to battered women, some men were seen in counseling. Services to men were always voluntary, never part of a court-mandated program. The men were referred to the agency in the following ways:

- Women engaged in counseling would request that their husbands or mates be seen in counseling separately from them.
- At times it was appropriate that couple counseling take place.
- Each month several calls would be received from abusive men seeking help, who were responding to AWAIC'S outreach offering services to women.

The awareness grew at AWAIC, as self-referred abusive men called the agency, that there was nothing being offered to this population in the way of counseling services. Men who had exhibited violent outbursts within the family have not been welcomed by most of the traditional social service agencies dealing with domestic violence, where the primary service is to provide a safe refuge for women. No agency in the New York metropolitan area was reaching out specifically to abusive men who were aware of their problem, who wanted help but needed the encouragement to come forth, who needed a place to go where professional, nonjudgmental help was available and where confidentiality would be guaranteed.

AWAIC had to take a long, hard look at the issue of how the expan-

---

* Martin, Del. Battered women: Society's problem, In *The Victimization of Women,* Vol. 3, Jane Chapman and Margaret Gates, (eds.) Beverly Hills, Cal.: Sage Publications, 1978.
** Roy, Maria. A model for services, In *Battered Women: A Psychosociological Study of Domestic Violence,* Maria Roy (ed.) New York: Van Nostrand Reinhold, 1977.

sion of services to batterers might affect its first priority which was, and is, the provision of services to abused women. It had to determine if expanded services would be consonant with this priority. It was decided that in line with the agency's concerns regarding the preventive aspect of domestic violence, this new direction would be relevant and productive to the agency's goals. It was realized that working with the abuser is a critical component of an effective delivery system. Helping battered women who are the victims of abuse to leave or resolve their relationship is just one side of the coin. If the woman decides to leave the relationship, the chances are that the abuser goes on to form new relationships where the same dynamics leading to abuse are operational, thus continuing his patterns of violent behavior and claiming new victims. It was decided, therefore, that working with the abuser, · particularly the self-referred man who is ready to seek help, presented an important and relevant area of service.

HOW THE PROGRAM WORKS

Outreach Strategies

The key factor in launching an effective outreach program (January, 1980) is the use of the media: radio, television, and the press. Calls were made to public service directors of local radio and TV stations explaining AWAIC's new thrust to reach men who batter and to let them know of the availability of counseling services. These calls were received with a high level of interest and positive response. They were followed up by sending timed "spots" for airing to each person contacted. Spots are usually 10, 30, or 60 seconds in length, depending upon the guidelines of the particular station or channel.

Sample of a 10-Second Radio Spot Developed by AWAIC.
"Men, can you control your temper? Do you hit instead of talk? If you want to change your violent behavior towards your family, we can help. For professional confidential counseling call _____," (repeat number).

A slide photograph of two men seated, facing each other, was taken at the agency, and was sent along with the above spot to TV stations. It received many months of exposure by major networks.

As a result of contacting feature editors and writers at city news-papers, several articles appeared detailing AWAIC's services for bat-terers. A caution here concerns the propensity of the press to highlight the more sensational aspects of domestic violence. Based upon the ex-perience of the agency,* it would be wise to address this issue when discussing publicity with newspaper and magazine staff.

The media campaign led to appearances on several TV talk shows by AWAIC staff, which permitted a discussion of the services to men and the issues of domestic violence in general. While these appearances were helpful in the outreach thrust, the question of clients appearing on the shows (or being interviewed by the press) came up repeatedly. Agencies must be prepared to deal with the need for respecting the con-fidentiality of their clients and the effect of interviews on the treatment process.

In addition to these outreach strategies, a wide mailing was sent to social service agencies and organizations in the field of domestic violence, to inform them of the availability of AWAIC's services for batterers and to encourage referrals to the agency.

Results of the Outreach

By fall of 1980, 9 months after starting its outreach campaign, over 100 calls had been received on the AWAIC hot line from men seeking counseling services who identified themselves as batterers. (Paren-thetically, it may be of interest to note that 1% of these calls were made by men who were themselves victims of battering by their spouses).

One-third of the callers came to the agency for counseling. Over two-thirds of those who came for counseling remained in treatment for more than 3 months.

Who Responded to the Outreach

The abusive men who called for help reported the following intake in-formation: they ranged in age from 23 to 71. More than 50% of the callers were married and slightly more than 30% had children. The average length of the relationship with the mate was 6 years. All the

---

* Roy, Maria. op. cit.

men who called were (with one exception) gainfully employed (i.e., banker, teacher, stockbroker, pilot, computer programmer, marketing manager, correctional officer, bus driver). The nature of the physical abuse was mainly slapping and punching, with the victim not requiring hospital treatment.

Treatment Approach

The program at AWAIC is geared towards self-referred males who have an awareness of and a discomfort in relation to the violence they exhibit toward their mates. Unlike the stereotypical image of the cruel, sadistic, macho male, batterers engaged in treatment at AWAIC have been bright articulate men with deep underlying shallowness, severely impaired egos, and unresolved conflicts between the desperate need for the mate yet the fear and anger this brings. Their lack of impulse control and inability to deal with anxiety particularly when their limited sense of self is attacked, results in the release of aggression. This aggression is often the tie that protects the ego. The main task of therapy becomes assisting the batterer in beginning to feel and cope with the depression that accompanies any frustrating experience.

Treatment begins with a look at the violence and reconstructing a healthier sense of self. Insight-oriented therapy such as that practiced at AWAIC is a long process. The forces behind the behavior are examined, with less time spent on the spousal relationship per se.

The focus of the first session is developing a contract to work based upon the recognition that the client has deep-rooted internal problems which are vented aggressively. The violent behavior is exposed in an attempt to provide the man with an opportunity to drop his facade in a safe environment where he need not fear the impotency or threat of the spousal relationship. Most of these men have never spoken to anyone about their feelings in relation to their violent spousal relationships. This process in itself will create anxiety, therefore a foundation must be laid in the therapeutic relationship so that in time the underlying depression can surface. Sharing with the patient the fact that the work is going to be hard and painful helps to lay the needed groundwork.

As Fleming points out in discussion regarding counseling the abuser, "Critical to working with abusive men is finding a basis for identification with them, their goals, aspirations, frustrations and being empathetic with their plight. In general, men are conditioned to believe that the need for counseling or therapy is a sign of weakness or inadequacy, so that it is vital to establish a basis for trust. . ."*

Several therapeutic techniques are used at AWAIC and all are geared to the special needs of men. Short-term focused treatment (hourly sessions held once a week) is offered with an option to renegotiate the treatment contract after 8 weeks. Treatment of this kind focuses primarily on the battering and how one can change the communication patterns. After 8 weeks, plans for continued treatment based on the work done during those weeks are presented to the client.

Intensive, reconstructive psychotherapy is the primary form of treatment used at AWAIC. This long-term process is geared for men who are ready and motivated for this insight-oriented treatment. The emphasis is on reconstructing the impaired ego and working through the early developmental conflicts.

REPLICABILITY OF THE MODEL

"How-To" Steps

The AWAIC Model for counseling services to batterers presented in this paper is appropriate for those agencies dealing with the provision of counseling services to battered women which are seeking to expand their services to the men who are batterers. It is a model which can be successfully replicated with attention to key points.

Briefly the "how-to" steps involved in implementing such a program include the following:

• Determine agency readiness for the program
• Plan the outreach campaign
• Anticipate the response

Determining Agency Readiness

Determining agency readiness for providing services to batterers is perhaps the most critical step in launching the model, and can play a

---

* Fleming, Jennifer B. *Stopping Wife Abuse: A Guide to the Emotional, Psychological and Legal Implications for the Abused Woman and Those Helping Her.* Garden City, N.Y.: Anchor Press/Doubleday, 1979, p. 308.

vital role in its successful implementation. In order to determine agency readiness there are three important areas of consideration which should be addressed namely: (1) the attitudinal reactions of the professional community; (2) of the staff, and (3) of the women clients at the agency.

Reactions of the Professional Community

AWAIC's primary goal and focus since its inception has been and continues to be the provision of services to battered women. The question has been raised by concerned professionals in the field as to whether the emphasis on providing service to batterers in any way dilutes the concern for helping battered women in crisis. Agencies must be prepared to deal with this reaction on the part of colleagues outside (as well as within) the agency.

At AWAIC it is believed that the services to abusers enhance its ongoing programs for women and indeed add a much needed dimension to the spectrum of clinical services which the agency already provides. In no way are the services for batterers detracting from the primary goal of serving battered women. As stated above, counseling batterers is viewed as focusing on the preventive aspect of domestic violence—a necessary component in breaking the cycle of intrafamilial violence. The introduction of men to the client population at AWAIC was initially in response to women clients who asked that their abusive mates be seen in counseling. From the AWAIC experience, it behooves agencies interested in implementing this model, to be aware that questions and concerns may be forthcoming from the network of providers of services to women and women's organizations regarding its impact on existing programs.

Reactions of Staff

It is important to obtain input from agency staff on how serving abusers is viewed. Do the workers feel judgmental towards the abusers? To what extent might this interfere with the counseling treatment? Is there a fear of violence by batterers coming to the agency, on the part of the staff? Todate, there have been no untoward incidents reported at AWAIC. However, it is critical to the success of the treatment process that these and other concerns on the part of the staff are explored and dealt with before implementing the program.

Reactions of Clients

Agencies which specialize in services for battered women usually have literature, posters, and other printed materials displayed in the reception area, dealing with the terrors of abuse. If the agency has been viewed as a "women's" center, it is important to consider whether the atmosphere is conducive to making male clients feel comfortable? Might the women clients feel apprehensive at seeing men in the waiting room? These concerns should be elicited from the women clients and dealt with by their counselors. A fine line must be walked between not disturbing the women clients and yet encouraging the male clients. Perhaps providing the services for men on another site or at times when women are not being seen may provide a solution if these factors present a problem.

Planning the Outreach Campaign

This step has been detailed above. The dissemination of the news regarding the availability of services to batterers should be distributed to the media as well as to social service agencies. Continuing follow-up and reinforcement is imperative to keep the information before the public. The AWAIC experience indicates that there is considerable receptivity toward the topic, and cooperation should be readily forthcoming. There is no cost to nonprofit agencies for public service announcements.

Anticipating the Response

It is critical to the smooth functioning of the program to anticipate the response to the outreach campaign by having the agency's facilities ready and in place. Some of the mechanics to be addressed are as follows:

- Development of an appropriate intake form for the men who call for services.

- Assignment of a special phone number (if possible) to handle the incoming calls, with specially trained workers who are aware of the psychological dynamics of the sensitivities of the abuser who is making, what is for him, a difficult call—perhaps a first admission of his abusive role.
- Make sure that an adequate number of staff workers and space is available to implement the counseling services.
- It would be counterproductive to the outreach effort, if men who respond to it are told to call back or are put on a waiting list for counseling appointments.

IMPLICATIONS FOR FUTURE DIRECTIONS

When this program was launched at AWAIC there were many questions to be answered as a new target population was being addressed, namely the self-referred male abuser. Would these men respond to the outreach strategies? Would they engage in treatment? How long would they stay in treatment? Are the treatment techniques effective? What would be the effect of the program on the agency's work with women?

At the end of 9 months a retrospective consideration gave some answers. Yes, there was a response to the outreach from the target population, with substantial numbers of men coming for counseling and committing themselves to long-term treatment. While it was too soon to determine the long-term effects of treatment, the short-term goals of the cessation of violence were accomplished. Based upon the AWAIC experience so far, the responses of the staff and the women clients have been supportive to the new services.

FUTURE DIRECTIONS

AWAIC anticipates expanding its counseling services to batterers to include groups. At the time of this writing a media campaign is underway again, this time disseminating news that Batterers Anonymous Groups are being formed. It is anticipated that these groups will be designed on a 6-week model, open to extension, led by a professional counselor. Group counseling will also be recommended for those men currently in individual counseling for whom the experience is deemed appropriate by their therapists.

A body of data is being collected at AWAIC concerning self-referred male abusers, which it is anticipated will be of value to the field. The records will provide previously unavailable information on the demographics, psychodynamics, and responses to treatment for this specific population of abusers. It should provide the basis of a blueprint on which to plan future programs to deal effectively with batterers' programs which can prevent the victimization of countless women in our society.

17. Developing Operational Procedures For Police Use

Nancy Loving
Police Executive Research Forum
Washington, D.C.

Many police officials are becoming more sensitive to the severity of spouse abuse and wife beating problems and to the need to respond to these calls more effectively. An important part of this awareness should be a decision to develop and implement formal written procedures for patrol officers' use. The purpose of these standards or procedures is to provide officers guidance on the range of successful intervention techniques for handling any criminal violation, protecting the victim, and ensuring officer safety, including:

- the alternatives available for dealing with a given situation;
- the factors to consider in choosing among the available alternatives; and
- the relative weight each factor should have.[1]

By limiting police discretion to a certain range of responses, police officials help patrol officers perform with maximum efficiency and effectiveness by focusing their efforts on responses that have proved to be successful. Many police practitioners believe that any limits on discretion are harmful because every family violence case is different, but the same may be said for every type of police call for service. Each case *is* different, but generalizations are possible.

A balanced and practical description of ways to respond to spouse abuse and wife beating cases should enable the officers to make intelligent judgments in a variety of volatile situations. With proper guidance, officers can respond in a manner that will prove useful and effective; be free as possible of personal prejudices and biases; and achieve a reasonable degree of uniformity in handling similar incidents in the community.[2]

Formal procedures should represent a balanced combination of acceptable standards of conduct with the rules of law and due process. They should be general enough to allow the officers freedom to exercise their unique talents and skills, but specific enough for them to know which actions they should not take.

Police officers interviewed for this report consistently mentioned their need for "greater direction" and "more specific guidance from top brass" on how to handle spousal violence calls. Rather than viewing procedures in a negative light, these patrol officers seemed to welcome advice and guidance. Several officers said they felt poorly equipped with only "seat of the pants" skills and were eager to receive any available materials on the subject. The rest of this chapter presents a summary of operational procedures for step-by-step successful intervention in spouse abuse and wife beating cases. These sample procedures are a composite developed from many written sources[3] and from interviews with more than 150 police officials, training officers, and patrol officers. The procedures should be considered suggestions, and police agencies should review, test, add to, modify, or eliminate provisions that are irrelevant or inappropriate for their communities.

The outlined procedures are divided into two categories: the intervention process and the disposition process. The intervention process extends from the receipt of the call by the police operator to the interviewing of witnesses. The disposition process includes action plans for felony crimes, misdemeanor crimes, and threatened assaults. Many of the steps mentioned often occur simultaneously, but they are presented in sequence to provide a manageable "check list" for police officers. Many of these steps will strike some police as elementary and mundane. They are mentioned as a reminder that often the most basic and obvious precautions are overlooked or forgotten. Furthermore, it must be emphasized that these steps were composed to assist officers in domestic conflict calls involving the use of violence or the threat of violence.

THE INTERVENTION PROCESS

Receipt of the Call

When a police operator receives a call involving a domestic conflict, he or she must determine if police presence is required at the scene and how quickly it is needed. To make these decisions, the operator should ask the caller if violence or a weapon is involved in the conflict. If either is involved, the operator should then gather as much information as possible about when the assault occurred, the whereabouts of the victim and assailant, and the seriousness of any injuries. Threats of violence are to be regarded as serious precursors to physical assault, as has been shown to be true for domestic homicides and aggravated assults.[4] The operator also should try to determine whether children are at the conflict scene and if either party has been drinking alcohol or using drugs. Precise questions should be asked, such as:

- Has anyone been injured? How severely? Is he or she still at the scene?
- Has any property been destroyed?
- Is a suspect still at the scene?
- How long ago did the suspect(s) leave the scene? In what direction did they go? How were they traveling?
- Was a weapon(s) involved? What type?
- Are there witnesses? Where are they located?

This information should then be relayed to the police dispatcher. His or her decision about dispatching a patrol car to the scene should be made according to the seriousness of the injuries or threatened harm, and whether or not the assailant is on the premises. Evidence of an assault in progress, such as screams or an interrupted or incomplete phone call, should be assigned an immediate response.

The dispatcher should then assign the call to one of the following responses:

- Immediate Response—immediately dispatch the beat unit, if available; immediately dispatch the nearest available unit if the beat unit is not available; if no unit is immediately available, pull the nearest unit off a low priority call and dispatch.
- Expedited Response—dispatch the nearest unit which is not handling a call.
- Routine Response—dispatch the beat unit as soon as it is no longer handling a call.
- Appointment—schedule an appointment with the caller.

It is extremely important that the dispatcher or operator inform the caller of his or her intended actions and how long these actions will take, such as "I'm sending a patrol car out to you immediately. Someone should be there in three minutes."

In wife-beating cases, the operator may try to keep the victim on the phone until responding officers have arrived, to allow the police department to monitor the situation and to provide comfort and reassurance to the victim. In many jurisdictions this practice would be impossible because of the large number of incoming calls and the need to keep police lines open. If the assailant is still on the premises, the operator may ask the victim to meet the officers at a safer location, such as a neighbor's house.

Arrival at the Scene

Unless a weapon is involved, the officers should proceed to the scene promptly without using lights or sirens. It a weapon is involved, lights and sirens should be used, but they should be turned off when the officers enter the block of the conflict scene to reduce commotion in the neighborhood, to protect the officers against ambush or assault, and to avoid aggravating an assailant who is already out of control.

Officers should park the patrol car as close to the scene as possible, but not directly in front of the residence. They should lock the car before approaching the scene, and take a minute to review with each other what they know about the incident and its participants.

Two patrol officers should respond to spouse abuse and wife-beating calls. If personnel shortages or a busy shift prevent such a response, the calls should receive priority backup status. The first officer to arrive at the scene should wait in or near the patrol car until a backup officer arrives. No more than two officers should respond to these calls unless the officers clearly would be endangered without additional support.

The officers' arrival at the conflict scene should be as discreet as possible. If neighbors or relatives have gathered near the premises, they should be asked to leave unless they made the call or witnessed the conflict. Anyone directly involved should be taken aside, identified, and questioned briefly. Witnesses should also be advised to remain close by for further questioning.

Next, the officers should make an external assessment of the premises, checking for danger signals such as double parked cars, broken glass, and people leaning out of windows. If possible, a quick survey of the side and back of the property should be made to identify possible exits. In rural areas, a pen of hunting dogs may suggest the presence of weapons in the house, as would a gun rack in a pick-up truck, or a National Rifle Association membership decal posted in any vehicle window. Officers should look for toys, bicycles, sandboxes, swings, and other evidence that children may be present.

Approaching the Conflict Scene

Officers should approach the scene cautiously and quietly, as much to avoid aggravating the assailant as for their own safety. If they are approaching a house by a front sidewalk, the officers should walk apart, with one officer preceding the other in order to minimize the effects of an ambush. If it is night, flashlights should be held away from the body and pointed toward the ground, rather than toward either officer or the household.

If entering an apartment building, the officers should try to speak with the resident manager before approaching the apartment where the conflict was reported in order to determine if he or she knows anything about the nature of the incident and whether past assaults have occurred. The officers should not permit the manager to accompany them to the conflict scene. Next, they should proceed to the scene by a stairway or elevator to the floor above the apartment, and walk down. If the conflict apartment is on the top floor, officers should proceed to the next lower floor and walk up. When using a stairwell, the officers should stay to the left side of the stairs, with one officer preceding the other by half a flight. On the designated floor, officers should note the exits and check any open doors. All these measures are taken to ensure the officers' safety.

At the door, officers should listen for 10 to 15 seconds for any sounds. If possible, one of the officers should look through a window to see what is going on in the house or apartment. Such action is covered by the plain view doctrine. It can establish probable cause that a crime is in progress or has been committed, a necessary requirement especially if officers must make a forced entry. If there is a screen door, officers should try to see if it is locked.

If the victim and assailant are in a corridor or lobby, they should be escorted to a private area. Officers should keep them separated, one officer walking between them and the other officer behind all of them.

Gaining Entry

Before knocking on the door, the officers should position themselves on either side of the doorway. If a window is near by, one officer should stand by it to observe the person who will answer the door. The other officer should knock on the door, making sure to resume a position to the hinge side of the doorway as a protection against possible gunfire.

The next few seconds are critical for the officers and they must be prepared for several developments. Most likely, someone will come to the door and ask who is there. The officers should identify themselves and explain they have been notified that someone inside may be hurt and they want to come in and make sure that there is no problem. At this point, the person at the door may invite the officers to come in or may refuse them entry. If they are refused admittance, the officers should consider a forced entry if they have reasonable cause to believe the victim is in danger. Evidence of such danger would be cries of distress or for help, signs of a struggle, or weapons displayed. (Although the Supreme Court ruled, in *Payton v. New York,* that police may not make a warrantless and nonconsensual entry into a suspect's home to make a routine felony arrest, such an entry was approved for "emergency and dangerous situations." Immediate physical harm to a victim appears to qualify as an "exigent circumstance" and, thus, permits police to make a warrantless forced entry.) Police should not enter if someone yells, "Come in." Rather, they should wait for someone to open the door. Once inside, the officers should close the door behind them.

Another possible response to the officers' knock is that someone will open the door immediately. If it is the person who has made the call to the police, usually the victim or a third party, the officers, probably will be invited in without argument. In most of these instances, the assailant has left the premises.

If the assailant opens the door, the officers may have a difficult situation to handle. Depending upon the assailant's composure and state of sobriety, he may either become more hostile at the sight of the officers or more controlled and complacent. If the former, the officers must be alert to possible physical assault or use of a weapon and, in the latter case, that they might be dealing with a "walking time bomb." Also, since many assailants frequently deny or minimize the seriousness of the violence, they may appear in perfect control and convince officers that there is no need for their presence. They may also state that the victim is drunk, on drugs, or just fell down the steps. Officers should always interview the victim in these cases in a private setting where she cannot be directly intimidated by the assailant.

Officers should take great care at this point not to confuse the *effects* of the violent behavior, i.e., a disheveled, unkempt hysterical victim, as the *cause* of the violence. Her physical and emotional deterioration are usually the result of abusive behavior, as are her feelings of guilt and self-blame.

In all cases, the officers should wait to be invited inside but should not hesitate to make a forced entry if necessary to protect the victim. In those cases in which the officers determine that an entry is required and envision no immediate danger to the victim or no potential for violence, a warrant should be obtained before making a forced entry.

If no one person responds to the officers' knock, one officer should knock on a back or side door. If again no one answers, they may consider a forced entry if there is convincing evidence that the victim is in danger. On the other hand, someone may answer the door but refuse to speak with the officers or insist that they leave. Before the officers leave the scene, they should resolve for themselves that no crime has been committed, that no crime is in progress, and that neither party has been intimidated into silence. They may make these determinations by inspecting the premises and by interviewing family members and neighbors. Following their decision to leave the scene, the officers should depart promptly, lest they become targets for citizen complaints of police harassment or officer officiousness.

Handling Violence in Progress

In many instances, especially those in which a third party has called the police, the assault may be in progress when the officers arrive at the scene. If the officer hears or see signs of this situation, they should first knock on the door to gain entry, but quickly enter the scene to interrupt the assault. Both officers may be needed to restrain the assailant, and a call for additional officers should be made as soon as possible.

In those cases which are particularly out of control, the victim may assault the officers who are attempting to subdue the assailant. The victim may fear that the officers are harming the man or she may wish to demonstrate her loyalty to him. Often the victim has called the police for a specific purpose—to stop the violence—and becomes resentful or panicky when the officers use force against the assailant and/or indicate their intention to arrest him. It is important for the officers to be aware of the victim's reaction to their use of force and to try to keep her in view at all times. Equally important, officers should take care to prevent either individual from grabbing their service revolvers from their holsters. This most often happens when the officer is leaning over an individual.

If both parties have been assaulting each other, each officer should be responsible for subduing one of the parties. This is an extremely volatile situation because both parties may turn their aggression on the officers. In this case, force may be needed to restrain the parties. Officers should use the minimum amount of force necessary so as not to escalate the violence. In some instances, both parties will need to be handcuffed until order is restored.

Officers must be alert to possible use of a weapon by either party. This may be difficult if the officers' immediate attention is focused on restraining them. Nevertheless, they must disarm either party holding a weapon, or confiscate any weapon displayed in plain view, and hold it for evidence if an offense report is prepared. In some jurisdictions, unless the weapon belongs to the victim, the officers cannot legally take it for safekeeping if the victim only fears that it will be used. Blunt objects which may be used against the victim or the officers should also be removed from reach.

In some cases, the assailant may barricade himself in a room, usually a bedroom or bathroom, when the police arrive. Often he refuses to come out and says he is armed with a knife or firearm. The responding officers should first attempt to coax him to come out peacefully. If this approach fails, the officers should radio for their department's tactical unit, establish a perimeter around the household and, if necessary, use the public address system in their patrol car to warn neighbors to remain in their homes or apartments, or to evacuate the immediate vicinity. At no point should the responding officers attempt to enter the room in which the person is barricaded or to use tear gas to flush him. Barricade situations sometimes require several hours to resolve and are best left to the tactical units which have both the time and the training to handle them properly. Use of tactical units is essential if the barricaded person is holding a hostage, such as a child or relative. Extreme caution and patience are required in these situations and the assistance of a trained negotiator is usually necessary.

Order is restored only when the officers have located and calmed every person in the household and eliminated all sources of noise and commotion from the scene, such as interfering neighbors, a blaring stereo or television set, or a barking dog. The household must be quiet and calm before the officers proceed.

Establishing Control

Once the assault is stopped, the officers should then assert control of the situation by acquiring information and evidence about the nature of the violence. If the officers do not speak the language used in the household, they should try to locate an interpreter. The whereabouts and identities of all persons at the scene must be established first, followed by a determination of the extent of any injuries suffered and of any weapons in the household. If a barking dog is present, the officers should ask someone to remove it from the household. The parties involved should be visually frisked by the officers. If one of them is to be physically frisked, he or she should be informed of the officer's intention. The frisking should be conducted while the other officer is in the same room. The victim and assailant should then be separated out of hearing range of each other but close enough so that the officers can maintain eye contact with each other. If possible, the couple should move to separate but adjoining rooms, and the officers should refrain from touching or crowding them. Many individuals will react violently in these situations if they feel physically trapped or closed in.

If a third party or children are present, they should be sent to another room and asked to shut the door. Bedrooms should be avoided due to the likely presence of handguns in these rooms. If only small children are present, they should be placed in a crib or playpen.

No person should be taken to the kitchen because the availability of knives could escalate the violence. The officers should avoid removing either party to a bedroom because it is not only the primary storage place for handguns kept for self-defense, but may also symbolize the most intimate and, therefore, volatile part of the couple's relationship.

Assessing the Situation

If the officers agree that the situation is under control, they should begin to determine if a criminal violation has occurred, and what emergency services are needed. They should focus their attention on what happened, and not why it happened. As they do this, it is extremely important that the officers convey a professional attitude and not permit their personal feelings about the people involved or their life-style to control their actions.

The officers should first determine the seriousness of any injuries and summon medical assistance if necessary. This procedure can be particularly difficult in wife-beating cases for several reasons. The victim is often suffering from shock or trauma when the officers arrive and cannot accurately answer inquiries about the nature and extent of her injuries. Other victims, fearing retaliation, deny the seriousness of the beating. This situation, as noted earlier, can be aggravated by an assailant's inclination to minimize or deny the seriousness of any violent episode or injuries.

In many cases, these situation, are further complicated because many assailants beat their victims on the chest or back with fists. Injuries from such a beating, such as bruises, internal injuries, or cracked ribs, are not always intially apparent. The officers should make every effort to ask specific questions about the beatings, especially the location of the blows, and should look for signs of internal injury, such as abdominal pain or tightening, as well as for any blood or clear (spinal) fluid flowing from the nose, mouth, or ears. In addition, the woman should be asked if she is pregnant, as the assault may have injured the developing fetus and could result in a miscarriage without proper medical attention.

Officers must try to get clear account of what happened, avoiding humorous remarks, moral pronouncements, or judgmental statements about the couple's lifestyle or behavior. Realizing the people may be embarrassed and ashamed, the officers should not humiliate them further. After each party has had an opportunity to explain his or her version, each officer should help the individuals focus additional remarks or descriptions on specific behavior rather than on recounting past incidents or problems. It is important to remember that a person should be stopped and advised of his or her rights when he or she becomes the subject of direct police questioning or begins to incriminate himself or herself.

In determining whether a felony or misdeameanor criminal violation has occurred, the officers must be familiar with a wide assortment of assault, weapon, civil protection, and disturbance statutes. Efforts must be made to determine "probable cause" that this individual intentionally committed a crime, using the following indicators:

- Seriousness of the injury;
- Use of weapon;
- Threats to the victim;
- Violent actions of the assailant;
- Disarray of the household and damaged property;
- Level of intoxication; and
- Existence of a valid protection order.

It is also important to evaluate the emotional state of the man and woman to make proper judgments about what actions to take. Special attention should be given to nonverbal behavior indicating stress; eyes blinking, playing with hair or clothing, excessive smoking, covering face with hands, crossing arms and legs.

As noted earlier, many victims may be suffering from trauma and appear dazed. Others may break down into sobbing and become disoriented, while others may become angry and hostile. Assailants react to the officers' presence in different ways, such as increased submissiveness or hostility. If either person seems quiet or in complete self-control, special attention and care should be given to help the person express feelings, lest the person suddenly explode or release the tension much later.

All of these reactions are exaggerated fear and anxiety responses and should be met with calm, reassurance, and patience. At this point, especially, the officers should avoid acting as if they are rushed, bored, or unconcerned. They should make every effort to give the individuals enough time to regain their composure at their own speed. If one or both of the parties need more time than usual, the officers should inform the police dispatcher that they will be tied up longer than expected.

Caring for the Victim

The officer who tends to the victim should make special efforts to care for her physical and psychological well-being. In wife-beating cases the woman will need to be reassured of her safety and security, and that of her children. She will also need a calm, secure atmosphere in which to vent her feelings of helplessness, fear, anger, embarrassment, and anxiety. Victims should be encouraged to express whatever feelings they are having, but many times their true feelings will be covered over by a nervous laugh or extreme composure. These are defense mechanisms the victim uses to buy time until she feels more in control. Officers should respond with empathy and reassuring statements, such as, "It's over now. You're safe," or "You've been through a lot, but it's over," and allow the victim to touch them or hold onto them if she needs a physical expression of support. If the victim is suffering from hysteria, she may be soothed by engaging in a conversation about something unrelated to the immediate problem or by performing a routine task, such as responding to the officer's request for an ashtray or a pen.

After assuring the victim of her safety and gathering basic information about the situation, the officer should tend to her medical needs. Since many battered women suffer internal injuries, their ability to diagnose their injuries is sometimes limited. In most situations the women should be encouraged to seek medical attention, unless there is convincing evidence of superficial wounds or scratches only and the victim strongly resists medical care. Verification of any injuries is, however, a necessity if the victim intends to press charges against the assailant.

If the victim's injuries are serious, the officer may decide to transport the victim to a hospital immediately or, if the victim is unconscious and suffering broken limbs, summon an ambulance. If the victim shows evidence of serious injury but refuses medical attention, the officers should summon an ambulance. If, on the other hand, the victim shows evidence of bruises or contusions and refuses medical attention, the officer should contact a neighbor, family member, or battered women's shelter staff and urge the person to make sure the victim receives medical care.

Sometimes the victim denies the beating for fear of reprisal or because of inability to admit the reality of the situation. She may attempt to reassure the officer that everything is fine and that police presence is no longer needed. If this happens, the officer could ask the victim to repeat the account of the incident or ask more questions about evidence that an assault has taken place. Officers must remember that many victims only want police officers to stop the violence and nothing more. If this is the case, officers should explain their law enforcement duties and emphasize the danger of repeated beatings to her and her children. They should tell the victim that domestic violence usually increases in severity and frequency, and that her marriage will not improve until steps are taken to change the man's violent behavior. Also, the officers may have to emphasize that the victim has suffered a criminal assault, not permitted between any two citizens, regardless of their relationship, and that the assault represents a crime against the community and it will not be tolerated.

If the officer is having trouble communicating or establishing rapport with the victim, it may be helpful to leave the victim alone for several minutes to collect her thoughts, or to ask if she would like to call a friend or relative to come over and stay during the rest of the police interview. (It is important to determine that this person is not someone who is the cause of or a contributor to the violent situation.) Often, the officer need not wait for the person to arrive before proceeding with the interview, because the victim may regain some composure from knowing the person is coming. If the victim does not want anyone to know about the assault, the officer might suggest that a staff person from a nearby battered women's shelter or social service agency be summoned.

The officer should clearly explain the procedures which are to be followed and what actions are involved in these procedures. First, the officer should make sure to elicit the following specific information:

- Nature and extent of injuries;
- Use of force or weapons;
- Threatening language or actions;
- Nature of the conflict leading up to the violence;
- History of past conflict violence, and of previous police interventions;
- Legal status of the relationship with the assailants;
- Previous attempts to sever the relationship with the assailant;
- Civil injunctions now in effect against the assailant; and
- Alcohol or drug-abuse problems of the assailant.

Once this information has been gathered, the officer should repeat a summary of the facts to the victim. This is a self-correcting exercise in which the officer should ask the victim to revise any wrong information, interpretations, or conclusions.

If the assailant has left the household, the officers should ask the victim for a physical description, as well as information about the possession of a weapon, use of and description of an automobile, and any suggestions about where he is likely to have fled. In situations requiring a felony arrest this information should be relayed to headquarters and a bulletin issued on the suspect. If the assailant is currently on parole or probation the officers should advise the victim to contact the probation officer as soon as possible.

Interviewing the Assailant

The officer who speaks with the assailant must be alert for an outburst of violence at the slightest provocation. For this reason, the officer and the assailant should go to an adjoining room and be seated as quickly as possible. If the assailant is still yelling, the officer should say nothing for several minutes; if he becomes threatening the officer should give him a specific and direct order to stop. Some assailants are calmed by the officer whispering to them; others will have to be handcuffed as a restraint measure. It is a good rule for the officer never to touch the assailant unless force is needed for restraint.

If the assailant appears to have calmed down, the officer should suggest taking several deep breaths to relax further. Giving the assailant the time to regain composure may minimize additional violent outbursts. Once the assailant is calm, the officer, sitting directly opposite, should explain what will happen next and why, emphasising that all the facts must be gathered before any decisions can be made. It is important that the officer convey a businesslike demeanor with the assailant and do nothing to aggravate the situation. The officer should not make the assailant feel inferior, powerless, or ridiculed, nor should the officer minimize the seriousness of the assault or indicate sympathy.

Questioning the assailant should be direct and concise, and should be conducted in a fact-finding manner, taking special care to ensure the assailant's constitutional rights of due process and protection from self-incrimination. Initial questioning should be general and aimed at allowing the assailant to give a description of the situation, without interruption, as long as there is no self-incrimination. Should self-incrimination occur, the officer should interrupt, tell the assailant what is happening, and read the Miranda warnings.[5]

The officer will need to establish probable cause and whether the assault was accidental, a matter of self-defense, or a criminal violation, by gathering the following information:

- Nature and extent of the violent acts;
- Nature and extent of the injuries;
- Nature and extent of property destruction;
- Use of weapon against the victim;
- Nature of the conflict leading up to violence;
- History of past conflicts and violence, and of previous police interventions;
- Legal status of the relationship with the victim; and
- Civil injunctions now in effect against the assailant.

In deciding to focus the questioning to an interrogation for incriminating information, the officer must inform the assailant again of the right to protection from self-incrimination.

The officer should pay close attention to any evidence of alcohol or drug abuse by the assailant, or if possible mental or emotional disturbances. The officer may want to try some "reality testing" by summarizing for the assailant what has been said, possibly purposely mixing up a minor detail or making erroneous conclusions to see if the assailant corrects him. These techniques, however, should never be tried on a significant issue that could lead to an escalation or to controversy.

The officer should be alert to areas of inquiry that make the assailant uncomfortable, as indicated by a sudden silence, moodiness, shifting the conversation, or a sudden outburst. The officer should remain silent or gently probe for more details. If the assailant resists, the officer should go on to other matters and return to the uncomfortable topic at the end of the interview.

Since many assailants have a tendency to deny or minimize the violent episode, or to shift blame for their behavior to the victim, the officer must take care not to reinforce these patterns by smiling or nodding in agreement. It is important to recognize that many assailants have a high need for control and to dominate others and that they use aggression and violence to do this. They also tend to express most all emotions as anger and are not able to identify the full range of emotions involved in conflict situations. The officer can help in this regard, by suggesting to the man that he seems "hurt," "anxious," "afraid," "guilty," or "sad," and take the focus away from the anger. The officer can also suggest that unless the man learns new ways of expressing his emotions, he will probably lose his family and friends, possibly his job, and certainly his self-respect.

Officers must be sensitive to the difficulty the assailant may have in coping with their presence and the power they represent, perhaps more so than the other criminal offenders they encounter. This may be particularly true if the assailant is a member of a minority group and both responding officers are white. Therefore, any unprovoked blatant show of police force (resting a hand on the service revolver, gruff commands, threats to arrest) should be avoided.

Interviewing Witnesses

As soon as possible, the officers should interview any people who witnessed the violent episode. If witnesses must be interviewed before a disposition is made, usually the officer who has been interviewing the victim should do so somewhere in the household. At no time should the officer leave the remaining officer alone in the household with the assailant.

The witnesses should be interviewed in the victim's immediate presence, but close enough so the officer can keep her in view. Having separated the witness from any group of people that may have gathered, the officer should establish the relationship of the witness to both the victim and the assailant and make an assessment of the person's reliability. The officer should ask the witness what he or she saw or heard, and attempt to verify that the person was in a position to see or hear what happened.

The officer should try to find out if the witness knows of any previous assaults within the household and if the victim has been seriously injured before. The officer should ask about the presence of weapons in the household.

Children who live in the household should be questioned carefully and gently. They may be extremely frightened, and should be asked only very general questions about the assault. If they show signs of trauma or distress, the questioning should stop. In addition, if the case involves weapon use, or if the officers think the children are exposed to a dangerous and traumatic situation, they should contact the protection services division of a child-welfare agency for follow-up evaluation.

Children should not be separated from the victim except in situations in which the victim requires medical attention. In these instances, the officers should help to make arrangements for the children to stay with relatives or neighbors. Moreover, if the children show any signs of fear of the assailant, they definitely should be removed from the household.

In many families which experience spouse abuse and wife beating, child abuse is also present. Officers should take note when they are speaking to the children to look for indicators of abuse, such as:

- *Bruises*—facial bruises (especially on an infant), bruises on the back side of the body or those appearing in unusual patterns that might indicate use of an instrument, or bruises in various stages of healing;
- *Burns*—immersion burns, cigarette burns, rope burns, or dry burns from a hot surface or hot implement, or scattered burns from spattering by hot liquid;
- *Head Injuries*—absence of hair, welts, or abnormal swelling; and,
- *Abnormal Behavior*—extreme passivity or aggression, hyperactivity, role-reversal behavior with parent, fear of adults, or withdrawal and wariness of strangers.

If any of these injuries or behaviors appear, the officers should ask the child about them if the child is old enough to respond, and then ask the parents about them. Officers should determine if the injuries are consistent with the explanations and if they are consistent with the child's age. If officers suspect child abuse or neglect, they should use proper agency procedures to protect the children.

THE DISPOSITION PROCESS

DEVELOPING A PLAN OF ACTION

After the officers have stopped the violence, restored order, and acquired the necessary information, the should decide how to resolve the case. At no time should they leave the assailant unguarded, to prevent a second attack.

The officers' first consideration should be the physical, emotional, and safety needs of the victim and children. Next, they should determine if the elements of a felony or misdemeanor offense are present. Third, they should consider what actions would be effective in preventing future assaults.

Several steps chosen in conjunction may work more effectively than one single action. For example, a victim may be advised to seek a protection order, and referred for medical attention and for emotional counseling as well. An assailant may be arrested, but may also be advised about how to find other living arrangements or referred to an alcohol abuse treatment program. However, in cases of acute stress, only one step—such as removal to a hospital or a battered women's shelter—should be taken. Officers should try to select from the range of alternative actions for the particular needs of each case. This requires extra effort, flexibility, and a knowledge of available services in the community.

Once the appropriate actions and referrals have been selected, the officers should decide who is to perform which tasks, such as calling for a paddy wagon, or contacting relatives, or a battered women's shelter.

FELONY ASSAULT

In cases involving intentionally inflicted serious injury or use of a weapon, many statutes require an on-view probable cause felony arrest.

Prosecution of these cases is difficult without the victim's cooperation, but it is possible. If there is strong circumstantial and physical evidence to establish probable cause that a felony assault or battery took place, some state statutes allow officers to conduct an investigation under their own authority and refer it for prosecution in the name of the state. If the officers decide to arrest without the victim's cooperation, they should explain carefully their duties and the requirements of the law. Such an explanation may result in long-term benefits for the victim, such as increasing the perception of the assault as a crime, encouraging termination of brutal behavior, and providing initial support and safety to make the transition to a new life. Also, officers should devise a plan to ensure safety from the assailant, such as securing an order of protection or finding temporary living arrangements elsewhere.

If the assailant has left the premises, officers should contact the communications officer and have a bulletin issued on the suspect.

Taking the Suspect into Custody

The officers should first inform the assailant of the charges on which they are making the arrest and then read the Miranda warning. The victim should be secured in another room while the assailant is escorted from the household. As in all arrests, officers should use a minimum of force, and should try to disperse any crowd that has gathered outside the household before escorting the assailant to the patrol car. The suspect should then be taken to the appropriate booking facility and, depending upon the agency's procedures, the officers should continue the interrogation, complete the necessary report forms, transport the suspect to a separate detention facility, or return to routine patrol.

Gathering Evidence

Collecting physical evidence is essential if the victim wishes to proceed with criminal prosecution against the assailant. It also may serve to establish a pattern of abuse if the victim decides to take legal action later on.

The most important evidence to collect is evidence of serious injury, which can be verified by an examining physician. Detailed information about each cut, bruise, scrape or fracture should be recorded, along with the physician's judgment about the type of weapon and amount of force needed to inflict the injury. The hospital or the police evidence unit should arrange to take color photographs of the injuries, with the victim's consent.

A second type of evidence is articles that tend to corroborate the occurrence of violence, such as a weapon, torn or bloodstained clothing, broken window-glass fragments, and broken furniture.

The condition of the household or apartment scene is the third type of evidence. A photograph or narrative description of the scene can help to establish that an assault took place. Officers should record any evidence of a struggle, such as a forced lock, broken windows, broken or overturned furniture, bloodstains, torn curtains or furniture, and thrown articles.

Report Filing

In domestic cases involving violence or serious injury, the officers should file an official report regardless of actions taken. The report helps to establish a case file on the household that will be useful to dispatchers and officers responding to future calls for assistance. This information also may be used to establish a pattern of abuse if one of the parties is subsequently killed by the other or commits an aggravated assault.

If an arrest is made, officers should complete the required forms with as much detail and precision as possible, recording information on the nature and extent of any injuries, as well as a description of weapons used. The brand name, caliber, and model of any firearms involved should be recorded, and whether the owner legally possesses the firearm. A description of the scene should note any broken windows, broken furniture, and damaged walls or doors. The officers should record any torn or bloodstained clothing on the victim or assailant, and any violent behavior of the victim and assailant in the officers' presence. Any threats that were made should be recorded, as well as the presence or participation of any third party in the conflict.

MISDEMEANOR ASSAULTS

A misdemeanor assault is one that results in physical injury involving substantial pain or impairment of a physical condition. The precise statutory requirements for these assaults vary widely among jurisdictions but usually entail less physical injury than a felony assault. Further, in many jurisdictions police officers cannot make an arrest for a misdemeanor assault unless it occurs in their presence. This requirement is changing in many jurisdictions as a result of new domestic violence statutes.

If it is appropriate, officers also may make an arrest for violations or civil injunctions, such as protection orders and restraining orders. In many jurisdictions, the victim must return to a court hearing to file a separate motion alleging violation of the order, after which a contempt of court citation and arrest warrant are issued. This practice is being modified in some jurisdictions to eliminate the court hearing and permit arrest if the officers' have reasonable cause to believe the assailant knew of but willfully disregarded the conditions of the order. Many jurisdictions now permit officers to verify the status of an order by telephoning a central police warrant unit rather than requiring the victim to present a copy of the order before a police action can be contemplated.

Taking the Suspect into Custody

If there is evidence of physical harm on the victim, the officers should make an arrest and the same procedures should be used as for a felony arrest. Following the arrest, the suspect should be taken to the appropriate court for processing. In certain cases, the officers may wish to negotiate a dismissal of the charges with the district attorney if the assailant agrees to enter a treatment program. Such an agreement would be nullified if the assailant were to be arrested for a subsequent assault, and the assailant would be prosecuted for both offenses.

If the assailant appears to be intoxicated or mentally unstable, officers may consider protective custody for observation before pressing formal charges. Usually the time allotted for this type of custody is limited to 1 or 2 days.

Making a Citizen's Arrest

If the officers do not have the statutory authority to make an arrest, but the victim wishes to press charges, a citizen's arrest may be made. The officers may first wish to establish that the charges are justified and then escort the arrested person to the nearest precinct station to assist the victim in processing the arrest.

Referral for Civil Action

If both the officers and the victim decide not to pursue criminal charges, the victim may file civil actions in the court having jurisdiction over family matters, usually the Family Court or Domestic Relations Court. Most often, the victim either obtains a temporary protection order or files for divorce or separation, sometimes both. Many jurisdictions no longer require the defendant to be present at a court hearing before issuing a protection order. Copies of these orders usually are filed with the local police department and can be renewed either monthly or annually.

Officers should explain the choices for action to the victim clearly and concisely, including the relative effectiveness of each measure, and the costs and logistics involved. It would be particularly helpful if officers were provided with a brief written description of these actions that they could review and leave with the victim. If such handouts are not available, the officers should write down the information, including directions and telephone numbers, and leave it with the victim.

Officers should encourage the victim to take whatever actions she can to ensure her safety. Although no civil injunction can guarantee safety, obtaining such an order may engender a sense of control and remove feelings of helplessness and passivity.

If the victim wants to file for a legal separation or a divorce, the officers should encourage visiting an attorney, the local legal-aid society, or a community legal services office. Women's rights groups and battered women's shelters can provide female victims with information about obtaining a divorce.

A final form of civil action the victim may want to take is to have the assailant commited to a mental institution as posing a continuing threat to himself and others. This may follow the officers' decision to take the assailant into protective custody and to admit him to a psychiatric facility. The victim should be informed that a psychiatric examination and a court hearing must be held in order to make a long-term commitment, and she should know that courts are increasingly viewing such commitments as violations of civil liberties and are denying a large number of commitment petitions.

Referral for Social Services

Many couples will need counseling and assistance, whether or not they stay together, even if they file criminal or civil legal actions. It is important for officers to refer the victim and assailant to the proper social services; this single action could prevent the offices from being summoned back to the household to handle subsequent assaults.

In order to make an effective referral, the officers must have diagnostic skills to evaluate what type of problems exist and what type of services are needed; and relevant and reliable information about available social services in the community. Without skills or information, the time spent making the referral will be wasted. To handle a domestic violence call quickly is tempting, especially if the officers are fatigued or annoyed at receiving repeated calls to the same household. After responding to several hundred spouse-abuse calls, the officers may not exhibit the sensitivity and interest that the victim and assailant expect. However tired or disgruntled, the officers should try to see the people before them as individuals with unique problems and social service needs.

Many victims and assailants will refuse either to accept or to follow through with a social service referral from police officers. Their resistance is a result of many factors, including their shame and embarrassment, a deep distrust of social service professionals, a tendency to minimize or deny their problems, or a desire to handle their problems without outside assistance. Whatever the reasons, the officers should not press the matter but should leave an agency name and telephone number on a piece of paper for possible future use. If appropriate, they should call the shelter or social service agency and put the victim on the phone before they leave. Some police go one step further and refer these cases to special crisis intervention workers or to victim/witness centers for a follow-up telephone call or visit.

If the officers do make a referral, they should recommend one agency—two at the very most—to avoid confusion. They should make a separate referral for the victim and the assailant if neccessary and should spend time describing the service to each of them. They should give precise information about the agency's address, how to get there by car or public tranportation, hours of business, telephone numbers, and recommendations about what kind of documents the agency will want to see. The person being referred should be told to ask for the "intake worker" when calling the agency for an appointment.

The officers should reassure the individuals that almost everyone needs some professional help or marriage counseling at some time and that they are free to refuse the services if they are found to be unsatisfactory. If possible, the officers should attempt to obtain an agreement from the individuals to a specific plan of action about who will make the call, how they will get to the agency, and what papers they will collect to take with them.

Officers should develop or participate in a formal network so that they can find out how effective the referral has been. Social services agencies should develop procedures to contact officers and tell them if their efforts were at all helpful to the individuals. Officers should not contact the social service agency directly, because many such agencies regard these inquiries as invasions of their clients' privacy. If the officer does not wish to contact the couple directly, the case should be referred to a victim/witness program for the follow-up.

Forms Completion

When the officers do not make an arrest, they should file a miscellaneous incident form so that the dispatcher has a record of their response. A description of the violent situation, the participants, and any injuries sustained should be included, as well as an explanation of why no action was taken. If the couple was separated or a referral made, the information should be noted on this form.

It is necessary to document the officers' response and role in these cases. If the victim chooses to file criminal charges or a civil action, the officers may be asked to testify to the condition of the parties at the time of the call and will need to refresh their memories with an accurate record of the incident. If recording this information on a written narrative is too time consuming, officers could be provided with a checklist type of reporting form or a small tape recorder to dictate the information.

THREATENED ASSAULT

In situations involving slapping or shoving, harassment, menacing, trespass, or endangerment which do not result in injury, officers should consider these actions as precursors of violence, especially if these actions are accompanied by verbal threats of increased violence.

Taking the Suspect into Custody

An arrest is appropriate if the threat occurs in the officers' presence and if the threat occurs within several weeks of a previous assault or threat. Also, an arrest would be appropriate if the threat required a call back to police officers during a 12-hour period, or if it is accompanied by trespass or other menacing behavior.

Issuing a Citation

In some jurisdictions, officers are permitted to issue summonses, appearance tickets, or citations for offenses that are either low-grade misdemeanors or violations, such as harassment or disorderly conduct, and which occur in their presence. They are urged, however, not to use this procedure if there is any reason to believe the violation will recur. If cited, the suspect either agrees to pay a fine or is taken to the precinct station where he may be scheduled for a future court appearance and released on his own recognizance. If the incident did not occur in the officers' presence, some jurisdictions allow the victim to inititate a citation or summons against the suspect at an appropriate summons court. In order to do this the officers must first file an incident report.

In some jurisdictions, where a suspected person has been cited and released, the officer is required to fill out a form with his or her signature, badge number, date, place, time of citation, and suspect's name. The form is given to the victim. The victim may show this form to officers who respond to subsequent assaults as evidence of prior assaultive behavior.

Separating the Parties

If there is no evidence of physical injury or harm and neither the officers nor the victim wishes to initiate misdemeanor charges, separation of the parties is recommended. In such cases, one or the other must be removed from the household to other living arrangements. The officers should remain on the scene until the separation is completed and, in some cases, should transport the departing person to the new living arrangements.

If the parties are to be separated, they should be interviewed separately by the officers to determine who is in a better position to leave. Accommodations with relatives and friends should be investigated first, followed by those offered by public service agencies. In cases where there would be little economic hardship, accommodations at a hotel should be explored.

If children are involved, the parent who is to care for them should be allowed to stay with them in the household. This consideration is especially important for women involved in wife-beating cases: many have left their homes following a beating and later lost child custody because they "abandoned their children," or have been charged with "desertion" in divorce suits and have lost their claim to jointly owned property. These judgments are becoming less frequent, but these factors surface in many fault divorce cases and in most child-custody suits.

A victim choosing to stay in the household, with or without children, should be encouraged to seek a protection order or restraining order from civil court directing the assailant to keep away from the premises. Some state laws grant such orders only if the couple is legally separated or has commenced divorce proceedings; others grant some form of protection order for assault victims. Many of these orders are ineffective and do little to deter the assailant, but they do provide the victim with a legal foundation on which to press charges if the assailant violates the order. It also shows a willingness to take self-protective actions and to end or change the relationship.

Many times, however, the victim will want to leave the household and stay with friends or relatives, or go to a battered women's shelter. Officers should help with the necessary arrangements and should make sure transportation is available. Officers should remind the victim to take only personal or co-owned property. No property solely belonging to the assailant should be removed from the premises. The officers should advise the victim to take a checkbook, credit cards, bank-account books, birth certificates, insurance policies, medical identification cards, and other documents necessary to establish eligibility for emergency services and credit.

Many shelters also have a 24-hour emergency telephone number, which may be used by victims as well as by police officers who need advice or assistance in handling a particularly difficult case involving, for instance, a traumatized victim or one who refuses to seek medical attention. Some of these service groups also offer counseling for couples and special group sessions for assailants. Even if the victim does not want to go to a shelter or counseling program at that moment, she should be told about it and encouraged to call them for advice and support. If the officers suspect she will not call, they can call the shelter themseleves and put the victim on the telephone. This way they are assured the victim is making contact with outside help. Many police departments are now distributing to battered women special referral cards or brochures describing these shelters.

Many assailants become extremely violent when they learn that the victim is leaving the household. Officers should be particularly careful with the assailant at this time and should not let him see or speak to the victim at all. The victim's destination should be kept confidential.

Officers may suggest that the assailant call a friend or relative to come over for a while. Many assailants are too defensive to acknowledge their need for support; others will agree to summon someone. Although the officers should not condone or minimize the serious nature of the assailant's behavior, they may try to provide support as he is confronted with the consequences of his behavior. At this point the assailant may be most susceptible to the officers' suggestion to seek some form of counseling to learn ways to handle stress and conflict. Officers should point out that violence is a learned response and that it can be changed through proper counseling. It is important to emphasize to the man that if he doesn't change his violent behavior, he will likely lose his family, friends, job—and even liberty if conviction and a jail term results. Officers should inform the man of available counseling programs. If possible, officers should call the counseling program and put the man on the telephone.

The situation may arise, however, in which neither the victim nor the assailant agrees to leave the premises. If the victim will care for the children and/or wishes to stay in the household, the officers should try to negotiate a solution with the assailant that includes one day away from home. If negotiation fails, they may issue a stern warning and urge the assailant to leave the premises. While the officers have no legal basis to remove the assailant from his home, they may make an arrest if the assailant threatens the officer or the victim.

Crises intervention and/or making a referral for social service

If the incident does not involve injury or harm, and the officers believe there is no likelihood of future violence, they should take additional, appropriate preventive actions. Many officers use the crisis intervention skills of negotiation or mediation in these situations to defuse the hostilities and to arrive at a mutual agreement. It is important that the officers act only as facilitators in these situations by clarifying issues or helping the parties to listen to each other. The individuals themselves must initiate the suggestions for any settlement and both agree to the settlement. Officers could become more active in the process by helping the citizens to focus on a specific problem, raising specific questions about the problem, and even offering general suggestions about what might solve the problem. The officers should remember that it is the couple—*not the officers*—who must be pleased with the settlement and believe it will work for them.

If the officers determine that the couple have poor communications skills and/or interpersonal problems, they should make a referral to an appropriate counseling agency. The officers should give the couple the agency's address, directions by car of public transportation, hours of business, telephone numbers, and recommendations about what kinds of documents they should take. They should be told to ask for the "intake worker" when calling the agency for an appointment.

REFERENCES

1. Goldstein, Herman. Policing a Free Society. Cambridge, Mass.: Ballinger Publishing Co., 1977, page 112.
2. Ibid.
3. Vandall, Frank. Police Training for Tough Calls. Atlanta: Emory University Center for Research in Social Change, 1976; International Association of Chiefs of Police. Training Key #246: Investigation of Wife Beating. Gaithersburg, Md.: IACP, 1976; Breslin, W. Police intervention in domestic confrontations, Journal of Police Science and Administration, September 1978; Valle, Jose and Axelberd, Mark. Police Training in Family Crisis Intervention. Miami, Fla.: Miami Police Training Center, 1978; Boxley, Russel, et al., Family Crisis Intervention. Boston: Boston Police Department, 1977; San Jose Police Department. Battered Women: Information of Police Officers. San Jose, Calif.: Police Department, 1978; Mallory, Jack and Gair, John. Domestic Crisis Intervention Training Manual: Skill Oriented Training for Police Who Handle Domestic Crisis or Disturbance Situations. Atlanta: Child Service and Family Counseling Center, undated; Silbert, Mimi. Crisis Identification and Management. Phoenix, Arizona: State Planning Agency, 1976; Ohio Peace Officer Trainning Academy. Domestic Violence Training Program Course Outline. London, Oh.: Ohio Peace Officer Training Academy, 1979; St. Petersburg Police Department. Conflict Management. St. Petersburg, Fla.: Police Department, 1976; New York City Police Department. Precinct Level Training Instructor's Guide: Husband and Wife Disputes. New York: Police Training Academy, Cycle 78-1, 1978; and Oakland Police Department. Domestic Violence and Domestic Disputes Training Bulletin III-J (Revised). Oakland, Calif.: Police Department, November, 1979.
4. Wilt, G. Marie, et al., Domestic Violence and the Police. Washington, D.C.: Police Foundation, 1977.
5. Proper use of the MIRANDA warning in these cases is as follows:

   While the initial "on the scene" inquiry may not necessarily require the giving of the MIRANDA warning, the police officer should always keep in mind that the MIRANDA warning must be given before any questioning or further questioning:
   (1) if the suspect, as a reasonable person under the circumstances, is led to believe that he is physically deprived of his freedom of action in any significant way, or
   (2) if the officer has probable cause to arrest. Probable cause to arrest, even in the field, is equivalent to "custody." When "probable cause to arrest" arises in this type of investigation will depend on the facts and circumstances of each case.

Appendix

Directory of Respondents to National Survey of Services for Batterers

Albert R. Roberts, D.S.W.

Alaska
Male Awareness Project
417 West 8th Street
Anchorage, AK 99501
(907) 279–9581
contact person: Keith Wiger, Program Director, or
Allen P. Price, Part-time Counselor

Arkansas
Family Service Agency
P.O. Box 500
N. Little Rock, AR 72115
(501) 758–1516
contact person: Mary Hasty, Social Work Supervisor

California
Santa Barbara County Family Violence Program
P.O. Box 1429
5689 Hollister Avenue
Goleta, CA 93017
(805) 964–8857
contact person: Roberta Foreman, Counseling/Diversion Coordinator

Youth and Family Services Bureau
Hayward Police Department
300 West Winston Avenue
Hayward, CA 94544
(415) 881-7048 or 7049
contact person: Elinor J. Marcelous, Family Counselor, or
                  Ann Leach, Director

YWCA Women Shelter—Men's Program
Alternatives to Violence
3636 Atlantic Avenue
Long Beach, CA 90815
(213) 426-1734
contact person: Alyce LaViolette, Men's Service Coordinator, or
                  Patricia Almaraz, Shelter Director

Stanislaus Women's Refuge Center (SWRC)
Counseling Connection
430 12th Street, Suite D
Modesto, CA 95354
(209) 578-1441
contact person: Wanda M. Hurley, Coordinator

Batterers Anonymous
P.O. Box 29
Redlands, CA 92373
(714) 383-3643
contact person: Jerry M. Goffman, Coordinator

Colorado
Abusive Men Exploring New Directions (AMEND)
144 W. Colfax, #302
Denver, CO 80202
(303) 575-3955—Office, (303) 289-4441—Intake
contact person: Chaer Robert, Project Coordinator

Connecticut
Men and Stress Control (M.A.S.C.)
YMCA
651 State Street
Bridgeport, CT 06601
(203) 334-5551
contact person: George Steinfeld, Director

Delaware
Family Violence Program of Child, Inc.
Box 4055
Greenville, DE 19807
(302) 655-3311
contact person: Joseph M. Dell'Olio, Executive Director

District of Columbia
Families & Children in Trouble (F.A.C.T.) Hotline
c/o Box C
1690 36th Street, N.W.
Washington, D.C. 20007
(202) 965-1900—Office, (202) 628-FACT (24-hour hotline)
contact person: Joan Cox Danzansky, Director

Illinois
Stop Abuse by Males (S.A.M. Project)
Men's Program Unit
University YMCA
1001 S. Wright Street
Champaign, IL 61801
(217) 337-1517
contact person: Steve Everett, Volunteer Organizer

Community Crisis Center
600 Margaret Place
Elgin, IL 60120
(312) 577-8917
contact person: Melodie Jawkowski, Case Manager or
                Mary Berg, Executive Director

W.A.V.E. Program
630 N. Church Street
Rockford, IL 61103
(815) 962-6102
contact person: Eve M. Stone, Director

Men's Program of the Sojourn Women's Center
P.O. Box 1052
Springfield, IL 62705
(217) 525-0371
contact person: Ronald W. Kanwischer, Coordinator

Indiana
Men's Group for Temper Control
South Central Mental Health Foundation
640 South Rogers Street
Bloomington, IN 47401
(812) 339-1691
contact person: Laurence R. Barnhill, Psychologist & Coordinator

Kentucky
Family Violence Project
Lansdowne Mental Health Center
P.O. Box 790
Ashland, KY 41129
(606) 324-1141
contact person: Cathy Waltz, Director

Maryland
Abused Persons Program
Community Crisis Center
4910 Auburn Avenue
Bethesda, MD 20014
(301) 654-1881
contact person: Cynthia L. Anderson, Coordinator

Good Neighbors Unlimited, Inc.
271 Thelma Avenue
Glen Burnie, MD 21601
(301) 761-7446
Another office is located at 1211 Wall Street
Baltimore, MD 21230
contact person: Patricia A. Erat, Director

Massachusetts
Domestic Violence Program
c/o Beacon Clinic
57 Beacon Street
Greenfield, MA 01301
(413) 772-6388
contact person: Ruth Yanka, Administrative Director, or
                John Elliott, Instructor/Counselor

Michigan
Batterers' Counseling Program
Domestic Violence Project, Inc.
202 E. Huron
Ann Arbor, MI 48104
(313) 995-5447
contact person: Lewis Okun, Counselor to Batterers or
Kathleen M. Fojtik, Executive Director,
Domestic Violence Project

YWCA Domestic Crisis Center—Assailant Program
25 Sheldon Boulevard, S.E.
Grand Rapids, MI 49503
(616) 451-2744
contact person: Susan Briggs, Center Coordinator or
Bob Vandenelst, Assailant Program Therapist

Muskegon Assailant Counseling Program
c/o Rape/Spouse Assault Crisis Center
23 Strong Avenue
Muskegon, MI 49441
(616) 726-4493
contact person: Anthony Senna, Assailant Counselor or
Sue A. Ashby, Assistant Agency Director

Catholic Social Services of Wayne County
2433 Van Born Road
Taylor, MI 48180
(313) 292-5690
contact person: Charles Geiger, Clinical Social Work Supervisor

Minnesota
The Violent Partner Program
Family Service of Duluth
424 West Superior Street
Ordean Building, Suite #600
Duluth, MN 55802
(218) 722-7766
contact person: Norm Herron, Therapist

Family and Children's Service
414 South 8th Street
Minneapolis, MN 55404
(612) 340-7467
contact person: Mae Hill, Coordinator of Family Violence Programs

Men in Violent Relationships Project
The Men's Center
P.O. Box 14299
University Station
Minneapolis, MN 55414
(612) 874-1985
contact person: Lance Egley, Chairperson

Missouri
Rape and Violence End Now (RAVEN)
P.O. Box 24159
St. Louis, MO 63130
(314) 725-6137
contact person: Craig Norberg, Coordinator or
                Hirsh Larhey, Volunteer

Montana
Family Court Services
#111 Courthouse Annex
325 2nd Avenue North
Great Falls, MT 59401
(406) 761-6700, ext. 257
contact person: Sally Meade, Receptionist or
                Diana M. Mann, Director/Social Worker

New Jersey
RESOLVE
Plainfield Area Chapter of the American Red Cross
332 W. Front Street
Plainfield, N.J. 07060
(201) 756-0900
contact person: Allan Reading, Director of RESOLVE

New Mexico
Esperanza—A Project for Battered Families
P.O. Box 5701
Santa Fe, N.M. 87501
(505) 988-9731
contact person: Dee Luijillo, Director or
                Magi Molt, Counselor

New York
Abused Women's Aid In Crisis (AWAIC)
P.O. Box 1699
New York, N.Y. 10116
(212) 686-1676

Couple Communications, Inc.
574 Metropolitan Avenue
Brooklyn, N.Y. 11211
(212) 387-6902
contact person: Donato Lamonaca, Director

Partners Anonymous
159-34 Riverside Drive
New York, N.Y. 10032
(212) 568-6525
contact person: Claudia M. Sissons

Referral Outpatient Service
Erie County Medical Center
462 Grider Street
Buffalo, N.Y. 14215
(716) 898-3368
contact person: Edith Murray, Program Manager or
                Marilyn Shine, Psychiatric Social Worker

Spouse Abuse Educational Workshop of the Volunteer Counseling Service
151 S. Main Street
New City, N.Y. 10956
(914) 634-5729
contact person: Beverly D. Houghton, Research Specialist or
                Phyllis Frank, Project Director

Victims Information Bureau of Suffolk, Inc. (V.I.B.S.)
496 Smithtown Bypass
Smithtown, N.Y. 11787
(516) 360-3730
contact person: Carolyn Lamberg, Clinical Supervisor or
                Lucette VonHalle, Executive Director

North Carolina
RESOLVE
108 Highland Avenue
Fayettville, N.C. 28301
(919) 323-4187
contact person: Peter Verabee, Counselor

Oregon
Men's Resource Center Counseling Service
3534 S.E. Main
Portland, OR 97214
(503) 235–3433
contact person: Don Anderson, Director or
       Brad Woodworth, Social Worker

Tennessee
Alpha
5796 N. Foxburrow Circle
Memphis, Tenn. 38118
(901) 362–0295
contact person: Maxine L. Bernard, Co-Director

Texas
Family Service Association of Lubbock
1220 Broadway, Suite 1405
Lubbock, TX 79401
(806) 747–3488
contact person: Margaret Elbow, Caseworker, or
       Betty Lowder, Director

Washington
Hay & Nickle Associates
1702½ East Fourth Avenue
Olympia, WA 98506
(206) 357–8293
contact person: Norman Nickle, Partner, Private counseling group

Men's Counseling Program
c/o OB42A
Bureau of Community & Residential Care
Department of Social & Health Services
Olympia, WA 98504
(206) 754–2870
contact person: Frances Purdy, Volunteer Consultant

Abusive Men's Project
Family Services of King County
107 Cherry Street
Seattle, WA 98104
(206) 447–3883
contact person: Jules Rosanoff, Social Worker

Domestic Assault Program
American Lake Veterans Administration Medical Center
Tacoma, WA 98493
(206) 582–8440, ext. 6822
contact person: Anne L. Ganley, Staff Psychologist

Index